PROFESSIONAL KNOWLEDGE IN MUSIC TEACHER EDUCATION

Professional Knowledge in Music Teacher Education

Edited by

EVA GEORGII-HEMMING
Örebro University, Sweden

PAMELA BURNARD
University of Cambridge, UK

SVEN-ERIK HOLGERSEN
Aarhus University, Denmark

ASHGATE

Published by
Ashgate Publishing Limited
Wey Court East
Union Road
Farnham
Surrey, GU9 7PT
England

www.ashgate.com

Ashgate Publishing Company
110 Cherry Street
Suite 3-1
Burlington, VT 05401-3818
USA

Educ

MT
1
.P774
2013

British Library Cataloguing in Publication Data
Georgii-Hemming, Eva.
  Professional knowledge in music teacher education.
  1. Music teachers–Training of. 2. Music–Instruction and study–Philosophy.
  I. Title II. Burnard, Pamela. III. Holgersen, Sven-Erik.
  780.7'1-dc23

Library of Congress Cataloging-in-Publication Data
Professional knowledge in music teacher education / edited by Eva Georgii-Hemming, Pamela Burnard and Sven-Erik Holgersen.
     pages cm
  Includes index.
  ISBN 978-1-4094-4111-3 (hardcover : alk. paper) – ISBN 978-1-4094-4112-0 (ebook)
1. Music–Instruction and study. I. Georgii-Hemming, Eva, editor. II. Burnard, Pamela, editor. III. Holgersen, Sven-Erik, editor.
  MT1.P774 2013
  780.71–dc23

                                                                    2012026995

ISBN 9781409441113 (hbk)
ISBN 9781409441120 (ebk – PDF)
ISBN 9781409473022 (ebk – ePUB)

Bach musicological font developed by © Yo Tomita

Printed and bound in Great Britain by the
MPG Books Group, UK.

Contents

List of Figures and Tables

Figures

Tables

Key Terms Used

Didactic knowledge – is used in two different meanings: 1) knowledge about how to teach, referring to the Anglo-American curriculum tradition, and 2) pedagogical content knowledge, meaning different kinds of knowledge forming the basis for teaching a subject (e.g. Chapters 3 and 9). In the German-continental tradition of *Bildung*, pedagogical content knowledge is called Didaktik (Chapter 3).

Pedagogy – may refer to the pedagogical practice or to pedagogical theory (as a subject in teacher education) (Chapters 3 and 9). Pedagogy may also refer to models of organizing teaching (e.g. classroom pedagogy) or to conceptions such as constructivist pedagogy (Chapter 6). Pedagogy as professional knowledge may include responsibility for developing an understanding of otherness (Chapter 12).

Pre-service music teacher – see Student music teacher.

Professionalism – According to recent educational theory, professionalism in music teaching depends on the music teachers' ability to integrate different kinds of knowledge as a basis of continued professional development (Chapter 3). In the tradition of apprenticeship learning, professionalism is a social phenomenon rather than a kind of de-personalized skill or expertise (Chapter 11). Professionalism is discussed throughout the book.

School-based in-service teaching – Teacher training based on experiences in school practices in addition to theoretical studies. See Chapter 1: 'students were surprised at how little their supervisors in the school-based, in-service phase of their education seem to have reflected on the reason for having music in schools' (Swedish context).

Schooling – Doing school. Two positions are described, one focusing on the objective of school teaching in terms of efficiency and measurability, the other focusing on students as subjects and their individual needs. In this sense, schooling may have divergent and often problematic connotations as described in Chapters 5 (Swedish context) and 7 (German context).

On the other hand, schooling can just refer to education, through which students 'make connections between theory and practice, and have a greater understanding of the musical competence of school students', Chapter 6 (US context).

Student music teacher – Music teacher student who practises teaching as part of his or her study programme. See for example Chapter 1: 'In their practice teaching, student teachers learn by example and are socialized into the profession'. There is a similar use of the term in Chapter 9. Cf. school-based in-service training (both examples reflect a Swedish context).

Teacher educator – Those training teacher students in study programmes. Most often, students' teaching practice is mentored by experienced teachers that are not educators. An example of an educator taking on both roles is described in Chapter 6.

Teacher researcher / teacher educator – Most often the two functions are combined, and it is suggested that student teachers should also be trained as practitioner-researchers under the supervision of the teacher educator (Chapters 3, 5, 6, 8, 9 and 11).

Notes on Contributors

Pamela Burnard (co-editor) (BMus, MMus, MEd, PhD) is a Reader in Education at the University of Cambridge, UK where she manages higher degree and postgraduate courses in music, arts, culture and education, and in educational research. She is co-editor of the *British Journal of Music Education* and co-convener of the British Education Research Association's Creativity in Education special interest group. She is editor of the 'Creativity Section' in the *International Handbook of Research in Arts Education* (Springer, 2007), and the 'Musical Creativity as Practice' section of the *Oxford Handbook of Music Education* (Oxford University Press, 2012), and author of *Musical Creativities in Practice* (Oxford University Press, 2012).

Suzanne L. Burton is Associate Professor of Music Education, Director of Graduate Studies, and Coordinator of Music Education at the University of Delaware. Burton specializes in music-teacher preparation in authentic contexts, early childhood and K-12 general music, and is on the certification faculty of the Gordon Institute for Music Learning. Her research interests are music acquisition and the development of music literacy, school–university partnerships, intercultural music teacher preparation, and effective professional development. Dr Burton is on the editorial board of *Visions of Research in Music Education*, is widely published in professional journals, and has contributed book chapters for *Applications of Music Learning Theory and Collaborative Action for Change: Selected Proceedings of the 2007 Symposium on Music Teacher Education*. Known for her editorial work, she is lead editor and contributor to the book *Learning from Young Children: Research in Early Childhood Music* (Rowman & Littlefield, 2011), and editor and contributor for *Engaging Musical Practices: A Sourcebook for Middle School General Music* (Rowman & Littlefield, 2012). Dr Burton is the NAfME National Collegiate Chair and chair of the NAfME Early Childhood Special Research Interest Group. She also chairs the Community Engagement Committee of the College Music Society.

Kirsten Fink-Jensen is Associate Professor of Learning and Music Education in the Institute of Education, DPU, Arts, Aarhus University, Denmark. She received her PhD in music education from the same institution in 1996. She teaches masters students in aesthetic learning processes and qualitative research methods from a phenomenological perspective, and masters and bachelor students in music education. Research interests include questions about how to educate students in the understanding of the relation between theory and practice, children's listening experiences in music lessons and aesthetic learning processes. She has presented several papers in international conferences in Europe, especially in the Nordic countries, and published articles in *Philosophy of Music Education Review*, *Raime Proceedings* and *Nordic Yearbook of Research in Music Education*. She has been a member of the board of the Nordic Network of Research in Music Education.

Eva Georgii-Hemming (editor) is Professor of Musicology at the School of Music, Theatre and Art, Örebro University, Sweden. She received her PhD in musicology with music education orientation from Örebro University in spring 2005. She teaches undergraduate courses in music education, and qualitative research methodology, and graduate courses in philosophy of music and sociology of music. Research interests include questions about *Bildung* and the concept of knowledge, as well as the value and role of music in education and in people's lives. Professor Georgii-Hemming has contributed to international anthologies such as *Learning, Teaching and Musical Identity: Voices across Cultures* (Indiana University Press, 2011) and *Future Prospects for Music Education: Corroborating Informal Learning Pedagogy* (Cambridge Scholars Publishing, 2012). She has also published articles in Scandinavian as well as international research journals, such as *British Journal of Music Education*, *Research Studies in Music Education*, *Music Education Research* and *Nordic Research in Music Education*. Her research interests have led to frequent presentations at international conferences in Europe and USA.

Sven-Erik Holgersen (co-editor), MA in musicology and pedagogy, PhD in music education, Associate Professor in the Department of Education, Aarhus University, Denmark. Publications include book chapters and articles about early childhood music education; music teacher education; music psychology and research methodology in particular from a phenomenological perspective. Currently, Holgersen is serving as chief editor of *Nordic Research in Music Education Yearbook*. Holgersen is head of masters studies in a number of educational subjects and teaches MA and PhD courses in music pedagogy, music psychology and research methodology. He is past chair of the ISME Early Childhood Commission (ECME); co-founder of the European network of Music Educators and Researchers of Young Children (MERYC); past chair of Research Alliance of Institutes for Music Education (RAIME) and of the Nordic Network for Research in Music Education.

Finn Holst, MA in music education and MEd in general education, PhD fellow in music education at the Department of Education, Aarhus University, Denmark. The research area for his PhD is music teacher competences and professional knowledge with special reference to music teacher education. Holst teaches MA courses in general pedagogy, music pedagogy, music psychology and research methodology. Publications include reports, articles and book chapters about development projects, classroom research, music education and new technology, conditions of music education and pedagogical theory.

Andreas Lehmann-Wermser studied music education, German literature and educational sciences at Hanover University of Music and Drama and the Hanover Technical University. For the following 20 years he taught music and German in various high schools. For six years he was head of the Department of Aesthetic Education at an experimental school project. Returning to Hanover he received his PhD in music education with a prize-winning thesis on historical music education. Since 2006 he has been Professor of Music Education at University of Bremen; during this time the Institute of Music Education has developed to become one of Germany's most successful institutions in third-party funding. Andreas Lehmann-Wermser was appointed Director of the Center for Teacher Education in 2010.

Teresa Mateiro is Associate Senior Lecturer at the School of Music, Theatre and Art, Örebro University, Sweden and Associate Lecturer in the Music Department at the State University of Santa Catarina, Brazil. She carried out her PhD in music education at University of the Basque Country, Spain. Before that she studied at Federal University of Rio Grande do Sul, Brazil, where she completed the arts licentiate (degree in arts education – orientation music) and the masters degree in music – qualification in music education. In 2008 she was awarded a grant from CAPES, a foundation of Brazil's Ministry of Education, to develop her research as a visiting scholar at Lund University, Sweden. Her research interests comprise teacher education, teaching practice in music education, curriculum development and evaluation, and cross-cultural studies. Her work has been presented in national and international conferences and published in journals from different countries. She is principal editor of two books published in Brazil: *Práticas de Ensinar Música* (Sulina, 2006; 2008) and *Pedagogias em educação musical* (IBPEX, 2011).

Rosie Perkins is a Research Associate in the Centre for Performance Science at the Royal College of Music London (RCM). Having completed her doctorate at the Faculty of Education, University of Cambridge, Rosie works widely across music education and psychology. Current research interests include musicians' career development, musicians' wellbeing and identity, the learning cultures of conservatoires and the role of music-making in enhancing wellbeing. Additionally, Rosie teaches at undergraduate and postgraduate level at the RCM, with particular input into the newly founded MSc in performance science. Rosie sits as a commissioner to the International Society of Music Education's Commission for the Education of the Professional Musician and is a member of the Dutch research group Lifelong Learning in Music and the Arts.

Jonathan Stephens is Professor of Music and Music Education at the University of Aberdeen, Scotland. He holds a PhD in composition and musicology from the University of Wales. His compositions have been performed in the UK, Scandinavia, the USA and Canada, and include two works for the late Elisabeth Klein – an international concert pianist and former pupil of Béla Bartók. Over the past thirty years, Professor Stephens has been a regular international conference speaker, lecturer, workshop leader and consultant on music and arts education. He has led classes in universities and conservatoires and participated in conferences in the UK, Europe, USA, Canada, Australia and Asia. His articles, papers and book chapters have been published in many countries and languages. Jonathan Stephens has held key positions on several national and international committees, served on editorial boards and examined at universities in the UK, Scandinavia and Canada.

Angeliki Triantafyllaki is a postdoctoral research fellow at the Department of Music Studies, University of Athens, where she works on the European Project *MIROR* (FP7-ICT). Angeliki initially trained as a pianist and as a secondary school teacher before completing her doctoral thesis in music education (PhD, University of Cambridge, 2008), which focused on the construction of instrumental teachers' professional identities and knowledge in the workplace. Since then she has worked on a range of education research projects on improving the quality of teaching and learning in performing and creative arts higher education (e.g. student creativity and work-related learning, University of the Arts London; e-portfolio use in masters courses, University of Cambridge; community music modules in university curricula, University of Athens). More recently, Angeliki was awarded funding by the Greek State Scholarship Foundation (Postdoctoral Scholarship, University of Athens) and by the British Academy (Visiting Fellowship, Institute of Education, University of London) to conduct research on novice music teachers' classroom experiences and their initial teacher education. She is an active member of BERA, ISME and SEMPRE.

Øivind Varkøy is Professor in Music Education at the Norwegian Academy of Music (Oslo, Norway), and visiting professor in Musicology at Örebro University (Sweden). He is trained both as a musicologist and as a music educator, with a masters degree in musicology from the University of Oslo, a masters degree in music education from the Norwegian Academy of Music, and a Phd in musicology from the University of Oslo. Previously, Varkøy worked as a music teacher in secondary schools for ten years. His research interest is in the philosophy of music education, and he has published a number of books and articles in this field (in publications such as *Nordic Research in Music Education* and *Philosophy of Music Education Review*). Varkøy has participated in a number of international research conferences both in Europe and North America giving keynote speeches as well as papers, and has visited a number of institutions of higher music education in Europe as guest lecturer. Varkøy is even a composer, and has for instance written theatre music and songs for Morten Harket (A-ha).

Maria Westvall is a Senior Lecturer at Örebro University, Sweden. She completed her PhD at St Patrick's College/Dublin City University, Ireland, in 2007, and she also has a doctoral degree from Örebro University in Sweden. Since 1999 she has taught undergraduate courses in curriculum music to pre-service generalist teachers in Sweden and in Ireland. Presently she teaches music specialist teachers, lectures in music pedagogy and the sociology of music and supervises graduate students. She has taken part in several European teacher exchange programmes, and in the 1990s she taught music for one year in the Middle East. She has presented her research in national and international conferences and has published internationally. Her research interests focus on intercultural issues and cultural diversity in the area of music and music education. Her present research interests encompass collaborative studies concerning cultural comparative perspectives in music education as well as student music teachers' reflections concerning the transition from student to teacher. She is currently carrying out a study among retired professional musicians in Sweden who commenced their musical schooling and education in the 1940s.

Preface

What is the nature of different forms of knowledge? What is the function of different forms of knowledge for the music teacher profession and how does professional knowledge develop? The way we view these questions is influenced by our experiences, our culture and the traditions within which we live and work. However, it is possible to challenge our understanding through experiencing other views and ideas. These are important underlying thoughts throughout this book.

This book examines understandings of 'knowledge', the changing nature of professional knowledge and its significance for professionalism in music teaching. The texts are written by authors from various parts of Europe and the USA. The authors are active researchers as well as qualified teachers. They are working within countries, and/or come from countries, with different pedagogical and academic traditions and ways of interpreting the concept of knowledge. Several different theories and viewpoints are being offered in the book, which illustrate a range of educational settings that create professional knowledge in various ways. Thus, the book contains contrasts. The aim is to show the breadth and complexity involved in the concept of knowledge as such, as well as in music teacher education and the teaching profession.

Through questions at the end of each chapter, you as a reader are invited to critically reflect your own perspectives as well as the perspectives offered in the book. The aim of the critiquing exercise is to illuminate well-known culture and practices as clearly as possible, but also to emphasize other perspectives on music teachers' professional knowledge.

It is possible for those who use the book for educational purposes – for example, within music teacher education programmes – to work with the chapters by using the questions for reflection in the end of each chapter. The intention is to deepen thoughts about the content in each chapter, but also to give the opportunity to further reflect on similarities and differences between the chapters.

The book consists of three parts. After the introductory chapter – 'The Context for Professional Knowledge in Music Teacher Education' – Part I, 'Understandings of Knowledge', discusses the nature of knowledge. The main contribution in this section lies in demonstrating the power of diverse theoretical concepts and perspectives to explore, analyse and engage with professional knowledge. Empirical studies are used to highlight and develop continental epistemology and theoretical perspectives.

Part II, 'Professional and Pedagogical Practice', deals with how professional knowledge is constructed and developed over time, but also how it is culturally sensitive. The particular contribution in this section is to demonstrate how theory can inform professional practice and vice versa.

Part III, 'Re-Thinking Professionalism in Music Teacher Education', deals with the implications and challenges of contemporary pedagogic practices. The central contribution in this section is the demonstration of how these can be analysed and understood in the context of reform.

Music teacher education poses many challenging questions. The complexity of various forms of knowledge and practices that we encounter, as teachers, university lecturers, teacher educators, student teachers, policy-makers or researchers, demands careful thought and reflection.

All around the world there are courses that develop professional music teachers with significant teaching skills and qualifications to create good learning environments. Yet, many music teachers are striving to achieve improved social status and legitimacy. In other words, the professionalism and professionalization of teachers are two sides of the same coin, even though they may not necessarily go hand in hand. We hope that this book will lead to reflections and actions that can contribute to both.

Eva Georgii-Hemming, Pamela Burnard and Sven-Erik Holgersen
October 2012

Introduction
The Context for Professional Knowledge in Music Teacher Education

Pamela Burnard

Music teaching – in the broadest sense, the practice which makes use of the professional knowledge and skills of music teachers for teaching music in multiple learning contexts, including both formal and informal settings – can be characterized as a profession which, although recognized as a specialized discipline, is generally not considered to be a high-status occupation with firmly bounded, scientific and standardized professional traits (Comte 1988; Russell-Bowie et al. 1995) (see also Chapter 12). With the aim of better preparing pre-service teachers for the multiple contexts that they may face in the future, and for developing the power of the profession and the professional self, this chapter takes the reader to the heart of the quality and standards debate on initial teacher education (ITE) and continuing professional development (CPD) for music teachers.

There is reason for concern. Teachers are usually outsiders in the policy process, and so we ask how music teachers, at the *initial* and *ongoing* professional career development phases, can participate more actively as subjects and agents for change to enhance their professionalism. Little wonder that many music teachers lose sight of the reasons why they came into teaching in the first place, and become disenchanted or lose their enthusiasm for their betterment and for raising their professional status.

The professional significance of music and music teacher education is concerned with *professional knowledge* and *knowledge specializations*, and questions of what constitutes *pedagogical content knowledge and skills*; how this knowledge grows; and what this means for the way in which teachers (and their students) learn and why they change (or do not change), what motivates them, and what factors help or hinder their development.

It is important to society that schools and parents are aware of and support the increasing research focus on the knowledge of teachers generally. Building an understanding of music teachers, music teacher thinking and music teacher education has been accompanied by an increasing recognition by teacher educators (usually academics developing professionally focused courses in increasingly beleaguered higher education institutions), policy-makers as well as the community at large. They have begun to recognize that the quality of teachers and our understanding of teacher knowledge and teaching in music education (including community music and arts settings) are key factors in students' learning and achievement Music educators can significantly influence attitudes towards music learning and learners' motivation to learn, not only through their content knowledge, general pedagogical knowledge, curriculum knowledge, pedagogical content knowledge, knowledge of learners and their characteristics, knowledge of educational contexts and knowledge of educational ends (see also Chapter 3), but – and equally important – through their capacity to inspire and their passionate commitment to using their professional knowledge creatively for the renewal and implementation of music teacher education programmes.

As professionals, music teacher educators are engaging in the development of professional teacher practice. At the *initial* and *ongoing* professional development phases of music teachers, the traditional higher-education concern with disciplined, codified, propositional knowledge (which comes closest to traditional academic discipline-based theories, practical principles and propositions about particular cases in the applied field of professional action) has usually triumphed, together with the emphasis on one or more of the kinds of teacher knowledge (as suggested by Eraut 1994). *Professional knowledge* and *personal practical knowledge* (or self-knowledge of performance) *of teachers and teacher educators* and the distinctions between them are important for the music teacher profession because they provide insights into what it is that teachers need to know; they develop and grow scholarly understanding of what teacher knowledge is. This is a result of personal growth in the context of educational work and social interaction with the teaching and learning community (see also Chapters 4, 6, 9 and 10). While the customary focus on the 'what' questions is important, so too are questions of 'how', 'where', 'who' and 'why' when learning to teach music (see also Chapters 1, 3 and 12).

What Kinds of *Professional Knowledge* Are Valued by Music Teacher Educators?

Central to any discussion of *professional knowledge* is the role of theory and the generalizability of practical knowledge. Making theories explicit in practice (for both espoused and established theories) (see also Chapters 1, 6, 8 and 9) and reflecting on them are commonly accepted as essential components in the process of becoming a reflective teacher (that is, a professional who is creative and conscious of the multifaceted and multicultural locus in which they work).

The validity of the discipline-based form to the body of knowledge we call 'music', and its relevance to professional training, is often considered by music teacher educators as difficult to decide, especially when the experts who teach it may not even be members of the profession concerned (that is, not music specialists) and crowded syllabi and job pressures force prioritization. Another difficultly is that the functional relevance of a piece of theoretical knowledge may depend less on their presumed validity than on the ability and willingness of teacher educators to use them. High-quality learning depends on highly qualified teachers and teaching. Where policies advocate school-based pre-service training (as with US and, increasingly, UK policies), where the process of teacher certification and becoming a professional involves circumventing university-based systems and preparing new teachers in quick-fix school-based programmes (see 'Teach First' in the United Kingdom or 'Teach for America' in the USA) this seems hard to accomplish.

High-quality teachers are trained in Finland by properly accredited courses that require pre-service teachers to meet the rigorous practical and intellectual standards that are becoming of a demanding profession. In Finland professional knowledge learning starts after graduating with a first degree, when highly motivated applicants are more sure of their career choice and when the probabilities of subsequent dropout are reduced. This increases quality, reduces training costs and contributes to stability and sustainability within the system.

There are no quick fixes for creating quality music teachers and music teaching. The approach followed in Finland shows how to get and keep the best. In contrast, the UK and USA seem to be advocating 'tearing down the wall' of teacher certification by making it easy for applicants to circumvent university-based systems for preparing new teachers, by offering performance-based pay, and by relabelling qualifications as master's degrees so as to draw teachers by extrinsic rewards.

So, how the term *professionalism* in music teacher education comes to be defined depends upon the political landscape and the particularities of any government's educational reform process (see also Chapter 3). Evidence from national and international research studies shows teachers as being continually in the grips of educational change and rapid reform, as observed by Lang et al. (1999, p. 11) over twenty years ago:

> Teachers do not work in isolation. Those who work with them are caught up in the reform process. The professional self is developed in a community of persons involved in teaching and learning as colleagues, students, researchers, teacher educators, administrators, parents or politicians in an environment of openness, mutual help, trust and understanding. But there are also many pressures from diverse stakeholders. Many and conflicting good intentions exist for schools driven often by insecurities which flow from international testing and changes in the workplace. Conservative forces want productivity measures – liberal and socially oriented groups want autonomous and self-responsible developments and there is much in between. These many good intentions have the power to influence teacher practice. The means are embodied in curricula, syllabi, standards, financial incentives, school structures, teacher and student assessment systems, textbooks and computer purchases. Researchers, no less than others, contest the nature of education and its assumed contribution to a good life, and all involved have a point of view and an agenda.

In music teacher education, there is much evidence, in research of innovative practices, which contests the nature of the profession's claim to a specialist knowledge base, in, for example, developing values, determining cultural norms, participating and linking with communities and drawing on the expertise of community musicians. As Jorgensen (2011, p. 71) argues:

> One of the most pervasive models underlying music education is that of community. Whether it be the Hindustani sitarist instructing his disciple in traditional manner, the Western classical pianist conducting her masterclass, the Australian Aboriginal songman teaching his young kinsmen a love song, or the Balkan mother singing her daughter a lament, all participate in a community in which music making and taking plays a central role.

Hence, in relation to school-based and service-learning programmes, the community stakeholders see music, music educators and students as valued resources. The education stakeholders involved in initial (or pre-service) teacher education in the higher-education system, are starting to value and incorporate collaborative partnerships, including the nurturing of community partnerships, in order to bring together the classroom and the broader community in ways which recognize the diverse lenses with which we are now coming to view music education (see, for example, Ballantyne and Bartleet 2010; Pitts 2010), where practice and knowledge are brokered in intergenerational and intercultural contexts (Larkin et al. 2004; Schippers and Cain 2010; Tait et al. 2010).

Traditionally, educational institutions have been responsible for providing ITE and CPD, and for steering how the quality of the profession's intake and degree-entry routes are judged. Professionally focused courses are, however, increasingly disappearing. All around the world there are courses that develop professional music teachers with significant professional knowledge and skills, qualifications and practices to create effective learning environments. In spite of this, there is considerable evidence that CPD is, all too often, under-supplied, and is, therefore, minimally effective in advancing and developing new professional knowledge. Music teachers and music educators continually strive to achieve improved social status and legitimacy (see also Chapter 12). Yet the framework for promoting and facilitating professional learning depends upon the professional knowledge of teacher educators themselves and how they help teachers to acquire professional knowledge.

My central argument is that *there are conflicting conceptions of professional knowledge* and *in failing to articulate (and decide what constitutes) a distinctive knowledge base* music teachers have suffered from the profession being undervalued in school music reform policies. Reform agendas embody images of professional ideals and models of practice. Problems arise from the implicit nature of many professional models of practice, the process of 'know-how' in music taking very different forms (see also Chapter 10). We see this through analyses of such activities as curriculum planning, assessing and professional decision-making, and the actions of generalist and specialist practitioners. The former group can bypass theory by teaching methodic procedures with non-technical knowledge from a theoretical perspective, and its academic status remains correspondingly low; the latter group is likely to emphasize the primacy of musical skills, specialized knowledge and the nature of that knowledge, and its mode of organization is well constituted. The music teacher is concerned not only with the communication of specialist skills but with explaining concepts of particular significance and complexity.

Moreover, the debates and ideas about the need for CPD for generalist practitioners in primary schools and the role of specialist music teachers at secondary or high schools reflect ideas about knowledge. Knowledge, to quote an English head teacher, is like a 'tangle of spaghetti', a metaphor similar to Gilles Deleuze's idea of *rhizomatic knowledge*:

> Something which shoots in all directions with no beginning and no end, but always *in between*, and with openings towards other directions and places. It is a *multiplicity* functioning by means of connections and heterogeneity, a multiplicity which is not given but constructed. Thought, then is a matter of experimentation and problematization – *a line of flight* and an exploration of *becoming*. (Rinaldi 2006, p. 8: original emphasis)

We can think about professional learning and particular ways of conceptualizing knowledge as a process, like creativity, which is co-constructed and shared, questioned and reformed in relationship with others and without the necessity of known outcomes; which requires openness to the new and unexpected, listening to ideas and theories, and invention; and which emphasizes connectedness to learning and to conditions which enable learning, involving the questions and answers of children and adults alike; a process where knowledge is relational and provisional, representing something that can be continuously reworked; a process of construction by the individual in relation to others (Burnard 2012).

Such a relational view of knowledge, however, conflicts with the complex web of state regulation which constrains specialist primary teacher numbers, salary levels and social status. There is an historical imbalance between music teachers and music services, compared to the fields of literacy and numeracy, in school sectors. The agendas outlined above – and especially the conflicts that inhere in them – require us to reflect on the concept of *professional knowledge*, the state of *music teacher education* and the possibilities for improvement (Lee and Wilkes 1999).

With a focus on understanding the nature of knowledge and the need for defining what constitutes music teacher education's *professional knowledge base*, we are reminded of Johnson (1972, 1984) who argues that instead of defining what constitutes a 'profession' we should regard 'professionalism' as an ideology and 'professionalization' as the process by which an occupation – in this case, music teaching – seeks to advance its status and progress towards full recognition within that ideology. Irrespective of what professionals actually do, as music teachers our *knowledge claims* are strongly influenced by the need to sustain the ideology of professionalism and further the process of professionalization, as the process by which our occupation seeks to gain status and privilege in accord with that ideology. Within this mix, and in the context of professional education and development at the initial teacher training level and ongoing phases of professional development of music teachers, a central question for music teacher education and teacher educators is: How do we come to comprehend more clearly the *professionalism* and *professional significance of music teachers* in society? And, given that *conceptions of teacher education* and understanding about learning to teach are changing rapidly: What are the implications of these changes for the professional knowledge of teacher educators themselves? How can teacher educators create professional learning communities where leaders pull responsible, qualified and highly capable teachers together in pursuit of improvement?

Reconceptualizing Professional Knowledge: Reconstructing Professionalism

There is general agreement that governments are increasingly taking control of the teaching profession (Alexander 1992, 2004). Teachers are expected to perform in specific and regulated ways. While forms of knowledge provide variation, within pedagogic practices knowledge determines the way that the 'what is to be learnt' is written and taught. We know that a specialized language specializes consciousness – specialist music teachers determine and realize a more skills-based music pedagogic discourse (where elements of professional knowledge are presupposed by the curriculum), and generalist teachers develop de-specializing 'content-rich' pedagogy (Moore et al. 2006) – and that allegiance to a discipline, such as music, specializes teachers' identity and strongly classifies and frames teachers' confidence and claims to specialist knowledge (i.e. expertise) (see also Chapter 7). In other words, professional knowledge and professional learning matter a lot. Possession of specialist knowledge (and the basis of specialization as a music teacher) is having the right kind of knowledge, and this is perceived by teachers as important in defining identity and achievement. But within the field of education, generally speaking, Alexander (1992) proposes that although teaching is a complex and unpredictable activity, 'good' practice lies within the intersection of five overlapping considerations which are particularly relevant to the context of the continuing professional education of teachers:

1. the *policy-making context*, where the concept of 'standards' and assertions about standards and accountability are defined in political discourse by policy milestones;
2. the *academic context*, where theoretical knowledge may be related to practice and practical knowledge may be used to generate theory, and where professional knowledge can be validated by research;

3. the *school context*, which corresponds with these educational discourses, debates and discussions of accountability and school improvement aligned with what initial teacher training and teacher education say, and do about (as well as what shapes) professional knowledge;
4. the *curriculum context*, which corresponds to knowledge about curriculum, and wider questions of value and purpose of how and what children should learn and what knowledge matters; and
5. the *classroom context*, which corresponds with locally devised contexts.

How knowledge use is depicted in these contexts is what shapes teachers' expertise, and within them normal professional practice can be produced in a relatively routine, situated manner (which can be described as richly elaborated and tacit knowledge about curriculum, classroom routines and students that allows them to apply and dispatch what they know as professional knowledge) with or without questioning the assumptions on which it is based. In this way also, questions about what constitutes good teaching for different teachers can be distinguished by the way in which people learn to operate, grow and develop as professionals (by writing, talking or doing) and by the way knowledge is validated (by expertise, by stakeholders' support, or by personal knowledge). The overlapping considerations for professional teaching are (Figure I.1):

1. CULTURAL: What practices do the teacher value and believe in?
2. POLITICAL: What practices do ministry officials and school leaders advocate/not advocate?
3. EMPIRICAL: What are the most important prerequisites for the continued development of professionalism in music teachers?
4. PRAGMATIC: What practices work best (or do not work) for the teacher?
5. CONCEPTUAL: What are essential elements constituting music teaching and music teacher education?

Important research conducted by Woods and Jeffrey (1996) identified teachers coping with tensions surrounding reforms and negotiating the interface between the rhetoric of policy and realities of practice. Ideas about knowledge reflect ideas about learning and becoming. The problematization and implementation of educational policy into professional knowledge and pedagogic practice is neither straightforward nor unproblematic. The conflict between reform agendas, political imperatives, reformulation of theory resulting from empirical evidence and teachers' professional learning from practice-based research in education causes tensions for teachers. The process of learning as co-construction, in relation with others, is aggravated by the effect of all the tough talk of standards (Ball 2003).

There is wide acceptance that good, professional music teaching is a complex task involving a person acting professionally in education and developing an occupational self with well-founded educational values and a high degree of expertise (Bauer 1999). There is general agreement that good, professional music

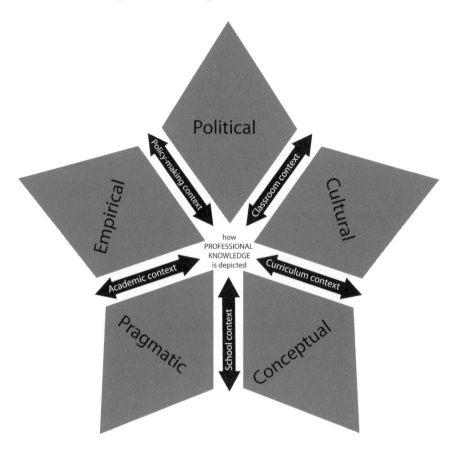

Figure I.1   A framework for understanding professional knowledge

teaching is well organized, reflective and planned; is based on sound subject knowledge; is dependent on effective classroom management; and requires an understanding of children's developmental needs. Most importantly, however, professionalism in good music teaching uses exciting and varied approaches (Alexander 2008; Finney and Harrison 2010; Harrison and McCullough 2011).

With the exception of some countries[1] (see also Chapter 3), a collaborative culture involving university–school partnerships has become a global delivery model in many initial teacher education programmes. In the United Kingdom, as with Norway, the USA and Australia, there is a long history of collaboration between teachers and professional artists in participatory arts activities, in both

---

[1]   For example, in Germany, although standards are set through nationwide state exams and entrance regulations, Bauer (1999, p. 193) has reported that one cannot speak about a collaborative culture because the institutions responsible for schools, teachers and teacher education do not really cooperate.

schools and communities. Models of practice in partnerships between artists and teachers vary considerably. However, effective partnerships between artists and teachers in schools suggest it is in the act of creativity itself that empowerment lies. Teaching is a subtle and complex art, and successful teachers, like artists, view their work as a continuing process of making and participating, reflecting and learning, in high-level arts-based knowledge communities (see also Chapters 4 and 7). The political climate and policy, in one way or another, shapes the propensity to exercise more or less *knowing agency* with regard to experiences of initial teacher education and continuing professional development. What happens to professional knowledge in the context of working in classrooms collaboratively with artists? Inclusion, exclusion, alienation, disruption, ambivalence and critical autonomy all work to co-create opportunities for *knowing* and *being* in ways that find significance in understanding learning to teach. Collaboration with artists is especially important in bringing an alternative perspective to initial teacher education and teacher development.

Whether universities or a competitive training market without the involvement of universities are the main provider of ITE, teacher–artist partnerships (as with school–arts organization partnerships) directly benefit students. They also have the potential to indirectly benefit students by increasing professional knowledge (i.e. teacher expertise). There is a consensus that educational partnerships are dependent on the help, trust and openness of the individuals involved (Jeffery 2005). For a partnership to work well, either for students or for professional teacher development, Wenger et al. (2002) argue that there must be genuine collaboration, dialogue, openness and mutual tuning. Under these conditions, a collaborative partnership can develop, where teachers and artists are engaged in a dialogue and are dialogic in their teaching. For this to happen, they need to have time for thinking, to encourage and maintain ambiguity, and to share understanding about what they are doing and what this means within the professional learning community (Galton 2008).

Teachers and artists co-construct knowledge when their collaboration encompasses 'the act of teaching, together with the ideas, values and collective histories that inform, shape and explain that act' (Alexander 2008, p. 38). When teachers and artists collaborate, they often have different conceptions concerning the professional knowledge that brings the purpose of teaching into focus. Some see teaching as imparting knowledge and others maintain a focus on the *act* of teaching, perceiving teaching as the preparation of pupils to use old and create new knowledge. The visiting artist typically uses a more improvisational, open-ended approach, whereas the classroom teacher typically uses a more structured style. Teacher–artist partnerships provide researchers with an opportunity to study the paradox of teaching knowledge and creation in action: How does the teacher–artist dyad resolve this paradox in balancing the more unpredictable, improvisational approach of the visiting artist with the more predictable, normative and accountable style of the teacher? (See Burnard 2011; Sawyer 2011.) Research tells us how important it is to meet the standards required of teacher professionalism (a process of educational growth or *Bildung* in the context of educational work, Bauer 1999) (see also Chapter 7). This is a policy issue in many countries. It presupposes a professional language which enables knowledge to be shared with other members of the professional community, where common knowledge is constructed through interaction with colleagues.

Hitherto the emphasis of my discussion has been on professionalism and professional knowledge – this being part of teachers' accountability to students. Music teacher educators cannot afford to ignore the policy agendas (as, for example, in England, of professional accountability) which underpin political imperatives. Developing professional knowledge through collaborative partnerships with visiting professionals, promoting creativity and innovation in teaching, and raising standards of attainment across the curriculum, all form part of a music teacher's commitment to the continuing development of teachers' professional knowledge base. Music teacher educators need to develop practices that emphasize enjoyment and inclusion, but do not undermine music teachers' professionalism and self-worth, their professional learning, skills, knowledge, understanding, confidence and commitment to pedagogic and curriculum change.

Music teacher educators need to become sophisticated analysts of socio-cultural politics, an essential skill in the cultural realm and the political terrain. The ways in which different forms of cultural capital interact within the social production of 'school music' (and 'school composition') are informed by how music is seen at the level of collective and individual policy trajectories (see also Chapter 10). Indeed, the issue I am raising here is not about what an artist brings to pedagogic practice but what it *means* for different groups of teachers and teacher educators/ mentors whose deeply ingrained perspectives, experiences and dispositions may or may not be shared. It is essential that music teachers *engage* in this debate.

While governmental demands for improved standards and calls for new professionalisms may appear to be complementary and balanced agendas, the general consensus is that government intrusion has diminished the professional autonomy of teachers (Jeffrey and Woods 2003; Jeffrey 2006; Burnard and White 2008). There is little research on whether music teachers experience productive or conflicting tensions. We know that perceived shortfalls in the teaching of music and the political pressures to raise standardized test scores contribute to the isolation that music teachers feel; this results in uncertainty and rising tensions in the profession of music teaching. Some writers suggest tensions arising from the professional discourses stimulate teachers to rise to new challenges through creative mediation (as a necessary and integral component of becoming professional change agents) despite the discomfort and destabilization that these tensions engender (Burgess 1995). Other writers emphasize the challenges faced by teachers (particularly those involved in educational partnerships) (Jeffrey 2006) and find little evidence of teachers incorporating artistic elements into their curriculum and pedagogic programmes beyond one-off events.

More than for any other subject teacher, music teachers are being controlled and driven by concerns for uniformity, accountability and educational standards.

Their ability to provide a creative response and take control of appropriate reforms, adapting them to ensure a higher level of learner involvement, will determine, to a large extent, their success in becoming professional change agents (for practices and insights that support real change) (see also Chapter 12). If music teachers are not professionally sustained, then the distressingly high numbers of teachers leaving the profession can be predicted to continue. In evaluating the significance of the current impulse by government to engineer creative partnerships in formal education, it becomes apparent that the loss of power and control by music teachers (with pedagogic interventions by practising artists) leaves the profession at its most vulnerable.

Music needs to be repositioned in the mainstream curriculum, in ways that go beyond funded arts 'one-off' activities. We need to encourage new music pedagogies which step outside the boundaries of traditional assumptions, allowing teachers to balance creative mediation and accountability against the requirements to teach in different (rather than certain) ways. We need a transforming professionalism where music teachers become convinced of their own 'can-do-ness' (Hartley 1997, p. 119) and, in that realization, re-balance the rhetoric of performativity with creativity through innovation in classroom practice (Furlong et al. 2000).

We need to analyse and articulate the principles, purposes and theoretical foundations of national standards in music. We need to explore how they can be reconstructed so as to be interpreted and understood as a non-linear interacting system, the ultimate goal being a synergy that embraces curriculum, pedagogy and assessment in counterpoint with the continuous development and self-renewal of music teachers and better teaching.

The serious challenge is not what music teachers *won't* do. Rather, it is in the professionalism and agency of what music teachers *can* do to implement and support real change. This means rethinking the role of practising music teachers and their students in the creation, application and dissemination of professional knowledge about what works in their schools and classrooms. Doing so needs to be an intentional activity with the purpose of influencing how music educators see music teachers' potential for transforming music teacher education. Teachers and teacher educators need to work together to establish what it means to be 'good at' music, and investigate the validity of judgements as to what quality looks like in music. They need to do this as members of a community, working together in a collaborative attempt to better understand and transform their shared musical worlds.

The tensions between conflicting policies can be used to provide music teachers and music teacher educators with an opportunity to construct a value based professionalism that includes creative values, progression and achievement values, and holistic educational values (see also Chapters 1, 2, 3, 7 and 12). However, we need to analyse in more detail what kind of music teacher professional knowledge is being produced and in what way this is affecting teachers and students alike (see also Chapter 1). We need to identify how others have researched professional knowledge and reflect on what that means in practice. We need a clearer understanding of professional knowledge, shared by all those involved in music education, so that professional knowledge and knowledge creation comes to underpin music teaching and learning. At the same time we need to show that crude instrumental performativity strategies are less effective and generally debilitating. We need to move into a period dominated by developing professional knowledge, with tensions that are both positive and complementary.

Concluding Thoughts

Finally, we come to the most important quality of the pre-service, newly qualified and experienced professional music teacher, the disposition to both theorize and become the ultimate arbiters of educational change in the field of music. If our trainee music teachers acquire and sustain this disposition they will go on developing their professional knowledge, their theorizing capacities and their potential as drivers of sustainable educational change throughout their teaching career. But music teacher educators need to insist on more than just compliance from music teachers. In response to the pervasive problems that have been identified above, the 'who' and the 'how' questions need to concentrate on developing:

1. High-quality, motivated music teachers who are encouraged and engaged in initial and continuous professional learning and renewal of professional knowledge using their professional energy not to bolster government control, but to create a powerful sense of shared professional responsibility to collectively raise standards.
2. Proactive and powerful music teachers' associations, which go beyond collective bargaining and professional development provision and address the public's desire for a profession that places the musical interests, development and achievement of children at the heart of its vocation. Funding should be given to support more positive union involvement in professional development and strengthen a culture that deals with the professional knowledge and development of music teachers.
3. Lively networked music learning communities and collaborative cultures, which prevent the classroom and studio alienation and isolation of cocooned music teachers (which, in turn, leads to non-innovative cultures of conservatism, individualism and apathy). These should be linked to learning and achievement in music. Collaborative cultures are strongly associated with increased student success and improved retention among new music teachers. They provide the mutual learning and moral support that stimulate teachers and sustain them through the difficulties of change. These elements can be observed in Finland's professional teaching culture of trust, cooperation and responsibility, and in the lateral learning networks of sharing between schools (Hargreaves and Shirley 2009).

References

Alexander, Robin (1992). *Policy and Practice in Primary Education*. London: Routledge.

— (2004). Still No Pedagogy? Principle, Pragmatism and Compliance in Primary Education. *Cambridge Journal of Education*, 31(1), 7–33.

— (2008). *Essays on Pedagogy*. Abingdon: Routledge.

Ball, Stephen J. (2003). The Teacher's Soul and the Terrors of Performativity. *Journal of Education Policy*, 18(2), 215–28.

Ballantyne, Julie and Bartleet, Brydie-Leigh (2010). Navigating Context Based Learning in Pre-Service Teacher Education. In Julie Ballantyne and Brydie-Leigh Bartleet (eds), *Navigating Music and Sound Education*. Newcastle upon Tyne: Cambridge Scholars Publishing, 1–15.

Bauer, Karl-Oswald (1999). On Teachers' Professional Self. In Manfred Lang, John Olson, Henning Hansen and Wolfgang Bünder (eds), *Changing Schools / Changing Practices: Perspectives on Educational Reform and Teacher Professionalism*. Louvain: Garant, 193–228.

Burgess, Lesley (1995). Human Resources: Artists, Crafts eople, Designers. In R. Prentice (ed.), *Teaching Art and Design: Addressing Issues and Identifying Directions*. London: Cassell.

Burnard, Pamela (2011). Creativity, Pedagogic Partnerships and the Improvisatory Space of Teaching. In Keith R. Sawyer (ed.), *Structure and Improvisation in Creative Teaching*. New York: Oxford University Press, 51–72.

— (2012). *Musical Creativities in Practice*. Oxford: Oxford University Press.

Burnard, Pamela and White, Julie (2008). Creativity and Performativity: Counterpoints in British and Australian Education. *British Educational Research Journal*, Special Issue on Creativity and Performativity in Teaching and Learning, 34(5), 667–82.

Comte, Martin (1988). The Arts in Australian Schools: The Past Fifty Years. *Australian Journal of Music Education*, 1, 107–115.

Eraut, Michael (1994). *Developing Professional Knowledge and Competence*. London: The Falmer Press.

Finney, John and Harrison, Chris (2010). *Whose Music Education Is it? The Role of the Student Voice*. Solihull: National Association of Music Educators.

Furlong, John; Barton, Len; Miles, Sheila; Whiting, Caroline and Whitty, Geoff (2000). *Teacher Education in Transition: Re-Forming Professionalism?* Buckingham: Open University Press.

Galton, Maurice (2008). *Creative Practitioners in Schools and Classrooms*. Final report of the project: The Pedagogy of Creative Practitioners in Schools. Cambridge: Creative Partnerships/Faculty of Education. www.educ.cam.ac.uk/people/staff/galton/Creative_Partnershipfinalrept.pdf

Hargreaves, Andy and Shirley, Dennis (2009). *The Fourth Way: The Inspiring Future for Educational Change*. London: SAGE.

Harrison, Chris and McCullough, Lis (2011). *Musical Pathways*. Solihull: National Association of Music Educators.

Hartley, David (1997). *Re-Schooling Society*. London: Falmer.

Jeffery, Graham (2005). *The Creative College: Building a Successful Learning Culture in the Arts*. Stoke-on-Trent: Trentham.

Jeffrey, Bob (2006). Creative Teaching and Learning: Towards a Common Discourse and Practice. *Cambridge Journal of Education*, 36(3), 399–414.

Jeffrey, Bob and Woods, Peter (2003). *The Creative School: A Framework for Success, Quality and Effectiveness*. London: RoutledgeFalmer.

Johnson, Terence J. (1972). *Professions and Power*. London: Macmillan.

— (1984). Professionalism: Occupation or Ideology. In Sinclair Goodlad (ed.), *Education for the Professions: Quis Custodiet?* Windsor: SRHE and NFER Nelson, 17–25.

Jorgensen, Estelle (2011). *Pictures of Music Education*. Bloomington: Indiana University Press.

Lang, Manfred; Olson, John; Hansen, Henning and Bünder, Wolfgang (eds) (1999). *Changing Schools/Changing Practices: Perspectives on Educational Reform and Teacher Professionalism*. Louvain: Garant.

Larkin, Elizabeth; Friedlander, Dov; Newman, Sally and Goff, Richard (eds) (2004). *Intergenerational Relationships: Conversations on Practices and Research Across Cultures*. New York: Haworth Press.

Lee, Shirley and Wilkes, June (1999). In What Ways Do Student Teachers Contribute to Teaching and Learning in the Classroom? Views from some Schools in England. *Teacher Development*, 3(2), 249–61.

Moore, Rob; Arnot, Madeleine; Beck, John and Daniels, Harry (eds) (2006). *Knowledge, Power and Education Reform: Applying the Sociology of Basil Bernstein*. London: Routledge.

Pitts, Stephanie E. (2010). Musical Education as a Social Act: Learning from and within Musical Communities. In Julie Ballantyne and Brydie-Leigh Bartleet (eds), *Navigating Music and Sound Education*. Newcastle upon Tyne: Cambridge Scholars Publishing, 115–28.

Rinaldi, Carlina (2006). *In Dialogue with Reggio Emilia: Listening, Researching and Learning*. London: Routledge.

Russell-Bowie, Deirdre; Roche, Lawrence and Marsh, Herbert (1995) Wow, I Can Do Music! A Study of Self-Concept of Student Teachers in Relation to Various Subject Areas. *Australian Association for Research in Music Education (AMEL) Conference* 1995, Wollongong.

Sawyer, Keith, R. (ed.) (2011). *Structure and Improvisation in Creative Teaching*. New York: Oxford University Press.

Schippers, Huib and Cain, Melissa (2010). A Tale of Three Cities: Dreams and Realities of Cultural Diversity in Music Education. In Julie Ballantyne and Brydie-Leigh Bartleet (eds). *Navigating Music and Sound Education*. Newcastle upon Tyne: Cambridge Scholars Publishing, 161–74.

Tait, Anja; Musco, Edel; Atfield, Megan; Murrungun, Leonie; Orton, Catherine and Gray, Tony (2010). Weaving New Patterns of Music in Indigenous Education. In Julie Ballantyne and Brydie-Leigh Bartleet (eds), *Navigating Music and Sound Education*. Newcastle upon Tyne: Cambridge Scholars Publishing, 129–60.

Wenger, Etienne; McDermott, Richard and Snyder, William M. (2002). *Cultivating Communities of Practice: A Guide to Managing Knowledge*. London: McGraw-Hill.

Woods, Peter and Jeffrey, Bob (1996). *Teachable Moments: The Art of Creative Teaching in Primary Schools*. Buckingham: Open University Press.

PART I
Understandings of Knowledge

Chapter 1

Music as Knowledge in an Educational Context

Eva Georgii-Hemming

Being a music teacher involves so many kinds of knowledge … To be able to describe them, or say in words what music is … Well, isn't that one kind of knowledge? Probably the most difficult, at any rate for those of us who work with music. That's why it's so important we try. (Student music teacher Linda, in an interview, 2010)

Introduction

This chapter discusses the concept of 'knowledge', and what it may mean in the context of music education. It has often been said that we live in a *knowledge society*. Knowledge is invariably singled out as an important factor in national or regional success, and is a buzzword in the political rhetoric of education (UNESCO 2005), yet the nature of knowledge seems largely to be taken for granted and is rarely problematized. The idea that education is an important ingredient in national success has led to educational priorities that are expressed in terms of efficiency and measurability (Peters and Olsen 2005). However, people as seekers of meaning, equipped with qualities such as imagination and curiosity, are rarely visible in the education debate; neither are the questions of the content, meaning and worth of *different* kinds of knowledge, whether for individuals or for a democratic knowledge society as a whole. The way in which we use, understand and value 'knowledge' influences the education system. Therefore, reflecting upon epistemological matters is important for anyone who is involved in education.

'Knowledge' is used and understood in a variety of ways depending on where we live, what we do for a living and how we interpret our surroundings. Yet the roots of our Western perspective on knowledge can be traced back to antiquity. This chapter will discuss Aristotle's treatment of the meaning of knowledge. The starting point is that knowledge exists in different forms, and this text is constructed on the basis of Aristotle's distinctions between *episteme*, *techne* and *phronesis*.

My aim in this chapter is to facilitate discussion about what 'knowledge' means. By doing so, two objectives can be achieved. Firstly, such facilitation can help to structure and identify differences in, and relationships between, the ways in which knowledge is understood in modern society. Aristotle's distinctions are still topical and are mirrored in learning outcomes such as 'knowledge', 'understanding', 'skills' and 'attitudes'. Secondly, the discussions can give a voice to different forms of knowledge and, by doing so, these voices can be respected and valued as well as being critically observed and developed.

In order to *illustrate* how we can understand the three forms of knowledge, I use material from a study of Swedish student music teachers. The students were asked, individually, as well as a part of a focus group, to consider what *knowledge* means in the context of music education: What is the nature and what are the characteristics of different kinds of knowledge, and how do they manifest themselves in teacher education? The students' deliberations address a whole series of themes in music and art, in school and beyond – themes that are being discussed within music education, music pedagogy, music philosophy and artistic research. Some of the responses can only be touched on in this chapter. To redress at least some of the imbalance, the references in this chapter can be viewed as suggestions for further reading.

I will first explain the theoretical assumptions that underpin this chapter, before briefly presenting some information on the kind of empirical material that I have used to illustrate Aristotle's ideas about knowledge. I will then discuss these ideas in separate sections, and illustrate how they can be beneficial, either when thinking about music teacher education, or in music teaching and/or in discussions about music and 'musicking' (Small 1998) in general.

Theoretical Assumptions

The text, like the study, is grounded in a hermeneutic view of knowledge, which holds that knowledge evolves in the encounter between the familiar and the unfamiliar (Gadamer 1994), and presupposes people to be historical beings who exist in a social and cultural context. In order to understand and create meaning, we interpret the world. This is something which we do in the everyday setting in which we feel most at home – our lived world – where there are traditions, notions, and accepted ways of acting (Georgii-Hemming 2007). Whenever 'we ourselves' – our understanding and earlier experiences – encounter the Other – the unknown, others' experiences, or new ideas – there is the potential for us to change fundamentally. Yet for such an encounter to lead to new understanding, it is necessary that we change perspective. Understanding the Other also requires us to have the courage to view the ingrained or familiar with different eyes (Schuback 2006). In this way, thinking beyond what is now to what might be means that knowledge combines experience and fact with imagination (Bernstein 1983; Gustavsson 2009, pp. 91–107).

The concept of knowledge used here also differentiates between knowledge and fact or information. Information provides the building blocks that can be refashioned as knowledge, but is not identical with knowledge. Information is something we gather from outside, from the Internet or books, while knowledge is borne within people. Information can be repeated, replicated, and learned by rote. In order to utilize information and transform it into knowledge, we have to interpret, process, evaluate and understand it. In the process of transformation, information must be related to an individual's existing knowledge or experience, and be set in a meaningful context. The historian of ideas Sven-Eric Liedman has described this distinction between information and knowledge as 'the necessary detour taken by knowledge' (Liedman 2001, p. 24).

Aristotle separated knowledge into three distinct kinds: *episteme* (knowledge), or certain knowledge; *techne* (craft), or practical, creative knowledge; and *phronesis* (sense), or practical judgement. The classic definition of knowledge to be found in reference books, and as much used in philosophical debate as in everyday discussion, derives from Plato (427–347 BC). His criteria for the distinctions between true and certain knowledge (*episteme*) and subjective belief or opinion (*doxa*) are still useful. There has never been full agreement on Plato's definition of knowledge as 'justified true belief', but arriving at certain and objective knowledge is widely believed to be the chief criterion of science (Gustavsson 2000; *Stanford* n.d.). Aristotle (384–322 BC), following in Plato's wake, broadened the discussion by introducing various forms of activity, but also by speaking of the various purposes of knowledge, thus asserting that 'truth is the aim of theoretical thought as action is of practical thought' (Aristotle 1998, p. 44).

In addition to Plato's *episteme*, he wrote of *techne* and *phronesis*, two forms of action. In *techne*, action exists to produce an end result, be it a house or a piece of music. Yet it should be noted that Aristotle rarely used the word 'practical' for this type of action, since for him *praxis* in the first instance was linked with *phronesis* – with ethics and wise actions between individuals. This latter form of action is desirable in itself. Aristotle, like Plato before him, believed that scientific knowledge is objective, and that the universal is all we can have hope to have knowledge of (Nordin 2003). At the same time, he argued that knowledge is anchored in different forms of human activity and groups. Aristotelian philosophy therefore provides a framework for discussing the knowledge implicit in music education without reducing it to the level of practice versus theory; art versus craft; verbal versus tacit; and so on.

Empirical Material Used

This chapter uses empirical material taken from the study *Music, Knowledge, and Teacher Education* (Georgii-Hemming 2008, 2011). The participants in the study were fifty or so students, with women and men in equal number, all of whom were training to become specialist music teachers. The length of the current music teacher education programme varies from four and a half to five and a half years, depending on the students' chosen combination of subjects. The degree qualifies them to teach music in compulsory school and, depending on choice of specialism, to teach singing or a musical instrument; students who specialize in music, instead of combining it with courses in, for example, history or mathematics, must also qualify to teach in a Swedish upper secondary school. The data was collected over a number of years (2008–10), and consisted of discussions in groups of eight to ten participants and a number of individual interviews. Each group met for three 60–90-minute discussions a year. The group discussions were thematized according to three main areas that the participants would be able to recognize from their music teacher education, and relate to art, scholarship and pedagogical practice (see Nielsen 1998). In the discussion of each theme, we attempted to identify what characterized these themes both as *branches of knowledge* and as *phenomena*, rather than trying to judge what constituted pedagogy or music as subjects per se. Candidates for the individual interviews were selected qualitatively on the basis of gender and educational background. All the participating students were in their third, fourth or fifth years.

Conversations about the nature of knowledge, conceptualizations and values are complex and do not provide immediate or precise tools for music education practice, in the same way as, for example, teaching can. Materials from the studies are used in order to make the different knowledge forms tangible and aid reflection by the reader. The forms of knowledge are tied to different activities, but they do interact and influence each other. Furthermore, it is difficult to attach the different knowledge forms to separate parts of the music teacher education. Therefore, the following sections are not entirely similar in their design. I have instead chosen to use the examples that provide the most useful illustrations.

Episteme – Scientific Knowledge

Episteme is scientific knowledge, comprehension, or that certain knowledge of how nature, mankind and the world are constituted and function. It is a theoretical pursuit intent on the things that, in reality, humans cannot change, but about which they can most certainly obtain knowledge by studying, describing and explaining. Although Aristotle's focus was fixed on universal and unchanging knowledge, he wrote that it is within our reach if we study the everyday world around us. In the specific there are qualities that are general. In order to explain natural phenomena or things (people, animals, statues, an octave) he therefore enquires as to their purpose and 'innermost being'. For example, he writes that 'man is a sensible animal'. This does not mean that all people are sensible, but that all people are meant to be sensible. In this manner, mankind's characteristics or 'innermost being' are evident in each individual while remaining true of all people (Nordin 2003, p. 99). In other words, Aristotle included 'why' questions – seeking cause and purpose – in his science (2003, p. 99). The modern natural sciences began to emerge at the start of the seventeenth century, and scholars within this area argued that these questions were impossible to answer scientifically, and therefore focused on the problem of how Nature functioned. They sought the immutable in Nature's Laws rather than the immutable in the nature of things (Alanen 2003).

Episteme: *Student Music Teachers' Perspective*

Our modern, Western way of viewing scholarly knowledge has been evolving over a long time period. How we view science varies according to country and epistemic tradition, and within that from individual to individual (Pritchard 2010). There is a time-hallowed dividing line between the natural sciences and technology on the one hand and the humanities and social sciences on the other. The difference is sometimes said to lie in the endeavour by the natural sciences to study Nature objectively, divorced from immediate human concerns. In this view, science is all that can be expressed about the world in true–false statements, while statements of right or wrong, beautiful or ugly, fall beyond its scope. The humanities and social sciences concern themselves with the questions of human ideas and experience, and the societies in which we live. This means that we study something of which we are a part, which gives us greater compass for individual interpretations (Gustavsson 2009, pp. 53–61).

The immediate response of the students participating in the study was that science was synonymous with the natural sciences; measurable and thus true knowledge. The question was whether qualitative and interpretive research on music education can be viewed as 'real' science. Certainly, the students saw a hierarchy of values built into the division between the various disciplines, a hierarchy that is equally evident in how people rate the importance of different school subjects. Their points of view varied considerably, but one relatively common notion crystallized when scientific knowledge was linked to the issues of its function and worth. One of the students, Louise, said indignantly:

> *Of course* research on music education is science! It's really important to try to grasp how teachers think and act when it comes to things like gender issues. After all, if we're going to change society as a whole, we also have to *understand* the problems. Properly. Numbers don't have much to say to us then, even if they say something else that is also important. I suppose we're simply dealing with different types of problem?

Exactly. The criteria for scientific knowledge are founded on different disciplines and are determined by how issues are framed in each. People's health problems can be studied, for example, by biologists, medical scientists or sociologists. The difference is that the explanations operate on different levels of human life – from the genetic to the physiological to the social and societal. In other words, we can obtain scientific knowledge about identical or similar problems, but from different perspectives. The different perspectives each demand their own theories and methods (Gustavsson 2009, pp. 47–61).

To summarize: students' thoughts on the differences between, and the value of, the natural sciences and the humanities as being a 'solution' to problems relate to a long-running debate. It is more useful to describe natural sciences and humanities as two differing scientific cultures, studying different objects, rather than arguing about which is superior. In literature on the theory of science, this is sometimes explained as the difference between wanting to *explain* and wanting to *understand*. Scholars in increasing numbers, both within the natural sciences and humanities as well as in philosophy, are increasingly interested in combining these perspectives (Bernstein 1983; Ricoeur 1984; Kincheloe and McLaren 2000, pp. 285–90).

Episteme*: In Music Teacher Education and Music Teaching*

For obvious reasons, scientific knowledge in teacher education is most in evidence in the theoretical pedagogical courses. This kind of knowledge, as the students saw it, is characterized by its framing of concepts and reflections on (and by means of) theory. In the pedagogical courses, students encounter texts by the likes of Dewey (1999) and Vygotskij (2001); they are expected to discuss themes such as marking, gender and ethnic diversity in the classroom. The teaching profession is addressed in the literature both in general terms and in more specifically musical terms (see, for example, Green 1997; Whiteley 1997; Froehlich 2007; Burnard et al. 2008).

Views on the value and function of such pedagogical courses differ considerably, but the present study shows that the value and functions became clearer when students approached the end of their studies. The students also became increasingly positive towards pedagogy. With greater practice and experience of theory comes greater awareness. Pedagogical studies have an important function that all the participants singled out in their comments: they allow music teachers to discuss work with their colleagues from other subjects on similar terms and using the same terminology. There is no risk of music teachers being left out of discussions in the workplace, while the ability to discuss and act upon pedagogical research means that music, as a subject, becomes more 'intelligible' to their colleagues. With a greater understanding of music's subject matter and function, the subject's status will be raised.

The students agreed that one learns to think theoretically by both 'theoretical practice and practical theory'. Michael (one of the students) explained why, adding that the intermingling of theory and practice was also worthwhile because it can help different educational traditions to evolve:

> It's one thing to sit in groups and discuss how things ought to be, and quite another to meet students every day. … The more those worlds collide, the better. It's good for both worlds.

The experience of 'reality' underscores and increases theoretical understanding. In school, this 'collision' results in music teaching that does not rely on ideas that are taken for granted or on *unreflecting* tradition. Each individual teacher has to reflect on where the subject should lead and therefore what its subject matter should be. (Georgii-Hemming and Westvall 2010b)

Reflection is an important tool for teachers to be able to make well-founded pedagogical decisions. But it is a complex concept that can equally refer to pedagogical, philosophical or cognitive ruminations. Dewey argues that reflection is by nature always theoretical and intellectual, but that in practical situations it demands action (Dewey 1999, p. 335). He also goes into the detail of the different phases of reflection, from 'perplexity, confusion, doubt' to a decision on the best course of action (Dewey and McDermott 1973, pp. 494–506).

Reflection also has a temporal dimension, which means that it takes different turns according to the circumstances. The form of reflection the students spoke of is generally forward-looking: what are the goals, and how should teaching be structured to achieve them? The students also discussed reflection in retrospective terms: why did things turn out as they did? Yet, the students did not mention reflection in the moment, or in the classroom, when perhaps there is no opportunity to pause and think things through. Schön (1983), known for his discussion of 'the reflective practitioner', writes of 'thinking on your feet', the ability to think *while* taking action (1983, p. 54; van Manen 1991); despite the importance in the students' discussions of the nature of reflection, this kind of thinking under pressure was not something they brought up.

Episteme*: In Music in General*

Where the notion of scientific knowledge is not limited to research, but is applied more broadly to evaluation, analysis and explanation – and being equipped with the tools to do these things – the students argued that it is integral to most parts of their music education (see Nielsen 2005). Caroline (a student music teacher) said in an interview that in creating 'your own understanding' of a piece, critical reflection, analysis, and the relation of its parts to the whole are not the only important issues, but so also is a comparison of interpretations from different periods. In these intellectual processes she attempted to alternate between artistic and technical problems. The mental exertions this requires are also described by established composers, musicians, and conductors (Meyer 1979; Stålhammar 2009).

In much the same detail, the students described cognitive processes – in the sense of the processing of information – as being involved in musical problem-solving, regardless of genre and regardless of their purpose. Analysis is demanded when learning a piece; it is there when listening to music, in the process of composition and when playing music (Swanwick 1994; Burnard and Younker 2004; Clarke 2005). The students, however, questioned whether verbal, reflective knowledge could be seen as being *characteristic* of artistic knowledge.

Techne – Productive Knowledge

Techne is associated with skill, with the processes of creating, manufacturing and producing. Its distinguishing feature is proficiency – knowing the tools and materials of the trade, knowing how to proceed. But that is not always enough. To build a boat or a house, you not only have to be able to follow a design, you also have to use your judgement (Gustavsson 2000). In classical *techne*, art and technique are synonymous. Indeed, both the English and French *art*, like the Latin *ars*, are translations of the Greek *techne*.

Art and technique later went their separate ways. The division first emerged during the Renaissance, and was a fully accomplished fact by the eighteenth century, when 'aesthetics', from the Greek *aisthesis* (perception), was established as a scientific discipline (Baumgarten 1954). This was the process by which the object itself came to be viewed as art, not only the knowledge and ability to create it. This concept of art, in conjunction with factors such as the rise of the bourgeoisie, formed the basis for the emergence of an autonomous artistic field (Goehr 1994; Shiner 2001; Edström 2008; Goehr 2008).

The separation of art and technique also had much to do with the distinction drawn between theory and practice. It is in this separation that the kind of knowledge embodied by art becomes problematic. The artist does not create immediately useful products in the way that other craftsmen do, but neither can their products be tested against the theories that hold good in science. The fruits of the artist's labours are achieved with the help of tools, just like the craftsman. And just like scientific knowledge, artistic activities are dependent on ideas. Art is thus not only neither–nor, it is also both–and (Liedman 2001, pp. 83–7).

Music, the subject, is bound to music, the phenomenon and the activity. This means that the subject displays both artistic and technically skilled elements. It is central to the nature of the subject that music addresses our senses and our non-verbal knowledge. This *ars* dimension is one reason why so many people believe that music, as a subject, has more in common with art than with science. In order for us to experience music, it must first be created or recreated, and in both these forms, proficiency, the element of craft, is crucial (Nielsen 1998, p. 106). In order to best illustrate *techne*, the students' thoughts are arranged along these two dimensions; craft and art.

Techne*: Music as Artistic Knowledge*

The most central characteristic of music as a subject is its artistic nature, according to the students. To 'master' your subject means possessing, understanding and being able to communicate artistic proficiency. In order to explain what this knowledge comprises – as distinct from other subjects – there was talk of creativeness and creativity, imagination and the expression of ideas and emotions. In their music courses, the students worked a great deal with reproduction – playing, singing or leading composed music, jazz standards, and cover versions – something which they saw as an important form of 'expressing yourself', although they thought that the teachers' education could centre to a far greater degree on innovation – improvisation and composition.

At one point, one of the participants felt that the group discussion had been far too much about individual *expression*. In speaking of the shifts between expression and *impression*, this student, Markus, introduced 'intuition' and the idea of a sense of 'flow' to the discussion (Csíkszentmihályi 2008). He was at pains to stress two correlative forms of interaction: the interaction between musicians in an ensemble, and between the ensemble and the listeners. In both situations he had experienced a strong sense of being very much present and yet at the same time completely divorced from time and place. A long exchange between Markus and Peter concluded:

> **Markus**: I mean that not all we do when we improvise builds on *either* feelings …
> expressions *or* skills. You listen too … inwardly, outwardly, in between. Absorb
> … intuition. You don't just stand there and *listen* and *do it*. But you understand
> what you're going to do before you know it.
> **Peter**: Some kind of alternative thinking, you mean?

This immediate, partly instinctive, insight into the direction that music will take is seen as one dimension of artistic knowledge. Similarly, Swanwick (1994) argues that there is a dialogical relationship between intuitive and analytical knowledge, and underlines the fact that this needs to be reflected in music teaching. Liedman (2001) shares the view that people can attain profound insights without being able to give a coherent account of the exact means by which they do so. At the same time, he believes 'intuition' does more to confuse the issues than it does to shed light on them; he also points out that it has more than a hint of gender prejudice about it, and suggests that it would be better to emphasize that people are physical, sensual and social beings long before they develop their full intellectual capacities.

Equally difficult to pin down is another side to artistic knowledge and the opportunities it presents for 'alternative thinking' that emerged in the study. The students talked of how art can bring together fact with imagination, and their own particular 'aha' experiences in musical contexts. Their descriptions touched on issues that verge on the existential, and more particularly on the fresh insights and greater understanding of the identity that music offers, or as one student, Sarah, put it in an interview:

> Several times I've hit upon things when I've been playing or listening to music.
> On my own or with others. Not that I could put my finger on it, but a sense of
> something I didn't know before. And I'm not talking about music as a mood
> changer, you know [referring to DeNora's research (2000)].

A profound musical experience can be an experience of a reality that goes beyond distinct words and conscious thought. Moreover, in art there is always something that lies beyond the reach of language and other means of expression. It is for this reason that music *as* knowledge, or as a path *to* knowledge, has often been dismissed. Among those who take the opposite line, we find very different ideas about *what* we can learn (Varkøy 2001). Some write of personal development, identity and a sense of community. Others hold that artistic expression opens the way to an understanding we can otherwise only glimpse; that we not only gain self-knowledge but also challenge the way we understand ourselves and the culture that shapes us (Reimer 2003; Nielsen 2006).

The philosopher Susanne Langer differentiates between two ways of thinking, reasoning and expressing ourselves. Colloquial language and scientific idiom are the products of words and logic in which signification and thought are built up lineally. In art, one works through a problem by presenting or depicting it. It is in this way that art, too, can be a path to insight and understanding:

> What it does to us is to formulate our conceptions of feeling and our conceptions of visual, factual, and audible reality together. It gives us *forms of imagination* and *forms of feeling*, inseparably; that is to say, it clarifies and organizes intuition itself. That is why it … inspires a feeling of deep intellectual satisfaction, though it elicits no conscious intellectual work (reasoning). (Langer 1953, p. 397)

There are not necessarily any contradictions between imagination, emotion and intellect, be it in the learning process generally or in the aesthetic field more specifically, and this is something that has been discussed by cognition researchers (Gärdenfors 2010), music educationists (Swanwick 1994) and philosophers (Langer 1942, 1953; Innis 2009).

Some path to deeper understanding seems to be offered by music, albeit an elusive one, and only to varying degrees recognized by the students (DeNora and Adorno 2003; Pitts 2005; McCarthey 2007). On the other hand, there is no general agreement that musical experiences become 'stronger' if they are compounded by reflection; indeed, it has been much discussed in the literature (Swanwick 1999; Reimer 2003; Nielsen 2006). Liedman (2001) believes that art and verbal language are two kinds of knowledge that have the potential to enrich each other. The contemplation of an artistic experience offers the chance to create 'an ever richer lattice of associations', and in so doing to develop nuanced tools with which to understand cultural expressions. 'Art is a field of knowledge both for its creators and its observers' (2001, p. 75).

Techne*: Music and Music Teaching as a Craft*

It was self-evident to the students that musical knowledge, as they understood it, is about skills and different forms of craft. Music as an activity, as 'musicking' (Small 1998), can be any number of things: playing or singing; improvising, arranging, composing or interpreting music; picking out a tune or transcribing music; or listening or dancing to music. All these activities have several building-blocks that through practice – if it is carefully prepared, at any rate – can develop the individual's motor skills, performance, breathing, or composition techniques (Jørgensen and Lehmann 1997). 'It has to be drummed into your body, head and all', said Frida (one of the students).

As well as the degree of skill inherent in musical activities of various kinds, the students also spoke of teaching per se as a 'craft', a kind of practical knowledge. The participants' discussions would seem to indicate that there are two dimensions to this. Firstly, the idea that teaching is a craft means having access to an assortment of possible methods and strategies that can be used in a variety of pedagogical contexts. Teaching strategies are something learned in pedagogical courses at university, sometimes in the course of school-based, in-service teacher education (the latter being the prime time for student teachers to learn by example, gathering practical tips for lessons and trying things out for themselves). Secondly, it was in discussing strategies that the students in the study touched on the issue of 'tacit knowledge' (see Polanyi 1983) and the importance of the body. They argued that the experience of being in the classroom, interacting with students by gesture and facial expression, is an important element in teaching *as* knowledge. It is in these bodily expressions that teachers convey their feelings and attitudes. This knowledge proved hard for the students to put into words. The same seems true of their supervisors, who were said to have found it difficult to explain why they acted as they did. The problem is well known, and is described in the literature (Molander 1992; van Manen 1995).

The other meaning of teaching as practical knowledge is the ability to make a (wise) choice from different strategies, and how teachers behave in their interaction with students (see the discussion of *phronesis* below).

Phronesis – Interpersonal Knowledge

Aristotle describes *phronesis* as practical knowledge. *Phronesis* is interpersonal, and is associated with ethical, social and political life. It is a matter of attaining 'good' for both individual citizens and the common weal, and its distinguishing feature is practical judgement, or wisdom, learned by example and practice in actual situations. Its quality lies in its actions, but it is more than the assimilation and communication of traditions and customs. The ability to judge a situation and determine a meaningful way in which to proceed demands critical reflection. *Phronesis* is the acquisition of knowledge that will influence how an individual's character will develop. To any onlookers, all that can be seen of *phronesis* is action; to the individual, viewing *phronesis* from within, it is a way of being.

Among the study's findings are a vast number of perspectives on the knowledge implicit in *phronesis*, both in terms of specifically musical encounters and interpersonal encounters in general. The reflections by the students became most versatile and rich when they spoke of ethical dilemmas, good judgement and reflection related to music education. Therefore, I have illustrated the '*phronesis* knowledge' only from the perspective of actions related to music education practice.

Phronesis*: Student Music Teachers' Perspective on Music Teaching*

To be a teacher means working with actual and everyday dilemmas as well as those that are abstract and more pronouncedly ethical. Common sense and a knowledge of the law tells student teachers that there are limits to what can be put on YouTube or Facebook; how best to divide their attention between disruptive students and others is problematic, but manageable nevertheless: both are forms of professional ethics that are discussed to some extent, if not as much as they should be, in their pedagogical courses at university and in their school-based, in-service education.

One clearly ethical problem is presented by marking, partly because its various principles, moral and legal, are sometimes felt to be at odds. The Swedish marking system is criterion-based: any student who meets the nationally determined criteria for top marks – for example, by playing a musical instrument to a high standard – must be marked accordingly, regardless of whether she or he attained this level during the course or prior to it, and regardless of her or his attendance rate. A different student who has no previous knowledge and who makes great strides thanks to hard work and commitment might still only barely scrape a pass. It goes against the grain in such circumstances to apply the legally correct marks. The student teachers were well aware that their musical judgement is contingent on fundamental issues of value, whether in their view of people or of music.

What is apparent from the study is the complex connection between norms and the ability to act in a discerning and ethical manner as a teacher. The students associated ethics and norms with several conceptual elements that are dependent on one another, integrated with one another, and, to some extent, unsorted: democracy, gender, ethnicity and views on music (Carr 2000; McLaren and Kincheloe 2007).

With regard to time, *phronesis* is a thing of the moment. In order to take apposite action at the right time, the music teacher must have at his or her command a large store of pedagogical and theoretical tools as well as the necessary musical references and competences on which to draw. Yet, wise action does not only come from conclusions based on a large quantity of factual material; finding solutions to an actual dilemma also requires experience, good judgement, the ability to interpret the situation correctly and an understanding of human reactions, which, together, increase the teacher's chance of acting in an appropriate manner in a real situation. Furthermore, in order to know what will be the most fruitful course in a given situation, we must also know what we wish to achieve in the longer term (Gustavsson 2000).

Many of the students were surprised at how little their supervisors in the school-based, in-service phase of their education seem to have reflected on the reason for having music in schools (see Georgii-Hemming and Westvall 2010a, 2010b). Witness the following exchange between three third-year students:

> **Philip**: … and for many teachers the goals seem a bit blurry at the edges.
> **Victoria**: Or just completely self-evident!
> **André**: … the teachers who've been around for ages couldn't care less about the curriculum. They carry on doing what they've always done.
> **Victoria**: Exactly! You have to define the curriculum yourself. Or else, as we all know, it becomes extremely prescriptive. Just having to stick to it.

The means of avoiding 'just having to stick to' tradition or 'doing what they've always done' is to think critically. By switching perspective, a teacher can take a fresh look at the subject and see it in its broader context. As another student, David, said, 'How do the media influence the picture of music, power, and gender?' It is something to be learned by 'bouncing your ideas' off scientific theories and concepts, using your judgement and your experience.

In Victoria's remark is the kernel of the great pedagogical issue of whether one learns by imitation or through dialogue (Gustavsson 2009, pp. 79–81). Experience is a central dimension in teacher competence. In their practice teaching, student teachers learn by example and are socialized into the profession (Lave and Wenger 2005). The students in the study would have liked to add critical thought to this, since it would contribute to teacher independence and improve the actual teaching on offer, but equally they did not dismiss the value of pedagogical role models out of hand. Learning by imitation not only feels safe, it provides a platform from which to develop one's own approach. The crucial factor is the dialogue. For there to be renewal there must be dialogue; the student must dare to criticize the 'master' and the traditions she or he represents (Kvale 2000):

> I'd be the first to say, 'think for yourself and think critically'. But I've got an example. … I was only allowed to use his [teaching] material, not at all how I'd have done it. But after *every* lesson we talked it through. Not only if I'd done well. We'd talk about why he works that way, why he'd chosen that repertoire. …
> I was very critical, but that was allowed and they were great conversations. I've got to say that was my best placement. I had something to get my teeth into, trying to understand how he thought and being forced to argue my case. (Louise, group discussion)

Meanwhile, for at least some of the students, a change in perspective also had a deeper meaning: to develop the *way* they thought. An ability to see with others' eyes, to put yourself in someone else's position, to see alternative approaches, and to shed your own preconceived ideas, means there is a greater chance you will act wisely, and ensures your personal and professional development throughout a long working life.

Kant was the first to take criticism as a philosophical starting-point (Kant 2003, 2004). To think critically means to think *differently*. By using the reason with which we are equipped, we can create our own views. We do not need to slavishly follow tradition, or do as others do or say. We can think and create our own opinions. In order to do so we need inspiration and ideas beyond those in our daily lives, but we also need the courage to stand up to different kinds of authority – for Kant's contemporaries, the power of the Church and the monarchy; for the students in the present study, supervisors and teachers.

With the globalization of society, specific situations become increasingly complex. In school, teachers and students encounter a diversity of experiences, norms, values, and cultural and social backgrounds (Giddens 1991), while teachers are expected to draw on their students' experiences in their work. The variations in possible pedagogical approaches would seem to be endless. The student music teachers were keen for students to feel involved and committed, for music to be something for them. One way of achieving this is to make the most of the students' own experiences of different musical genres or activities. But this is not always sufficient. In order to educate broad-minded people with the courage to engage with others – from different ethnic or cultural backgrounds, or of a different gender, or with different musical tastes – they must expose the students to 'the unknown'. Music teaching should point the way to the cultural riches available (Swanwick 1999; Stålhammar 2006; Green 2008; Georgii-Hemming and Westvall 2010a, 2010b). To do so without sticking to a musical canon or privileging some kinds of music as 'better' than others is tricky, but ethically needful. There is also the matter of the conflict between what is wisest at present for an individual student and what is best in the long run for groups of individuals or for society as a whole. Strategies to handle this cannot only be learned by studying theory. In order to both think and act wisely, a teacher has to have teaching practice and experience of life.

If experience is central to developing good judgement and wisdom, the question is whether one can acquire it in any other way than "just getting on with life and letting experience come", as one student said (Aristotle 1967). The students unwittingly described one tool themselves. They held that experience and concepts, practice and theory, are interlinked and interdependent. Yet in order to put yourself in someone else's shoes, or to view yourself as others see you, what you need is 'imagination', a theme to which the group discussions kept returning (Nussbaum 1997; Kant 2004).

Experience is not only subjective, it is intersubjective; while sagacity can only exist in the interpersonal. For there to be a meeting of minds, we must assume that our experiences are both comparable and unique (Liedman 2001). This, I would argue, is an important idea that has much to commend it to teacher education. The sharing, describing and comparing of real experiences can enrich the perspectives and ideas of all concerned. There are also indirect, but nonetheless important, means of obtaining human experience, for the experiences of others, as expressed in literature or art, contain the 'raw material' of wisdom (Nussbaum 1997; Liedman 2001). Multiple perspectives offer the chance to take an informed position on all that is available. This also requires that we scrutinize different perspectives (not least among them the views with which we grew up or have learned along the way) with a critical eye. This can only be achieved in comparison with something else, something unfamiliar (Gustavsson 2000).

Conclusion

The sources of knowledge used in music teaching are to be found in the music 'itself', in history and literature, and in the wider social context and the media.

The world of knowledge exists in art, word, hand and body – in combination. It is impossible to teach music without a judicious mix of the three forms of knowledge: *episteme*, *techne* and *phronesis*. Music and music education are *techne*, both by virtue of their craft and their artistry. Yet they are also *episteme*, for with their intellectual cast they can be used to systematize ideas, to prompt reflection – leaving music, even where it cannot explain, as a means of exploring the world. By the same token, music and music education are *phronesis* by dint of their interpersonal character. The sheer diversity of it all makes it no easy matter to teach, but this diversity must be viewed as resource rather than a hindrance.

To view knowledge solely as a means to a definite end, a tool to serve one specific purpose, is limiting in the extreme. Knowledge takes time, and should rather be seen as a lifetime project, and not limited to education. Knowledge presupposes interest, a degree of curiosity that recognizes no bounds within or beyond the particular specialism. Any form of knowledge that includes understanding will also include imagination. Thanks to our powers of imagination, we can switch perspectives and conjure up further opportunities on which to reflect. There is then a better chance that good decisions will be taken. In this way the diversity of knowledge available to music education is an *embarras de richesse*.

Questions for Reflection

1. In what ways are dimensions of *episteme*, *techne* and *phronesis* expressed in our understanding of music, music teacher education and music education, and in what ways can they shape our understanding of these contexts?
2. How may we best understand *episteme*, *techne* and *phronesis* in relation to the practice of music teaching in a range of contexts and settings?
3. What functions can conversations about *episteme*, *techne* and *phronesis* have in music teacher education?

References

Alanen, Lilli (2003). *Descartes's Concept of Mind.* Cambridge, MA: Harvard University Press.

Aristotle (1967). *Den nikomachiska etiken* [The Nichomachean ethics], ed. Mårten Ringbom. Stockholm: Natur och kultur.

— (1998). *The Metaphysics*, trans. Hugh Lawson-Tancred. London: Penguin Books.

Baumgarten, Alexander Gottlieb (1954). *Meditationes philosophicae de nonullis ad poema pertinentibus: Reflections on poetry.* Berkeley: University of California Press.

Bernstein, Richard J. (1983). *Beyond Objectivism and Relativism: Science, Hermeneutics, and Praxis.* Oxford: Basil Blackwell.

Burnard, Pamela and Younker, Betty Anne (2004). Problem-Solving and Creativity: Insights from Students' Individual Composing Pathways. *International Journal of Music Education*, 22(1), April, 59–76.

Burnard, Pamela; Dillon, Steve; Rusniek, Gabriel and Saether, Eva (2008). Inclusive Pedagogies in Music Education: A Comparative Study of Music Teachers' Perspectives from Four Countries. *International Journal of Music Education*, 26, May, 109–126.

Carr, David (2000). *Professionalism and Ethics in Teaching.* London: Routledge.

Clarke, Eric F. (2005). *Ways of Listening: An Ecological Approach to the Perception of Musical Meaning.* New York: Oxford University Press.

Csíkszentmihályi, Mihály (2008 [1990]). *Flow: The Psychology of Optimal Experience.* Harper Perennial Modern Classics; New York: Harper Perennial.

DeNora, Tia (2000). *Music in Everyday Life.* Cambridge: Cambridge University Press.

DeNora, Tia and Adorno, Theodor W. (2003). *After Adorno: Rethinking Music Sociology.* Cambridge: Cambridge University Press.

Dewey, John (1999 [1916]). *Democracy and Education: An Introduction to the Philosophy of Education.* New York: Free Press.

Dewey, John and McDermott, John J. (1973). *The Philosophy of John Dewey*, vol. ii: *The Lived Experience.* New York: Putnam.

Edström, Olle (2008). *A Different Story: Aesthetics and the History of Western Music.* Hillsdale, NY: Pendragon Press.

Froehlich, Hildegard C. (2007). *Sociology for Music Teachers: Perspectives for Practice.* Upper Saddle River, NJ: Pearson Prentice Hall.

Gadamer, Hans-Georg (1994). *Truth and Method.* 2nd rev. edn; New York: Continuum.

Gärdenfors, Peter (2010). *Lusten att förstå. Om lärande på människans villkor* [The desire to understand. About learning on human terms]. Stockholm: Natur & Kultur.

Georgii-Hemming, Eva (2007). Hermeneutic Knowledge: Dialogue Between Experiences. *Research Studies in Music Education*, 29, December, 13–28.

— (2008). Views of Music as Theory and Practice: Understanding Music within Music Teacher Education. *Research Alliance of Institutes for Music Education*, Proceedings IV.

— (2011). *Music Education as Practical Wisdom: Student Music Teachers' Views on Phronesis.* Conference paper. The 7th International Conference for Research in Music Education, 12–16 April. Graduate School of Education, University of Exeter.

Georgii-Hemming, Eva and Westvall, Maria (2010a). Music Education: A Personal Matter? Examining the Current Discourses of Music Education in Sweden. *British Journal of Music Education*, 27(1), 21–33.

— (2010b). Teaching Music in Our Time: Student Music Teachers' Reflections on Music Education, Teacher Education and Becoming a Teacher. *Music Education Research*, 12(4), 353–67.

Giddens, Anthony (1991). *Modernity and Self-Identity: Self and Society in the Late Modern Age.* Cambridge: Polity Press.

Goehr, Lydia (1994). *The Imaginary Museum of Musical Works: An Essay in the Philosophy of Music.* Oxford: Clarendon Press.

— (2008). *Elective Affinities: Musical Essays on the History of Aesthetic Theory.* New York: Columbia University Press.

Green, Lucy (1997). *Music, Gender, Education.* Cambridge: Cambridge University Press.

— (2008). *Music, Informal Learning and the School: A New Classroom Pedagogy.* Aldershot: Ashgate.

Gustavsson, Bernt (2000). *Kunskapsfilosofi. Tre kunskapsformer i historisk belysning* [Philosophy of Knowledge. Three forms of knowledge in an historic light]. Stockholm: Wahlström & Widstrand.

— (2009). *Utbildningens förändrade villkor: nya perspektiv på kunskap, bildning och demokrati* [Education's changing conditions: new perspectives on knowledge, education and democracy]. Stockholm: Liber.

Innis, Robert E. (2009). *Susanne Langer in Focus: The Symbolic Mind.* Bloomington: Indiana University Press.

Jørgensen, Harald and Lehmann, Andreas C. (eds) (1997). *Does Practice make Perfect? Current Theory and Research on Instrumental Music Practice.* Oslo: Norges musikkhøgskole.

Kant, Immanuel (2003). *Kritik av omdömeskraften.* Stockholm: Thales; originally published as *Critik der Urtheilskraft.* Berlin and Libau: Lagarde und Friederich, 1790.

— (2004). *Kritik av det rena förnuftet.* Stockholm: Thales; originally published as *Critik der reinen Vernunft.* Riga: J. F. Hartknoch, 1781.

Kincheloe, Joe L. and McLaren, Peter (2000). Rethinking Critical Theory and Qualitative Research. In Norman K. Denzin and Yvonna S. Lincoln (eds), *Handbook of Qualitative Research.* 2nd edn, Thousand Oaks, CA: Sage, 279–313.

Kvale, Steinar (ed.) (2000). *Mästarlära: lärande som social praxis* [Master–apprentice: learning as social practice]. Lund: Studentlitteratur.

Langer, Susanne K. (1942). *Philosophy in a New Key: A Study in the Symbolism of Reason, Rite, and Art.* Cambridge, MA: Harvard University Press.

— (1953). *Feeling and Form: A Theory of Art Developed from Philosophy in a New Key.* London: Routledge & Kegan Paul.

Lave, Jean and Wenger, Etienne (2005 [1991]). *Situated Learning: Legitimate Peripheral Participation.* Cambridge: Cambridge University Press.

Liedman, Sven-Eric (2001). *Ett oändligt äventyr: om människans kunskaper* [An endless adventure: on human knowledge]. Stockholm: Bonnier.

McCarthey, Sarah J. (2007) (section ed.). Composing. In Liora Bresler (ed.), *International Handbook of Research in Arts Education.* Dordrecht: Springer, 445–562.

McLaren, Peter and Kincheloe, Joe L. (eds) (2007). *Critical Pedagogy: Where Are We Now?.* New York: Peter Lang.

van Manen, Max (1991). *The Tact of Teaching: The Meaning of Pdagogical Thoughtfulness.* London, ON: Althouse Press.

— (1995). On the Epistemology of Reflective Practice. *Teachers and Teaching: Theory and Practice*, 1(1), 33–50.

Meyer, Leonard B. (1979 [1956]). *Emotion and Meaning in Music.* Chicago: University of Chicago Press.

Molander, Bengt (1992). Tacit Knowledge and Silenced Knowledge: Fundamental Problems and Controversies. In Bo Göranzon and Magnus Florin (eds), *Skill and Education: Reflection and Experience.* New York: Springer Verlag.

Nielsen, Frede V. (1998). *Almen musikdidaktik.* 2nd edn; Copenhagen: Akademisk forlag.

— (2005). Didactology as a Field of Theory and Research in Music Education, *Philosophy of Music Education Review*, 13(1), Spring, 5–19.

— (2006). On the Relation between Music and Man. Is there a Common Basis, or Is It Altogether Individually and Socially Constructed?. In Börje Stålhammar (ed.), *Music and Human Beings: Music and Identity.* Örebro: Örebro University, 163–82.

Nordin, Svante (2003). *Filosofins historia: det västerländska förnuftets äventyr från Thales till postmodernismen* [History of philosophy]. 2nd edn; Lund: Studentlitteratur.

Nussbaum, Martha Craven (1997). *Cultivating Humanity: A Classical Defense of Reform in Liberal Education.* Cambridge, MA: Harvard University Press.

Peters, Michael A. and Olsen, Mark (2005). 'Useful Knowledge': Redefining Research and Teaching in the Learning Economy. In Ronald Barnett (ed.), *Reshaping the University: New Relations between Research, Scholarship and Teaching.* Berkshire: Open University Press, 279–291

Pitts, Stephanie (2005). *Valuing Musical Participation.* Aldershot: Ashgate.

Polanyi, Michael (1983 [1966]). *The Tacit Dimension.* Gloucester, MA: Peter Smith.

Pritchard, Duncan (2010). *What Is this Thing Called Knowledge?* 2nd edn; London: Routledge.

Reimer, Bennett (2003). *A Philosophy of Music Education: Advancing the Vision.* 3rd edn; Upper Saddle River, NJ: Prentice Hall.

Ricoeur, Paul (1984). *Time and Narrative.* Chicago: University of Chicago Press.

Schön, Donald (1983). *The Reflective Practitioner: How Professionals Think in Action.* New York: Basic Books.

Schuback, Marcia Sá Cavalcante (2006). *Lovtal till intet: essäer om filosofisk hermeneutik* [A eulogy to nothingness: essays on philosophical hermeneutics]. Gothenburg: Glänta.

Shiner, Larry (2001). *The Invention of Art: A Cultural History.* Chicago: University of Chicago Press.

Small, Christopher (1998). *Musicking: The Meanings of Performing and Listening.* Hanover, NH: University Press of New England.

Stålhammar, Börje (2006). *Musical Identities and Music Education.* Aachen: Shaker.

— (2009). *Musiken tar gestalt: professionella tonkonstnärers musikskapande* [Music takes shape: professional composers' and musicians' music-making] Stockholm: Gidlunds.

Stanford Encyclopedia of Philosophy (n.d.). Available at http://plato.stanford.edu.

Swanwick, Keith (1994). *Musical Knowledge: Intuition, Analysis and Music Education* London: Routledge.

— (1999). *Teaching Music Musically.* London: Routledge.

UNESCO (2005). *Towards Knowledge Societies.* Retrieved from www.unesco. org/publications (accessed on 27 August 2009)

Varkøy, Øivind (2001). *Musikk for alt (og alle): om musikksyn i norsk grunnskole* [Music for everything (and everyone): views on music in Norwegian schools] dissertation; Oslo: Universitetet i Oslo.

Vygotskij, Lev S. (2001). *Tänkande och språk.* Gothenburg: Daidalos.

Whiteley, Sheila (1997). *Sexing the Groove: Popular Music and Gender.* London: Routledge.

Chapter 2

Technical Rationality, *Techne* and Music Education

Øivind Varkøy

In education there will be asked for technical solutions when one no longer has anything specific to tell... (Hans Skjervheim)

Introduction

Fundamental to music teacher education is the philosophical question: what is the justification for music education? In dealing with this question we soon realize that there is a trend that music education in general schools is justified by referring to its usefulness for general education. Here are four examples from the history of ideas:

1. In his thinking concerning how good music gives knowledge and understanding of the harmonic principles of the cosmos, and how this is followed by a process of *Bildung*[1] in children and young people, Plato focuses on how music helps to build a good personal character based on the good and harmonic principles of cosmos.
2. In Christian thinking concerning the utility of music during the first centuries after Christ, as well as in the Middle Ages, and, indeed, up to this very day, music is seen, on the one hand, as a means to knowledge of the Christian faith (for example, by singing psalms in church and school); on the other hand, music's beauty is seen (for instance by St Augustine) as a way of acquiring knowledge of the Divine Beauty.
3. At the end of the eighteenth century Friedrich Schiller (like Plato) connects the knowledge of the arts in education and upbringing to the process of *Bildung*; that is, to the development of a harmonic personality. In turn, harmonic personalities will be able to create harmonic societies.
4. In the German *Jugendbewegung* at the beginning of the twentieth century, singing and playing together with people from different social backgrounds and classes is seen as a means to overcome social differences and polarities.

---

[1]   See also Lehmann-Wermser, Chapter 7.

This tendency to justify music in education by referring to the usefulness of music teaching for general educational ends has also been documented in my own research on music education in general schools in Norway (Varkøy 2001). In 1790, in the very first curriculum for schools in the kingdom of Denmark-Norway, the justification of the subject 'singing', for instance, can be summarized in one word: 'God'. Throughout the nineteenth century, nationalist ideas are the main justification for singing in schools (in addition to religious upbringing). Modern curricula justify music as a subject on the basis of a number of general educational, social, health and political advantages. In some ways, music appears to have become a 'strategy for everything' in modern Norwegian curricula, through an ever-widening perspective on the value of music and its functions in education. It is viewed as a method or a tool in a number of pedagogical approaches and as a part of bringing up children in general. The National Syllabus for Primary and Secondary Education explicitly expresses the belief that teaching music has overall pedagogical, personal and social benefits. Music can be understood as a crossover between generations; it can create understanding and tolerance for foreign cultures, and it can contribute to the creation of a positive school environment. Music activities can, through the cooperation, wellbeing, and togetherness that they engender, create a sense of belonging and identity. It is maintained that music serves as a mirror for culture and society and that musical activities contribute to the development of social communities. Music is considered to be an important element in all-round pedagogical efforts, and can in many ways be regarded as a means for achieving non-musical results (Varkøy 2001, 2002, 2007).

At the same time, Scandinavian cultural researchers claim that there has been an instrumentalization of the concept of 'culture' as well. Cultural politics is, for instance, very often justified by being linked to economic growth. Art becomes the image of the nation's innovative audacity. 'Culture' becomes a means (or an instrument) for the production of adaptability, a pawn in a game of survival in the international market; it comes across as 'a strategy for everything'. If you have a problem, be it in education, in health, in industrial or commercial life, the medicine is 'culture'. In this way there is a blending of cultural politics and health and social politics. 'Culture' is valued as an element in technocratic social planning, an integral element in the large modern project of coordination.

I see this general instrumentalization as an expression of what is often called technical rationality. In this chapter I will discuss this technical rationality – a sort of rationality from the areas of technology and economy, which undoubtedly has become an important part of our modern society's ideals of life as a whole. To understand technical rationality on a deeper level, I will, after a while, turn my attention to the term *techne*, as we know it from Aristotle, given that it is quite commonly interpreted as some sort of technical knowledge concerning the development of technical skills. I will relate my discussions of technical rationality and the term *techne* to philosophers such as Aristotle, Immanuel Kant, Martin Heidegger and Hannah Arendt.

Technical Rationality

Few areas of education have been able to avoid the influence of the technical rationality of our time; this is also true for parts of the field of music education. Three examples of this situation are: (i) when musicality is seen as a measurable object; (ii) when we find a tendency in music teaching to focus on the outer, technical layers of the musical experience; and (iii) when we find instrumental thinking (as described above) within music education (Pio and Varkøy 2012). Let us have a look at the last of these three examples: instrumental thinking within music education. Instrumentalism is the tendency to look at everything and everyone as a means to another goal. An instrumentalist never values music as an end in itself. Neither does the instrumentalist appraise human development as an end in itself. Things, such as 'subjects' and 'people' are always seen as a means; as instruments. For the instrumentalist the school's aim is the production of useful citizens. To achieve this goal the instrumentalist is always hunting for better techniques. Concepts such as 'things', 'production' and 'techniques' show that this way of thinking is derived from industrial and business life. It's an approach where pupils and students are no longer primarily people or individuals, but rather products or things.

Closely related to this way of thinking is the concept of 'management by objectives' or 'goal-oriented management'. This is a management model where the task of the management is to define the main goals, while the employees' responsibility is to concretize the objectives into practice. The philosophy of 'goal-oriented management' can be said to be based on market principles. Market principles follow from a certain 'nervousness' of the market – anxiety that the profits will not be large enough – so justifying additional effort. Transferred to education, this means an emphasis on control over the degree to which the goals can be said to have been reached – in other words, the control of 'production results'. Many researchers in music education have discussed what they see as negative consequences of 'goal-oriented management' thinking for a subject like music. One, in particular, has focused on how the emphasis on measurable goals may lead the content away from that which cannot be measured, or is difficult to measure, such as musical experience and personal expression. This might result in music teachers that operate with technocratic attitudes to both pupils, school and community, and that move towards considering teaching as a collection of techniques that will ensure the best possible achievement (Varkøy 2007, 2010). Pedagogical thinking based on 'management by objectives' or 'goal-oriented management' thinking (based on market principles) is certainly related to technical rationality.

Max Weber – and Others

When focusing on technical rationality the 'academic classic' is the German sociologist Max Weber (2011). Weber points out that the very concept of 'rationality' is an historical term that contains a world of contradictions. Human life could be 'rationalized' based on very different values and in many different directions. The point is that what from one point of view is 'rational', may, from another point of view, be seen as 'irrational'. Weber's aim is to understand the character of modern Western rationality and to explain how it has been developed. In this context, it becomes clear that the rationality from the areas of technology and economy has become an important part of modern bourgeois society's ideals of life as a whole. Weber shows how the predilection for the mathematically founded, rationalized empiricism in Protestant asceticism is an important aspect of the Puritan spirit of capitalism. This implies, for instance, that sports are valued only if they serve a rational purpose; also, there is a general distrust of cultural goods that cannot be directly connected to religious values. Weber also highlights the well-known significance of these ideas for the development of upbringing.

Among other thinkers who focus on technical rationality in different ways in our time, we, for instance, find the American historian Christopher Lasch, the Canadian philosopher Charles Taylor and the Finnish philosopher Georg Henrik von Wright. Lasch (1991) focuses on the decline and trivialization of sports, from the valuing of 'useless play' to ideas of sports as service to education, character development or social improvement. Taylor (1998) speaks of the mastery of instrumental rationality, the kind of rationality we use when we calculate the most economical application of means to reach a given goal. And von Wright (1994) asserts that the manipulative and controlling kind of rationality of which modern science is originally a result, has been in such a dominant position that other forms of human spirituality – be it artistic, moral or religious – are deported to the field of irrational beliefs or the world of uncontrolled emotions.

The concerns of von Wright, Taylor and Lasch about the dominance of technical rationality seem to be a version of the criticism of the German philosopher and musicologist Theodor W. Adorno (Adorno and Horkheimer 2004) [relating to the objectification of the subject. According to Adorno objectification is spreading to other areas of society, damaging true and genuine human relationships and products. It is only avant-garde art that represents a possible defence strategy against this process of objectification. Modernist art is tearing itself away from the objectified society by denying it, by presenting alternatives, or by making itself strange and breaking with familiar aesthetical codes. When another thinker connected to the German 'Frankfurter school', the philosopher Jürgen Habermas, discusses technical-instrumental, hermeneutic and emancipatory aspects of knowledge, his discussion is also critical of the dominance of the technical-instrumental approach (see for instance Habermas 1968a and 1968b). Technical rationality is in many ways linked to a dream of a thoroughly rationalized society, closely associated with modernity, the modern project itself. A critical discussion of technical rationality is a criticism of modernity, as is extremely evident in the discussions of the Polish sociologist Zygmunt Bauman of the Holocaust as an expression of a perverted modernity and technical rationality (Bauman 1989).

It might be appropriate to emphasize that serious criticism directed against the total mastery, excrescences and perversions of technical rationality should not be mistaken for outpourings of reactionary political ideologies. This point becomes particularly evident in the writings of Hannah Arendt.

Hannah Arendt and Hans Skjervheim

According to the German-American philosopher Hannah Arendt (1996), there is a strong tendency in modernity to think of all human activity as focusing on 'productive work', and to speak, mostly, about what we do as humans in terms of labour or work. Labour is cyclical, and has no beginning and no end. We always have to labour – for example, in order to produce food. By working we use means to achieve an end, and work has in this way both a beginning and an end, as is the case, for instance, when a carpenter produces a chair. If we relate to life only as labour and/or work, however, we forget the form of human activity which Arendt names action. This third form of *vita activa* (active life; the first two forms being labour and production), action, certainly has a beginning, but it has no clear or predictable end. Actions are social activities, things people do together with other people. Things produced by labour and work have no end in themselves; they are means. Actions are, instead, characterized by being ends in themselves.

The modern understanding of the field of the active human life, is thus, according to Arendt, reduced to focusing more and more on productive work – labour and work – thereby forgetting action, or thinking about action as if it should be labour or work. Only activities that produce a product are seen to be important. They are useful. If an activity does not give rise to a product it is deemed useless. Following this kind of logic, labour and work are useful because they produce a product. Actions are not a means to produce anything, and this makes the activities of action useless. This kind of thinking embodies an anti-humanistic tendency. It does not take into account any activity that has no end beyond itself – any activity which is free and unfettered and which therefore expresses human freedom. Modernity's tendency to deny human freedom is, according to Arendt, a cornerstone of totalitarian ideology. According to Arendt's critique of modernity, thinking of life in terms of labour and work only, produces an experience of life as an unending chain of means. One is unable to distinguish between utility and the meaning of that utility. This points towards the dilemma of meaninglessness in the modern age. Everything is useful for something else. Even activities that traditionally have had 'intrinsic value' are given instrumental functions. In contrast to this, Arendt emphasizes the value of the form of activity that has its ends in itself: practical action; social activity (Arendt 1996; Pio and Varkøy 2012).

The Norwegian philosopher Hans Skjervheim (1996) has a similar criticism of technical rationality, which he regards as tending to lose 'the meaning of the utility'. The starting point for Skjervheim's educational thinking is the conviction that the current emphasis on technical education solutions, including teaching methodological issues, is increasing because in a cultural situation of general relativism we no longer have anything specific to tell the students. The educational philosophical questions of 'what' and 'why' are not only relativized, they are marginalized or even excluded. This implies a moving away from 'what' and 'why', to 'how'. Based on a statement of this problem, Skjervheim criticizes a technical understanding of education. In this context, he focuses on Jürgen Habermas' discussion of how the 'technical problem' today may seem to replace the 'interaction problem' (communication and interaction), and how this leads to a development from a 'political society' into a 'technocratic society'. The critical point is that people often misunderstand education and teaching, regarding both as being a question of techniques or methods. What Skjervheim calls 'the instrumentalistic mistake' of educational thinking is to make technical actions into basic models for rational actions in general. Skjervheim delivers a strong critique of any tendency to consider education mainly as technical reflections concerning teaching methods. He argues that technically oriented didactic reasoning should be done away with. Didactic reflection, according to Skjervheim, should avoid looking at all education as technique and all development of knowledge as being based on technical models.

Techne

When we, in our critical thinking regarding the dominance of technical rationality, turn our attention to the ancient Greek philosopher Aristotle for discussions on different forms of knowledge – amongst them *techne* – we have to start with an examination of his discussion of the concepts of *poiesis* and *praxis*. These concepts are related to the two different forms of practical knowledge: *techne* and *phronesis*.

Aristotle: Poiesis and Praxis – and Kant: Pragmatic and Practical Actions

Poiesis is about bringing something forth. *Poiesis* means to produce and create something, such as a house. In this way *poiesis* is an activity that has an end *outside* itself. The intellectual virtue that manifests itself in *poiesis* – in the good production of something – is *techne* (in English translated to *art*, in Scandinavian languages often translated to terms meaning a kind of practical knowledge).

Praxis, in contrast to *poiesis*, is an activity of action. An activity is an action when it has the end in itself. The intellectual virtue that manifests itself in *praxis* is *phronesis* (practical wisdom).

The distinction between human activities that have their ends outside themselves (*poiesis*) and actions that have their ends in themselves (*praxis*) is central. It is not just Aristotle who makes this distinction. The German philosopher Immanuel Kant, for instance, distinguishes between *pragmatic* and *practical* actions. *Pragmatic actions*, or technical actions, are actions which have an end, and, in addition, a calculation. A pragmatic action is defined as successful, when one reaches the end that has been set. *Practical actions*, however, are actions in the social world, in human relationships. In such processes, the thought of an end set by one part is less important. It is not ends or calculations, but universally valid moral norms that function as guidelines. Successfully achieved results are not the issue here. The point is that one's actions are based on moral principles, so that everyone can base their actions on the same principles. This is the content of what is often called *the Kantian categorical imperative*. On the basis of this imperative, Kant introduced the distinction between *things* and *persons*. A central point is that it is only legitimate to act pragmatically towards things or objects, never towards persons or subjects. The categorical imperative thus sets limits for technically oriented educational thinking. It is simply morally wrong to treat persons as things, and place them as factors in our calculations (Varkøy 2003).

Aristotle and Heidegger

> All art (*techne*) is concerned with coming into being, i.e. with contriving and considering how something may come into being which is capable of either being or not being, and whose origin is in the maker and not in the thing made; for art is concerned neither with things that are, or come into being, by necessity, nor with things that do so in accordance with nature (since these have their origin in themselves) …
>
> Art (*techne*), then, as has been is a state concerned with making, involving a true course of reasoning, and lack of art (techne) on the contrary is a state concerned with making, involving a false course of reasoning; both are concerned with the variable. (Aristotle 1999, p. 94)

The Aristotelian concept of *techne* is, in English, translated to 'art', as we have seen above. In spite of this, the Greek concept *techne* is often associated with technique, not least in the context of music education. One consequence of this understanding and interpretation of *techne* as technique is that the Aristotelian concept *techne* today very often is seen as technical knowledge or is associated with technical equipment in a modern sense. This understanding of the term technique is then, in turn, closely linked to thinking about knowledge as an instrument, and talking about instrumental knowledge.

In music education, it is very easy to relate this sort of thinking and talking to the *technical skills* that are needed to play an instrument. A skilled musician truly needs *instrumental knowledge*. That gives the term *techne* a double meaning in music education. It becomes, indeed, very ambiguous.

The German philosopher Martin Heidegger, however, underlines that *techne* in fact has nothing to do with what we today think about as *technical skills*. According to him the term is to be interpreted as *a way in which to have knowledge*. To have knowledge of this kind means *to have seen* – in the wide sense of 'to see' – *a perception of being as it is*, uncovering the truth of being (Heidegger 2000).

According to Heidegger, there has often been a focus on the fact that the Greeks used the word *techne* for both craft and art, and that the Greeks talk about the craftsman and the artist using the same term: *technítes*. Regardless of how common references to the Greek use of the word *techne* for both craft and art are, Heidegger still finds that this is a superficial understanding. To him *techne* means neither craft nor art, and certainly not *the technical* in the modern sense. *Techne* has absolutely nothing to do with a practical achievement. The word *techne* rather indicates a way to have knowledge. Having (this kind of) knowledge means having seen, in the wide sense of seeing, which means to perceive *being* as it is. The Greek understanding of knowledge as expressed by *techne*, Heidegger says, is that this kind of knowledge is the bringing forth of that which is. *Techne* should never be understood as *to produce something*. When art is called *techne*, this in no way means that we are experiencing the artist as a craftsman, according to Heidegger.

This, of course, makes it very interesting to discuss *techne* in a new way related to the other forms of knowledge: *episteme* (theoretical knowledge) and *phronesis* (practical wisdom) in music education. This discussion goes to the very heart of the thinking about what it means to make or to do music – *musicking* (Small 1998): focusing on *techne* as the knowledge to uncover and reveal the truth. And that's what it is very often about, isn't it? When we, for instance, discuss a musical performance, we do not often focus on the purely technical instrumental skills, do we? We focus on the musical interpretation; the uncovering and revealing of 'the musical truth'.

In general Heidegger emphasizes how a work of art holds the potential to evoke a new sensitivity to the world and to the basic conditions of life; the value of the artwork is closely connected with its world-opening force, and its potential to realize the truth of being. According to Heidegger, works of art have 'thingly' properties but are not things of use but *works – artworks –* that cannot be used for anything. They are *things* people have made that oppose use. *Useful articles* have a tendency to disappear in their use. They withdraw themselves in their application. For instance, we do not really think about the hammer when we are hammering. Works of art, however, possess a sort of stubbornness which makes them come forward. Therefore they do not let us pass by unconcerned. When works of art appear in this way, it is not just the artwork that becomes visible to us, but the entire world that these works of art are parts of, and to which we belong. The world becomes visible to us as such. Thus, Heidegger is critical of the modern idea of the self-sufficiency of art. In his line of thinking the work of art is not related primarily to itself, but to the world. So the value of art could be said to be that it enables us to stop and reflect on our being-in-the-world. In so doing works of art help us to realize aspects of our lives that we often do not notice.

Technical Rationality – Again

Thus, on the one hand, we have seen Heidegger's critical discussion of understanding *techne* as technique. On the other hand, we find in Heidegger a critical discussion of *the fundamental technical understanding of the world* of the modern era.

According to Heidegger, the modern technical understanding of the world is a new situation, which makes the world come present itself to modern man in a very particular way. The world becomes a resource that is possible to put into a calculation. And, as is the fact with all kinds of discourses, we are wrapped up in this discourse of *technical rationality* to a degree of which we are hardly fully aware (Pio 2011). Technical rationality is *The Way* of thinking; taken for granted. We don't see that we can exist as something more than producers, consumers and resources. The human individual is more and more perceived as a technical resource, both by others and by him/herself, characterized by endless optimization and development (i.e. lifelong learning).

The Danish music educator Frederik Pio (2011) points out how technical rationality today arrives in educational thinking in terms of buzzwords such as 'evidence-based', 'new public management', 'control' and 'measurable ends'. As an illustration of the technical rationality that pervades educational thinking, we can take a look at supranational institutions such as OECD, The World Bank, UNESCO and the EU, from which a discourse has developed which largely understands education as a game with people as resources (Pio 2011). Education and people are increasingly thought of in an instrumental way. Education is becoming a technical instrument for economic growth, and the people within education are at risk of ending up as merely a means for achieving the ends of that growth.

This is, of course, a discussion which goes beyond the discussion of *techne* as technical knowledge, meaning technical skills in today's music education. This is about *a way of thinking of the world and being* in general. This kind of general philosophical discussion of trends in today's society is also, however, of great importance when it comes to music education and music teacher education. In this situation, for instance, we have to ask questions such as: How can the school subject, music, be protected in an educational culture increasingly dominated by technical rationality? From this question we have to move on to focus on the importance of understanding how, and to what extent, our technical culture affects and shapes the way in which artwork appears to us. Then the question is: what is a work of art today (Pio 2011)?

So What?

A discussion of *technical rationality* and a reflection on *techne* raises many questions of interest to music education research. Let me conclude this chapter with three more examples of such questions.

The first question can be stated as follows:

> How can a reflection on the term *techne* have implications for thinking about
> teaching music? I mean, for instance: how is it possible to think and practice

music teaching in the tension between the learning of technical skills, on the one hand, and musical expression, on the other? This is about the relationship between 'craft' and 'art', the heart of the dual nature of the term *techne*. It's about working with relations between instrumental techniques and artistic interpretations. To what extent, and how, is it possible to focus on 'musical *techne*' understood as 'uncovering of musical truth'?

The second question can be posed as follows:

How can reflection on *technical rationality* in the light of a discussion of the concept of *techne* have impacts on thinking about education as a phenomenon? This concerns reflection on the relationship between the questions of 'what', 'why' and 'how' in educational thinking and practice. Not least, it's about saving the philosophy of education from being limited to the 'how' question – education understood as developing technical skills.

The third and last question might be:

How can reflection on *technical rationality* and a discussion of the term *techne* contribute to the discourse about music and music education in both primary and secondary school, in music and culture schools, and in everyday life?

Another version of this question could be: how can music educational philosophical reflection (including both music philosophical and pedagogical philosophical perspectives, as well as general, classical philosophical questions) contribute to an understanding of music education practice, illuminating discussions about the role and function of music and music education in today's society?

Central to such reflections and discussions is the Aristotelian distinction between *poiesis* and *praxis* – which has one parallel in the Kantian distinction between *pragmatic* and *practical* actions, a second parallel in the Heideggerian discussion of *things* and *useful articles*, on the one hand, and *works* (*artworks*) on the other, and a third parallel in the distinction made by Arendt between *labour* and *work* on one hand, and *action* on the other.

I think that reflections on, and discussions of, questions like these are necessary in the development of a *context-oriented critical philosophy* concerning music and humans, society and ideas – in a music teacher education the aim of which is to contribute to the development of reflective practitioners.

Questions for Reflection

1. How can reflection on *technical rationality* impact on thinking about (music) education as a phenomenon?
2. How can reflection on the term *techne* have implications for thinking about teaching music?
3. How can music educational philosophical reflection contribute to an understanding of music education practice, illuminating discussions about the role and function of music and music education in today's society?

References

Adorno, Theodor W. and Horkheimer, Max (2004 [1944]). *The Culture Industry: Enlightenment as Mass Deception.* London: Routledge.

Arendt, Hannah (1996 [1958]). *Vita activa. Det virksomme liv* (Original German title: *Vita Activa – oder vom tätiger Leben*). Oslo: Pax Forlag.

Aristotle (1999). *Nicomachean Ethics.* Kitchener, ON: Batoche.

Bauman, Zygmunt (1989). *Modernity and the Holocaust.* Cambridge: Polity Press.

Habermas, Jürgen (1968a). *Erkenntnis und Interesse.* Frankfurt am Main: Suhrkamp.

— (1968b). Erkenntnis und Interesse. In *Technik und Wissenshaft als 'Ideologie'.* Frankfurt am Main: Suhrkamp.

Heidegger, Martin (2000 [1935/36]). *Kunstverkets opprinnelse* (Original German title: *Der Ursprung des Kunstwerkes*). Oslo: Pax Forlag.

Lasch, Christopher (1991). *The Culture of Narcissism: American Life in an Age of Diminishing Expectations.* New York: Norton.

Pio, Frederik (2011). *Hvorfor er musikfaget i undervisning og uddannelse aktuelt præget af en generel krise? Heideggers begreb 'die Technik'.* Paper presented at Nordic Network of Music Education Research. Copenhagen, 1 April 2011.

Pio, Frederik and Varkøy, Øivind (2012). A Reflection on Musical Experience as Existential Experience: An Ontological Turn. *Philosophy of Music Education Review*, 20(2), autumn.

Skjervheim, Hans (1996). *Deltakar og tilskodar.* Oslo: Idé og tanke.

Small, Christopher (1998). *Musicking: The Meanings of Performing and Listening.* Hanover, NH: University Press of New England.

Taylor, Charles (1998). *Autentisitetens etikk* [The ethics of authenticity]. Oslo: Cappelen.

Varkøy, Øivind (2001). *Musikk for alt (og alle)* [Music for everything (and everybody)]. Dissertation, Oslo: University of Oslo.

— (2002). Music – 'Useful Tool' or 'Useless Happiness'? Ideas about Music in Norwegian General Education. In Ingrid Maria Hanken, Siw Graabræk Nielsen and Monika Nerland (eds), *Research in and for Higher Music Education.* Festschrift for Harald Jørgensen. Oslo: Norges musikkhøgskole, 121–34.

— (2003). *Musikk – strategi og lykke* [Music – strategy and happiness]. Oslo: Cappelen Akademisk Forlag.

— (2007). Instrumentalism in the Field of Music Education: Are We All Humanists? In *Philosophy of Music Education Review*, 15(1), Spring, 37–52.

— (2010). The Concept of 'Bildung'. *Philosophy of Music Education Review*, 18(1), Spring 2010, 85–96.

von Wright, Georg Henrik (1994). *Myten om fremskrittet* [The myth about progress]. Oslo: Cappelen.

Weber, Max (2011 [1904/05]). *The Protestant Ethic and the Spirit of Capitalism.* New York: Oxford University Press.

Chapter 3

Knowledge and Professionalism in Music Teacher Education

Sven-Erik Holgersen and Finn Holst

Introduction

The aim of the present chapter is to discuss core aspects of knowledge and professionalism in music teacher education and teaching practice in preschool, primary and lower secondary school. The overall theoretical orientation is phenomenological; that is, knowledge in music education is appreciated from the point of view of lived experience. Implications of this view are that any involvement with music is interdependently connected with a wide range of lived experiences and aspects of embodied knowledge.[1] Furthermore, different types of knowledge are not viewed as normative and ready-made constructs; rather, they are constituted through lived practices and therefore subject to change.

After a short introduction to the *educational context* for the present chapter, the second section will briefly introduce a few *basic concepts*: namely subject knowledge, pedagogical knowledge, pedagogical content knowledge, and the (German) concept of continental 'Didaktik'. An overview of educational content in different teacher educational contexts will be presented to highlight their different emphases on these different kinds of knowledge. These concepts form the point of departure for presenting the idea of *pedagogical genres* that will frame the discussion that follows.

In the third section, results from empirical research projects will be used to inform a *comparative analysis and discussion of knowledge and professionalism*, and their implications for pedagogical genres in music teacher education and practice will be discussed.

In conclusion, it is suggested that *professionalism in music teaching* depends on the music teacher's ability to integrate different kinds of knowledge and that, although professional knowledge differs across different music pedagogical genres, a particular kind of professional knowledge is shared across them.

---

[1]   Experiential and embodied knowledge is discussed from a sociological perspective by Perkins and Triantafyllaki, Chapter 10 in this volume.

Educational Context

The educational context for the following discussion is music teacher education and teaching practice in Denmark, though, hopefully, the core concepts and problems in question have explanatory power beyond the national context. As a background for the discussion, a short introduction is given to music education in preschool, as well as primary and lower secondary school, in Denmark.

Music education in Denmark, including teacher education, takes place in different kinds of institutions characterized by more or less autonomous educational cultures:

- Teachers for preschool settings (bachelor degree 210 ECTS[2]) are trained at university colleges and have received little musical training. Preschool teachers are less specialized than school teachers.
- Music teachers in primary and lower secondary school (bachelor degree 240 ECTS) are trained at university colleges (yet not in the same departments as preschool teachers) and they have received approximately half a study year of specialization in music. Teacher education includes two or three main subjects.
- Music teachers in music schools (voluntary) are trained at conservatories (master degree 300 ECTS) as musicians and music teachers. Music teaching in preschool is often provided by teachers trained for music schools.

The present chapter is based on empirical research on these three levels of music teacher education and teaching practices. In the following section, basic concepts of knowledge and competences will be introduced and discussed in relation to teacher training programmes and teaching practice.

Concepts of Knowledge and Professionalism

According to Benner (2010) professional practice is dependent on scientific theory through education, which everyday practice is not. Professional practice lies between everyday practice and scientific practice. The three areas are seen as being coupled with different types of knowledge and constitute three areas of practice and knowledge:

---

[2]   European Credit Transfer and Accumulation System (ECTS) is a standard for comparing the study attainment and performance of students of higher education across the European Union and other collaborating European countries. For successfully completed studies, ECTS credits are awarded. One academic year corresponds to 60 ECTS-credits that are equivalent to 1500–1800 hours of study in all countries irrespective of standard or qualification type and is used to facilitate transfer and progression throughout the Union. (Retrieved from 'Wikipedia' 28. February 2012)

1. everyday practice and experience
2. professional practice and professional knowledge
3. scientific practice and scientific knowledge.

According to Benner (2010) the need for a professional practice arises when everyday practice becomes too complex to be accomplished without a scientific and professional approach. The rationale of pedagogical professionalism is different from that of pedagogical practice on the one side and scientific practice on the other. On the one hand, the professional practice cannot be justified through the profession as a legitimate occupation, but in the pedagogical practice through which it is constituted (i.e. teaching music). On the other hand, pedagogical theory is needed in professional pedagogical practice, but pedagogical practice cannot be deduced from theory alone. Theories cannot be applied directly to practice but must be considered in terms of their relevance using reflection and judgement. This is a crucial feature of professional practice and cannot be delegated to science; it also distinguishes professional practice from everyday practice.

A general critique of music teacher education programmes is that there is a gap between the knowledge provided in teacher education and the knowledge required in teaching practice. A particular problem is how to integrate different kinds of knowledge or competence. We will now go on to explain the basic concepts used in this chapter, drawing on two understandings, one based on the American curriculum-tradition and one based on the European *Didaktik*-tradition.

Didaktik concerns the goal and content of education, whereas the English term 'didactic' refers to the teaching itself – in other words, 'meant to teach', or, in teacher training, 'directing how to teach'. The German and Scandinavian concept of *Didaktik* refers to a particular pedagogic tradition, even though, like the Anglo-American concept of curriculum, it deals with teaching/learning and its written basis' (Nielsen 2007, p. 266). A particular feature of the *Didaktik* tradition, however, is that 'the teacher is expected to be able to take part in discussions about educational aim and content and to contribute to developing them' (Nielsen 2007, p. 266).

In 1987 Shulman advanced his influential concept of pedagogical content knowledge[3] (PCK), which is included in the knowledge base for teaching. The claim that teaching is a profession is based on the belief that the professional practice of teaching is based on a body of knowledge (Shulman 1987) consisting of seven categories: (1) content knowledge, (2) general pedagogical knowledge, (3) curriculum knowledge, (4) PCK, (5) knowledge of the learners and their characteristics, (6) knowledge of educational contexts and (7) knowledge of educational ends, purposes and values. Grossman (1990, p. 5) summarizes how different researchers have proposed different components and combine these in four general areas of teacher knowledge: general pedagogical knowledge, subject matter knowledge, PCK and knowledge of context.

---

[3]   Elements of Shulman's construct of pedagogical content knowledge are further addressed by Mateiro and Westvall, Chapter 9 in this volume.

PCK can be characterized as 'the blending of content and pedagogy into an understanding of how particular topics, problems, or issues are organized, represented, and adapted to the diverse interest and abilities of learners, and presented for instruction' (Shulman 1987, p. 8).

Gudmundsdottir and Shulman (1987) showed that the important difference between a novice and an expert teacher is manifested in pedagogical content knowledge. It is not only a question of combining the two different kinds of knowledge; rather, they merge into a specific pedagogical content knowledge or didactic knowledge, and this type of knowledge is indispensable to the expert teacher.

Shulman's construct of PCK forms a parallel to the understanding of the concept of didactics in the *Didaktik* tradition. According to Wolfgang Klafki (1985, p. 36), didactics, with regard to a subject, evolves in the relational field between subject-matter knowledge and pedagogical knowledge. Didactics – as we use the concept in the present chapter – deals with the questions of why, what, how and so on, and thus with the same type of knowledge as PCK.

In the following we will compare the integrated professional knowledge described in the curriculum tradition and specified in Schulman's model of pedagogical reasoning and action with that in the *Didaktik* tradition and specified in a model of teacher professional competences by E. L. Dale (1998).

Shulman elaborates on the concept of PCK with a model of pedagogical reasoning and action (Shulman 1987, p. 15), describing the central concepts in the pedagogical process in five steps:

1. comprehension
2. transformation
3. instruction
4. evaluation
5. reflection.

We will compare this model to a concept of teacher competences developed by Dale (1998). Dale argues that teachers, as professionals, must have certain types of competences. The first type of competence (Competence 1 – C1) is concerned with carrying out teaching as such. The second type of competence (C2) is concerned with the planning, organizing and evaluation of teaching and learning. The third type of competence (C3) includes justifying, legitimizing and constructing/ reconstructing teaching/learning content, and carrying out theoretical reflection and argumentation.

These central concepts in Dale's three types of competences have been transformed to a model of the pedagogical process, a didactic process model (Holst 2008), with five steps comparable to the five steps in Shulman's model:

A. reconstruction (of teaching content)
B. actualization (organization and planning)
C. realization (interaction)

    D.   evaluation and practice reflection

    E.   analysis and theoretical reflection.

In Table 3.1, Shulman's five step model and the process model (Holst) based on Dale's three levels of competence are compared:

Table 3.1   Levels of the pedagogical process

	Didactic process model	Pedagogical reasoning and action model
'why'	A: Justifying, legitimizing and constructing/reconstructing teaching/ learning content (C3)	1: Comprehension (C3)
'what'		2: Transformation: preparation (C3)
'how'	B: Actualization: organization and planning (C2)	representation, selection, adaption (C2)
	C: Realization: the interaction of teaching and learning (C1)	3: Instruction
	D: Evaluation and practice-reflection (C2)	4: Evaluation (C2)
	E: Analysis and theoretical reflection (C3)	5: Reflection (C3)

The comparison shows that the same levels and functions are represented; however, they are differently grouped. In Schulman's model of pedagogical reasoning and action the first step is comprehension, which is a 'why'-type question (C3). Transformation in Shulman's model consists of preparation, representation, selection and adaption, which concerns methodical questions ('how' questions), such as selection from an instructional repertoire (C2), and questions of content ('what'), such as development of a curricular repertoire (C3). In the didactic-process model, reconstruction is concerned with the 'why' and 'what' questions (C3) and the actualization the 'how' questions (method).

The comparison of integrated professional knowledge described in the curriculum tradition (PCK), specified in Schulman's model of pedagogical reasoning and action, with the *Didaktik* tradition, specified in a model of teacher professional competences by Dale (1998), shows that the same central concepts are used in describing the third type of professional teacher knowledge, which is distinct from and related to subject knowledge and general pedagogical knowledge.

The need for different types of knowledge in teaching practice raises the question of how these are represented in music teacher education. We will compare the emphasis on the three types of teacher knowledge in different teacher education programmes in Denmark. Table 3.2 shows the ECTS points for the three knowledge areas:[4]

---

[4]   Music teachers trained at University Colleges are trained in three main subjects. Thus, the figure does not cover the entire study programme.

- subject knowledge
- didactical knowledge (PCK)
- general pedagogical knowledge.

These are shown for three Danish music teacher education institutions:

1. Royal Danish Academy of Music (RDAM)
2. Rhythmic Music Conservatory (RMC)
3. University College, educating music teachers in primary and lower secondary school.

Table 3.2   The emphasis on various kinds of knowledge in different study programmes (ECTS points only approximately represent the actual lessons taught)

		Subject knowledge	Didactical knowledge	General pedagogical knowledge	ECTS
RDAM	General music teacher, bachelor	152	25	3	180
	General music teacher, master	75	40	5	120
	Total	227	65	8	300
	Percentage	75%	22%	3%	
RDAM	Instrumental teacher (piano), bachelor	168	9	3	180
	Instrumental teacher (piano), master	97	18	5	120
	Total	265	27	8	300
	Percentage	88%	9%	3%	
RMC	Musician, bachelor	150	30	0	180
	General music teacher, master	92	17	11	120
	Total	242	47	11	300
	Percentage	80%	16%	4%	
	Conservatories, average	245	46	9	300
	Percentage	82%	15%	3%	
UC	Public school teacher Music, small main subject	30	30	30	90
	Percentage	12.5%	12.5%	12.5%	
	Public school teacher Music, big main subject	60	35	30	125
	Percentage	25%	15%	12.5 %	
	Total of public school teacher education				240

The overall picture illustrates the following:

1. Music teacher education at conservatories puts a great deal of emphasis on subject knowledge (music specialization) (82%), an average level of emphasis on didactical knowledge and an extremely low emphasis on pedagogical knowledge (3%). Generally, didactic subjects in programmes at the conservatories are focused on teaching methods based on practice; on the one hand, this is positive because this is a way to pass on the tradition, but, on the other hand, it means that there is little time for theoretical reflection. According to the syllabus of the bachelor programme at RMC, general pedagogical knowledge is not taught at all and didactics is teaching practice based solely on subject knowledge.
2. At the university colleges, teacher education with music as a main subject puts a very high emphasis on general pedagogical knowledge (three times the average for the conservatories), and an average level on didactical knowledge, which adds up to a high level for the three main subjects together. The emphasis on music as subject knowledge is extremely low (about one-eight of the average amount at the conservatories).
3. Here we have two types of institution with a strong polarization, which appears to be increasing, although the tendency is, to a degree, a traditional one.

Music Pedagogical Genres

As institutionalized practices, music teaching practices may be characterized as music pedagogical or music didactic genres. These are related not only to the age group of students, but to a number of factors such as: culturally (in)formed subject content and pedagogical content, practical and economic conditions, and, perhaps most importantly, the teachers' educational background. Music didactic genres do not refer to the teaching of different musical genres (classic, jazz, pop, etc.), nor does the concept of genre relate to different musical forms of activity, but to different forms of the practice of teaching music. Music didactic genres can be characterized as a cooperative repertoire of teaching practices in a specialized field of teaching music. It is assumed that the borders of such genres are, to some extent, fluid, and that the genres dynamically emanate from common aims and interest in the field.

Knowledge, Professionalism and Music Pedagogical Genres

This section discusses relations between different kinds of professional knowledge and different pedagogical genres identified in various music education settings. In the first subsection we will discuss how conservatory teachers and preschool music teachers trained at conservatories value (the necessity of) different kinds of knowledge. In the second subsection we will discuss how cooperation between music teachers with different educational backgrounds in primary and lower secondary school may further professional development both at an individual level and for the pedagogical genre.

Preschool

Music teaching for preschool children in Denmark is provided by music teachers who are, for the most part, trained at conservatories. Classes are given on a weekly basis for children and staff in the nursery/kindergarten (or in another suitable environment) or for children and parents in music schools. According to governmental regulations as well as local statements, music should be taught to young children in order to further musical development and/or general development, socialization and enculturation; sometimes more specific goals are suggested. Music teaching in preschool, though, is not provided according to a specified curriculum, and no specific teaching system prevails in Danish early childhood education. Some features, however, are shared across a variety of local practices in music teaching for young children, and thus music teaching in preschool may be identified as a particular music pedagogical genre. For example, most preschool practices are reminiscent of reform pedagogy in which music teaching is closely connected with a tradition which includes bodily activity. Trained music teachers have at their disposal a rich repertoire of songs[5] as well as children's own creativity (Holgersen 1997, 2008). Music teaching for kindergartens involves cooperation between preschool teachers with a general pedagogical education and music teachers trained at conservatories.

The following discussion is based on an investigation of music teacher education and teaching practice focusing on preschool, including: a) an analysis of study programmes in music teacher training at Danish conservatories; b) a survey of music teachers at conservatories (hereafter called educators) (n=58 educators); and c) a survey of music teachers trained at conservatories (n=36 teachers) and having at least two years of teaching experience (Holgersen 2010). One of the main questions for the investigation was: how do teachers and educators, as professionals, value different kinds of musical and pedagogical knowledge in music teacher education and teaching practice, respectively? Other questions tried to establish teachers' and educators' views on which kinds of knowledge are required for professional development.

Even though conservatories are, first of all, art-based educational institutions, music teacher training includes different areas of basic knowledge that may receive more or less attention or emphasis: music as an art form, musicology, music as craftsmanship, and music pedagogy as theoretical as well as practical

---

[5]   In addition to folk songs, Denmark has a rich tradition of songs including classical, popular and jazz music written by leading poets and composers through the last two or three centuries. Many of these songs have been written specifically for children.

knowledge. In order to compare the views of educators and teachers they were asked how much emphasis music teacher training should give to these basic areas of knowledge (Figure 3.1).

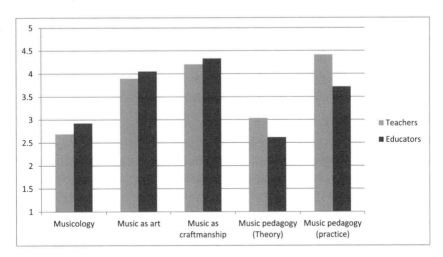

Figure 3.1   Responses to the question 'How much emphasis should music teacher training programmes give to the five areas of knowledge?' (Average values of ratings 1 to 5)

According to the responses, music teachers and educators have similar opinions about the emphasis that should be given to different areas of knowledge (Table 3.2). Music teachers, though, tend to appreciate music pedagogy – theory as well as practice – more than educators do, whereas music educators tend to appreciate music as craftsmanship, art and musicology more than teachers do. Music teachers think that most emphasis should be given to music pedagogy as practical knowledge, while educators have craftsmanship as their first priority and music pedagogy (practice) as their third. A relatively high emphasis on pedagogy as practice and a medium emphasis on pedagogy as theory are shared by teachers and educators, though educators give music pedagogy (theory) the lowest priority of all. As an educator commented:

> Pedagogy as a theoretical subject can hardly justify its relevance for the students. Connecting more closely to practical disciplines and to the main subject, it would be possible to motivate students to engage more deeply in pedagogy.

Study programmes (Table 3.2) include very little general pedagogical knowledge and a medium amount of didactical knowledge, but these concepts are not clearly defined in the programme descriptions. Responses in the two surveys, however, suggest that, from an insider perspective, pedagogical subjects include:

pedagogy (teaching method), pedagogical practice connected to the main subject (instrument), ensemble and choir instruction, arrangement of music (for teaching purposes), teaching groups of small children, and piano training for the purpose of choir instruction or demonstration. Some teachers also include ear training and other supporting disciplines.

Generally, practical knowledge is appreciated more than theoretical, and subject knowledge (music) is appreciated more than pedagogical knowledge. Considerations about subject didactics / didactical knowledge, on the other hand, tend to be ignored at the conservatories, because (educator's statement):

> Students must learn to play and understand music before they can pass it on. If they understand the music and the students they are facing, everything becomes much easier – theory or not.

In a practice-based educational culture it is a prevailing belief that years of experience as a musician and teacher proves its own infallibility, as many teachers at conservatories would say. Yet, experience is not a proof, not even an indicator of what actually works. Using inferential strategies in learning from experience reduces teaching to sheer behaviourism. On the other hand, generalized and theoretically based knowledge about learning is no more reliable, since it may not work in practice (Kvernbekk 1999; Jank and Meyer 2002, pp. 148–9). Nevertheless, the authority of firsthand experience tends to dominate pedagogical decision-making in music education and teaching practices. Furthermore, this tendency is self-affirming because, once a certain view has been established within an institution or educational culture, insiders tend to persistently maintain their view in the face of scientific knowledge (Kvernbekk 2003, pp. 182–5).

What teachers need is, therefore, reflective knowledge building on both experience and scientific knowledge as indicated above in the definition of pedagogical professionalism (Benner 2010).

Teachers' and Educators' Notions of Professionalism in Music Education

In order to establish teachers' and educators' personal beliefs about what constitutes pedagogical professionalism they were asked to respond to a number of propositions (Figure 3.2). Teachers and educators value most the ability to make students express themselves musically, which is obviously in line with their identities being closely connected to professional musicianship. On the other hand, it would have confirmed the general perception of the artistic conservatory culture if the teachers' ability to express themselves in musically adequate ways (2) had received most emphasis.

A distinctive, but maybe not very surprising, result is (9) that teachers and educators think that knowledge about teaching plans and curriculum regulations is not particularly relevant. The most obvious difference in their views is that teachers, considerably more than educators, tend to appreciate (general) pedagogical

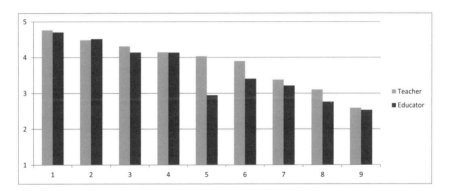

Note: The numbers given in the questions below link to the numbers in the figure.

1. The teacher is able to make students express themselves musically.
2. The teacher is able to express herself in musically adequate ways.
3. The teacher is able to make students express themselves (generally).
4. The teacher masters the disciplines of music as a subject matter.
5. The teacher can motivate, justify and reflect on her own and other teaching practice using music pedagogical theories and concepts.
6. The teacher can conduct and participate in pedagogical development.
7. The teacher can motivate, justify and reflect on her own and other teaching practice using theories and concepts about music as a subject matter.
8. The teacher can develop new theory about teaching music.
9. The teacher can motivate, justify and reflect on her own and other teaching practice using her knowledge about current teaching plans and curriculum regulations related to her teaching institution.

Figure 3.2   Responses to the question 'Which criteria should form the basis for the evaluation of professionalism of music teachers trained at a music conservatory?' (Average values of ratings 1 to 5)

knowledge, namely the ability 'to motivate, justify and reflect on her own and other teaching practice using music pedagogical theories and concepts' (5). Teachers also find it more important than educators that they 'can conduct and participate in pedagogical development' (6). This is a particular requirement for teachers in music schools, because they very often engage in pedagogical development across disciplines and institutional contexts such as music school, preschool, primary/ secondary school and other settings. (See also the following subsection.)

Surprisingly, subject knowledge (7) is relatively little appreciated. Since this is the kind of knowledge that is spoken and enacted in every teaching lesson, one could expect this to be highly rated. The explanation may be that the question emphasizes theory more than practice, and the most persistent attitude in both surveys is resistance to theoretical knowledge.

However, looking into the comments in the two surveys adds important nuances to teachers' and educators' view of pedagogical professionalism. Quite a few music teachers ask for more emphasis on didactical and pedagogical knowledge in music teacher education, because they have realized that they need it in teaching practice.

> My teacher education was not sufficient in this respect. This leads to lack of ability to reflect on your own and other's practice and to lack of development in music education. (Teacher's statement)

Many teachers face challenges in teaching practice which call for knowledge they have to develop through their practice. Sometimes they succeed: for example, through their cooperation with other music teachers or preschool teachers. But some problems simply call for theoretical knowledge which they do not have. This is the point in the following two teacher statements:

> Very often theory and music pedagogy can be an integrated part of musical practice in education.
> It is important that the theory and pedagogy is consciously reflected in musical practice, so that student teachers will recognize the connections. Considerations about planning, realization and evaluation of teaching should always be integrated.

This particular issue was addressed similarly in some of the comments from educators.

> I think it is important to work with pedagogical theory in order to inspire teacher students to more general considerations on pedagogical practice. But important, too, that supervisors can relate to pedagogical theory in their work with teacher students.

Differences between music teacher education based on artistic and practical knowledge, on the one hand, and on scientific and theoretical knowledge on the other, may be explained as characteristics of two different music pedagogical genres. For example, these two different genres may be recognized in music schools where preschool music teachers and instrumental teachers meet very different challenges and the conditions for teaching are very different. Preschool teachers have to deal with many participants in the classes, whereas instrumental teaching is most often a one-to-one relationship. It is a specific requirement for preschool music teachers to develop their practice, because their teacher training included very little teaching practice with children, and they realize that practical knowledge alone is insufficient to 'survive' a life as a preschool music teacher. In comparison, many instrumental teachers may teach in much the same way as they were taught at the conservatory, and their need for theoretical knowledge is less obvious. Furthermore, preschool music teaching is very often legitimated and appreciated in different ways by preschool teachers (concerned with children's musical and general development) and instrumental teachers (who may be more concerned with specific subject knowledge that can prepare children for instrumental teaching).

In summary, pedagogical knowledge in teacher education programmes at conservatories is almost entirely based on practice and experience. Generally, teachers and educators appreciate practical knowledge more than theoretical, and this is particularly evident with regard to pedagogical knowledge. However, music teachers often face challenges in their teaching practice – challenges which call for knowledge they did not acquire through their education and which they have to develop through their practice. *Experienced teachers ask for more emphasis on didactical and pedagogical knowledge* in music teacher education, because they have realized that practical knowledge alone is insufficient for them to 'survive' a life as a preschool music teacher.

Two Design Experiments in Primary School and Music School

Two parallel design experiments with special reference to music teacher education were carried out as continued professional development (CPD) projects. One project was carried out in two primary schools (music as obligatory subject) by primary school music teachers trained at university colleges (Holst 2011a). The other project was carried out in two music schools (voluntary) by music school teachers trained at conservatories (Holst 2011b). In both projects the music teachers carried out parallel lessons and subsequently shared their experiences around a common theme. The projects have much in common with cooperative action research in the Bath tradition (Reason and Bradbury 2001); however, the frame settings, as an intended part of the research, rather point towards a design experiment (Cobb et al. 2003). From the perspective of the participating teachers the projects were directed at challenges in the teaching/learning processes. In the primary school project, the teachers were concerned with teaching and learning processes, working with a theme in a classroom setting. In the music school project, the teachers were concerned with relations between teaching and learning processes in individual instrumental teaching. From the perspective of research the projects were directed at investigating processes in CPD and the comparative analysis of different types of professional knowledge applied by the teachers. For the comparative analysis a concept of genres of teaching music was developed in a didactic frame of understanding.

The institutional frames and the educational background of the teachers in the two projects were different:

- Primary school and lower secondary school are integrated in Denmark; music is a compulsory subject in grades 1 through 6 and is organized in a classroom setting with 20 to 25 pupils, and one to two weekly lessons of 45 minutes each. In the project reported here, there are two weekly lessons. The teacher is educated in, and teaches, several subjects, and the educational background is markedly different from that of the music school teacher.

- Music schools have a main focus on instrumental teaching, organized as one-to-one lessons of 20 to 25 minutes. Teachers have a conservatory education and the teachers in the project are trained as instrumentalists with teaching competences.
- The educational background and institutional settings of both projects can best be described as polarized. In a previous project, where the two types of music teachers worked together in an extended primary school music programme, an investigation of the teacher profiles showed a polarization to the degree that the areas of competence in which the one teacher profile had its strengths were the weaknesses of the other and vice versa (Holst 2008). This polarization can be observed at an institutional level in schools and music schools and in teacher education, and is related to a divide between the departments of education and culture. The institutional polarization is made up of a strong relation to the field of musical performance with a weak relation to the field of general education, on one hand, and a strong relation to the field of general education with a weak relation to the field of musical performance, on the other (Figure 3.3).

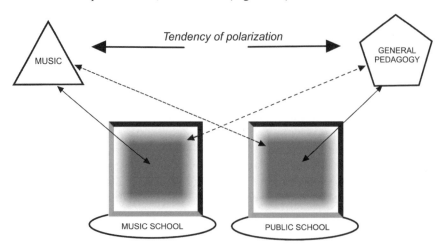

Figure 3.3   Institutional polarization

In the institutional frame of the music school the relation to the field of musical performance is dominant. In the institutional frame of the public school the relation to the field of general education is dominant.

According to Gudmundsdottir and Shulman (1987), the tendency to polarization does not support expert teaching. A blending of content and pedagogy necessary for expert-level teaching will be inhibited by either a low level of pedagogical competence or a low level of musical competence.

Both Shulman's concept of PCK and Klafki's understanding of didactics rest on the integration of subject matter and pedagogy. In the case of teaching music in public school and in music school, respectively, subject matter and pedagogy are seen from different positions with different perspectives, and different aspects are relevant. The instrumental competences of a cello teacher are different from those of a music teacher in primary school focusing on general music. Pedagogical theory relevant for teaching music to small children could well include knowledge about small children's cognitive and motoric development, yet this knowledge may not be relevant for instrumental teaching on an intermediate or advanced level.

According to Benner (2010) professional practice depends on scientific theory acquired through education, which everyday practice does not. Dale's (1998) differentiation of levels of professional competence (C1, C2 and C3) is central to an understanding of different types of pedagogical reasoning and action. It is a major point that theory is involved in C3. The three levels of competence can be analysed as levels of both action and reasoning (Holst 2011c), namely of interaction and situated knowledge (C1), reflection and methodical knowledge (C2), and theoretical practice and theoretical knowledge (C3). The relation between the levels may be described as both bottom-up (based on experience) and top-down (based on research), and on the third level this means that practical theory is constructed and scientific theory applied.

While following the projects in music school and in public school it has been possible to analyse which types of pedagogical practice and reasoning have been applied by the teachers. This has been investigated through video observation and interviews. The analysis of questions posed by teachers in the exchange and discussion of teaching experiences is of special interest, because it clearly shows how teachers use different types of concepts and reasoning.

In the music school project, more than thirty different didactical topics were identified as the teachers shared their experiences in dialogues and written descriptions. The majority of these topics were formulated in procedural terms based on methodical reflection. Some examples of the topics may illustrate this: how to include visual learning, how to have students working together, how to have students teach each other, listen-sing-play-notate, how to combine instrumental teaching with the use of notation programmes, and how to use creative processes as motivation. In the discussion between the teachers these topics were not related to more general categories or to theory. The practices and the building of a repertoire of procedures were of great value for the teachers in the project, and a subsequent analysis was able to categorize the many topics into four didactic themes linking to relevant theory. These didactic themes were:

- didactic design and modality
- improvisational and creative processes
- didactic scaffolding
- areas of teaching content.

A lot of valuable experience was gathered as experiments were carried out, but the teachers mainly conceptualized and reflected on a C2 level (methodical reflection) tending to regard it as personal experience. In the subsequent analytical phase of the project, the didactic theoretical aspects of the project were elaborated on the level of research. This provided a basis for implementing a future phase of the project in which theoretical considerations will be applied to establish teacher comprehension, including theory of particular relevance for the practice in question.

In the public school project, the sharing of experiences and knowledge was of great value for expanding the teaching repertoire, and a number of didactic themes were raised as the teachers presented and discussed their projects. The didactic themes were:

- the relation between different types of learning processes in the music classroom
- potential for applying different modalities (the multi-modality classroom)
- the relation between different forms of musical content especially technical skills and improvisational skills
- didactic scaffolding and musical resources in improvisational and creative processes.

These questions were discussed in relation to theories about didactic design and modality, didactic scaffolding and learning-processes, convergent and divergent processes and types of content in music. The teachers were evidently acting and reflecting at the C3 level.

It is interesting that the didactic themes in the two projects, to a large extent, overlap, and thus refer to the same complex of didactic theories. Despite the different perspectives of music school instrumental teaching and public school music teaching the didactic questions appear to be common to both, and thus shared across the music pedagogical genres. The difference between the two projects is that, in the public school project, the relation to theory was established through reflective practice relating to theory (competence level C3), whereas reflective practice in the music school project, which can be characterized as methodical reflection, was insufficient for establishing the relation to theory. The different ways in which music teachers in public school and music school conceptualize didactical problems concern the relation between didactic practice and didactic theory. This leads to an elaboration of the concept of didactics (*Didaktik*).

Nielsen (2005) has introduced the term didactology (*didaktologi*) to clarify different functions of didactics: The meaning of didactics (*Didaktik*) is normative and prescriptive and the approach is characterized by participation, nearness and involvement. The meaning of didactology is descriptive, analytical and non-normative, and the approach is characterized by having an analysing and inquiring distance. Despite the fact that didactics is oriented towards practice and didactology towards theory, Nielsen (2005) emphasizes that didactology, too, is directed towards practice, this being the object of the theoretical practice of didactology. In this way the theory and practice of a teaching subject (the subject of teaching music) can be seen as, at the same time, different *and* interdependent.

Nielsen's distinction also clarifies didactology as a particular area of research and theory. In the design experiment described above the theory in demand is precisely this type of theory – a type of theory developed with the (music) didactic practice in mind which subsequently is brought to use in the practical field.

This type of theory is different from a subject matter theory (theory about music, musicology) and a general pedagogical theory resting on psychology, philosophy, sociology and anthropology (and possibly more). In considering the theory–practice relationship there are thus three areas of practice knowledge and three areas of theoretical knowledge to be considered. This leads to a crucial point: music teaching does not only draw on theory borrowed from other areas. The professional practice of teaching music includes three theoretical fields: the field defined by the subject (music), the field defined by general pedagogy (theory) and the field of theoretical didatics (didactology). The professional practice of teaching music draws on the fields of music and general pedagogy, but apart from this it has its own practical and theoretical field and does not have to borrow its identity from the adjacent fields as part of a threefold theoretical base.

The comparative analysis of the parallel design experiments contribute to the understanding of this threefold knowledge base. The interesting point is the degree of coincidence of the relevant didactic theory in the two projects. In both projects there was an explicit interest in working with central aspects of music such as expression, improvisation and composition. In the two distinctly different music pedagogical genres of the two projects, the relevant subject knowledge and the general pedagogical knowledge were distinctly different, whereas the didactical themes and the theoretical base had much in common. The interesting point, which was unforeseen and turned up as somewhat of a surprise in the analysis of the comparative aspects of the projects, is that the variation of relevance and the autonomy of each music pedagogical genre seems to hold for only two of the three areas (Figure 3.4).

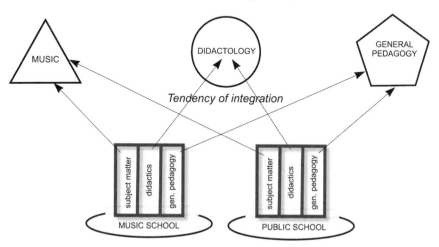

Figure 3.4   Didactical integration

The theoretical reference of music didactics – the didactology of music – appears to mainly be the same or at least have less variance across different music pedagogical genres. This could be described as an integrative tendency as opposed to the tendency of polarization.

In summary the comparative analysis leads to following main points:

1. It was possible for teachers to establish the relation between practice and theory.
2. Knowledge of relevant theory is needed to establish the relation.
3. The relevant subject knowledge and general pedagogical knowledge in the two different music pedagogical genres was distinctly different, whereas most of the relevant didactic theory was shared in common between the genres, thus representing an integrative tendency.

Summary and Conclusion

The aim of this chapter was to discuss what kinds of knowledge are required in professional practices of music teaching in preschool, primary school and music school settings.

A general point of departure for this chapter was the definition of pedagogical professionalism by Benner (2010) stating that professional practice is not legitimated in the profession as such, but in the practice through which it is constituted (i.e. teaching music). On the one hand, pedagogical theory is needed in professional pedagogical practice. On the other hand, theories cannot be applied directly to practice; rather, through reflection and judgement, theories must be considered with respect to their relevance.

In a continuation of Benner's notion of professionalism, basic concepts used in this chapter were explained by drawing on two understandings, one based on the American curriculum tradition and the other based on the European *Didaktik* tradition. The general idea was that teaching is based on a body of knowledge (Shulman 1987) consisting of seven categories.

Grossman (1990, p. 5) summarized components from different researchers and combined these into four general areas of teacher knowledge: general pedagogical knowledge, subject matter knowledge, pedagogical content knowledge (PCK) and knowledge of context.

The integrated professional knowledge described in the curriculum tradition (PCK), specified in Schulman's model of pedagogical reasoning and action, and in the *Didaktik* tradition, specified in a model of teacher professional competences by Dale (1998), were compared. The analysis demonstrates that the same central concepts are used, describing didactical knowledge as a third type of professional teacher knowledge distinct from, and related to, subject knowledge and general pedagogical knowledge.

A frequent criticism of music teacher education programmes is that there is a gap between knowledge provided in teacher education and knowledge required in teaching practice. The need for different types of knowledge in teaching practice raises the question of how these are represented in music teacher education. In order to shed light on this, study programmes from different music teacher educational systems were analysed; these showed a strong polarization between music conservatories and teacher training colleges. The analysis showed that pedagogical knowledge in teacher education programmes at conservatories is almost entirely based on practice and experience, whereas public school teachers with music as one main subject receive considerable training in pedagogy and didactics based on theory.

The concept of music pedagogical genres was suggested as a frame for discussing how different kinds of knowledge are related to institutionalized music teaching practices. Empirical data from different projects were discussed, one project related to preschool music education, and a double design experiment comparing music teaching in public school and music school.

In the preschool project, teachers and educators in the conservatory culture appreciated practical knowledge more than theoretical, and this was particularly evident with regard to pedagogical knowledge. However, music teachers often face challenges in their teaching practice, which call for knowledge they did not acquire through their education and which they have to develop through their practice. Many experienced teachers, therefore, ask for more emphasis on didactical and pedagogical knowledge in music teacher education, because they have realized that practical knowledge alone is insufficient for them to 'survive' a life as a preschool music teacher.

In the double design-experiment a polarization of pedagogical knowledge can be observed at an institutional level in schools and music schools and in teacher education at teacher training colleges and conservatories, respectively. The interesting point, which was unforeseen and turned up as somewhat of a surprise in the analysis of the comparative aspects of the projects, is that the variation of relevance and the autonomy of each music pedagogical genre seems to be true for only two of the three areas. The theoretical reference of music didactics – the didactology of music – appears to be mainly the same, or at least have less variance across different music pedagogical genres. This could be described as an integrative tendency as opposed to the tendency to polarization.

In the design experiments, a theory–practice relation was established between the actual practice and relevant theory in the one project, but not in the other. The difference was that, in the public school project, the reflective practice of the teachers related to didactic theory (didactology), whereas in the music school project the reflective practice related to methodical questions (didactics).

It is suggested that *professionalism in music teaching* depends on the music teacher's ability to integrate different kinds of knowledge and that, although professional knowledge differs across different music pedagogical genres, a particular kind of professional knowledge is shared across them.

In conclusion, it has been demonstrated that music pedagogical theory is needed in professional teaching practice, though it cannot be transmitted directly to practice; rather, through reflection and judgement, theories must be considered with respect to their relevance for practice.

Questions for Reflection

1. Referring to concepts in this chapter, how would you describe pedagogy as a subject in your music teacher education?
2 In your (education for) professional practice, to what extent do you draw on knowledge from the three different areas discussed in this chapter: subject matter, didactology, and general pedagogy? Can you give examples of each of the three categories?
3. Do you recognize your own education or practice as a particular music pedagogical genre? What are the characteristics of this genre?

References

Benner, Dietrich (2010). *Allgemeine Pädagogik*. Weinheim: Juventa.

Cobb, Paul; Confrey, Jere; diSessa, Andrea; Lehrer, Richard; and Schauble, Leona (2003). Design Experiments in Educational Research. *Educational Researcher*, 32 (1), 9–13.

Dale, Erling Lars (1998). *Pædagogik og professionalitet*. Aarhus: Klim.

Grossman, Pamela L. (1990). *The Making of a Teacher: Teacher Knowledge and Teacher Education*. New York: Teachers College Press, Columbia University.

Gudmundsdottir, Sigrun and Shulman, Lee (1987). Pedagogical Content Knowledge in Social Studies. *Journal of Educational Research*, 31, 59–70.

Holgersen, Sven-Erik (1997). Aims and Methods in Danish Preschool Music Education. In Bresler, Liora (ed.), *Arts Education Policy Review*. Washington, DC: Heldref Publications.

— (2008). Music Education for Young Children in Scandinavia: Policy, Philosophy or Whishful Thinking? In Lori Custodero and Lili Chen Hafteck (eds), *Arts Education Policy Review*, 109(3). Washington, DC: Heldref Publications.

— (2010). Appreciating Different Aspects of Professional Knowledge in Music Education. In Sven-Erik Holgersen and Frede V. Nielsen (eds) (2010). *RAIME Proceedings of the Tenth International Symposium*. Research Studies in Music Education Vol. 3. Research Unit Music Education, Department of Curriculum Research, The Danish School of Education, Aarhus University.

Holst, Finn (2008). *Ekstern evaluering af projektet: Musik til Alle – et samarbejdsprojekt mellem folkeskole og musikskole i Horsens Kommune*. Copenhagen: Musikpædagogiske Studier – DPU. Bind 1. Institut for Didaktik, DPU.

— (2009). Musiklærerkompetencer i et relationsfelt mellem pædagogik og fag. In Frede V. Nielsen, Sven-Erik Holgersen and Siw G. Nielsen (eds), *Nordic Research in Music Education Yearbook*. Oslo: Norwegian Academy of Music, Vol. 11, 237–54.

— (2011a). *Klasserumsstudier. Udvikling af professionskundskab i musik og billedkunst I folkeskolen*. Faglig Enhed Musikpædagogik, Forskningsprogrammet i fagdidaktik. København: Institut for Uddannelse og Pædagogik (DPU).

— (2011b). *Læringsrum. Et udviklingsprojekt i musikskolen*. Faglig Enhed Musikpædagogik, Forskningsprogrammet i fagdidaktik. København: Institut for Uddannelse og Pædagogik (DPU).

— (2011c). Musiklærerkompetence mellem teori og praksis. In S.-E. Holgersen and S.G. Nielsen (eds), *Nordic Research in Music Education Yearbook*. Oslo: Norwegian Academy of Music, Vol. 12.

Jank, Werner and Meyer, Hilbert (2002). *Didaktische Modelle*. Berlin: Cornelsen Scriptor.

Klafki, Wolfgang (1985). *Neue Studien zur Bildungstheorie und Didaktik. Beiträge zur kritisch-konstruktiven Didaktik*. Winheim and Basel: Beltz.

Kvernbekk, Tone (1999). Knowledge that Works In Practice [1]. *Scandinavian Journal of Educational Research*, 43(2), 111–30.

— (2003). *Pædagogik og lærerprofessionalitet*. Aarhus: Forlaget Klim.

Nielsen, Frede V. (2005). Didactology as a Field of Theory and Research in Music Education. *Philosophy of Music Education Review*, 13(1), 5–19.

— (2007). Music (and Arts) Education from the Point of View of *Didaktik* and *Bildung*. In Liora Bresler (ed.), *International Handbook of Research in Arts Education*. Dordrecht: Springer, 265–6.

Reason, Peter and Bradbury, Hilary (2001). *Handbook of Action Research*. London: Sage.

Shulman, Lee (1987). Knowledge and Teaching: Foundations of the New Reform. *Harvard Educational Review*, 57(1), 1–22.

Chapter 4
Artistic Knowledge in Practice

Jonathan Stephens

Being an artist means: not numbering and counting, but ripening like a tree, which doesn't force its sap, and stands confidently in the storms of spring, not afraid that afterward summer may not come. (Rilke 1903, p. 24)

Artistic Knowledge

In this chapter, 'artistic knowledge' will be considered primarily in relation to music, and applied to educational and professional identities of the musician (composer, performer) and music educator (teacher, lecturer). 'Artistic' can refer to a person, an object or a disposition; to the identities of the arts and their professional application. 'Knowledge' incorporates such aspects as scholarship, understanding, acquaintance and skill; it is more than the acquisition of factual information. Through considering a range of perspectives on music and education, an emerging practical model of artistic knowledge will be applied to musical and professional contexts. Twenty-first-century society places a high premium on scientific and technical knowledge. Whilst not denying the importance of such knowledge, or advocating an artificial division between different forms of knowledge, this chapter considers alternative ways of knowing that may be more appropriate for musicians and music educators.

Early in the twentieth century, Jaensch (1930, pp. 43–4) recognized a close relationship between human, artistic and scientific identities that is pertinent to our consideration of artistic knowledge:

the closest parallel to the structure of personality of the child is not the mental structure of the logician, but that of the artist ... Productive logical thinking, even in the most exact sciences, is far more closely related to the type of mind of the artist and the child than the ideal of the logician would lead us to suppose. That is shown in the loving attention to the matter in hand, in that close union of object and subject in children and artists, of which eidetic phenomena are merely a particularly evident expression.

During the process of formal education, the categorization of subjects into arts and sciences, core and secondary, may miss the potential of exploring the way human, artistic and scientific identities are related. The imaginative world of the child is close to that of the artist; sadly, for many, that world is diminished through an education process that considers the arts to be primarily for entertainment, a diversion from the serious business of preparation for life. In recent years, the field of music education research has been enriched by studies of musical and professional identity (Roberts 1991; Stephens 1995; Cooper and Olson 1996; Dolloff 1999, 2007; Beijaard, Meijer and Verloop 2004) and a growing interest in narrative research (Fulwiler 1997; Hinchman and Hinchman 1997; Winkler 2003; Chase 2005; Andrews, Squire and Tambokou 2008), which have opened up new ways of thinking and understanding for musicians and music educators. Such approaches recognize that imagination, life stories, literature and the arts offer ways of knowing that can be meaningful and valuable for individuals and communities; that science and technology are two amongst many ways of perceiving and knowing our world. Carl Rogers' theory of the 'self' and its application to student-based learning (Rogers 1951) underlined the importance of experience in the development of knowledge, understanding and skill – initially from a therapeutic rather than educational perspective. Abraham Maslow (1962) identified a pyramid, or 'hierarchy', of needs to represent stages of human development, from basic physiological requirements to the highest level of self-actualization, where peak experiences, creativity and problem-solving feature as ways of knowing and engaging with the world. Such aspects fit well into a model of artistic knowledge, where experience, creativity and making connections between sometimes disparate ideas and phenomena reflect deeper ways of knowing than the mere acquisition of facts.

For John Dewey (1934), art and life were integrated; the artificial division between practical and fine arts was seen by Dewey to be unhelpful, for even the functional could be beautiful. From earliest times, 'art music' has included a functional dimension, although often its purpose is beyond mere utility. Equally, Hindemith's 'Gebrauchsmusik' is meaningful as music beyond its original intended function. In a world where scientific method, analysis and categorization suggest sharp divisions between arts and sciences, education and training, beauty and function, there is much to be gained from Jaensch's (1930) perspective on the essential relationships that exist between human, artistic and scientific identities. Within the professional realm, contemporary music educators are expected to be not only proficient in a range of musical genres, but also cognizant of diverse educational theory and practice. At times the range of curricular possibilities and professional expectations facing teachers may present conflicting perspectives on artistic and professional knowledge. How should one reconcile, for example, the different musical values of classical and popular music, or the goals of formal and informal education? Is it possible to do justice to an indigenous musical tradition in the time allocated to music in schools? Seeking unity within diversity and potential conflict is essential to managing areas of knowledge, understanding and skill; considering ways in which musical and professional identities are connected rather than separated provides opportunities for students to synthesize diverse ideas and materials. My purpose in this chapter is to reflect on how different musical identities and professional roles combine subject knowledge and skills, where artistry is considered as both phenomenon and craft. It is hoped that the emerging model of artistic knowledge in practice will better inform our understanding of music and our approach to music education.

Practical Knowledge

Gadamer highlighted the importance of language, both in determining individual identity and as a vehicle for developing understanding and a sense of value (Abhik and Starosta 2001). For Gadamer, we arrive at the 'truth' of a text (for which we may interpose painting, musical score, poem) not by trying to capture the subjective meaning intended by its creator, but rather by relating closely with the text – almost like a conversation between the individual and the object – and retaining an open attitude to the various meanings it suggests (Chen 1987). Such personalization of a text is in the spirit of the 'I–thou' relationship proposed by Buber (1970), as opposed to the more objective and impersonal 'I–it' relationship. Arriving at a work's truth through subjective, artistic means contrasts with the objective, scientific emphasis that informs much thinking on what is significant and valuable in education and society. Practical knowledge that arises through dialogue and relationship humanizes understanding and allows for a richer learning experience:

> The challenge is to provide a suitable basis for considering the quality of ideas and to encourage appropriate techniques for developing students' musical thinking. If we as teachers do not rise to this challenge, we will have missed a valuable chance to engage students in vital learning opportunities. (Stephens 2003, p. 135)

Gadamer (1960) observed that subjective insight plays an important part in the way we construct meaning. The question of 'inherent meaning', like that of 'inherent beauty', continues to exercise philosophers. Kant's conception of artistic beauty highlights the importance of expressive character within a work's overall structure – relating the subjective with the objective:

> Above all the natural source of Beauty in Art is identified with expressive power rather than with formal excellence. (Gotshalk 1967, p. 253)

Stravinsky stated that:

> Music is, by its very nature, essentially powerless to *express* anything at all. (Stravinsky 1975, p. 51)

This is not to say that music cannot be expressive – or that musical performance should be unfeeling or sterile – but rather that the combination of sounds that make up a piece of music do not have a precise meaning. Music's power is not neutral, however; for all its apparent imprecision, its effect on individuals may be more immediate and persuasive than spoken language. When combined with visual images (as in film), music is significant in preparing, shaping and even determining response. Whilst music is not strictly a language (Graham 1997, p. 80), it does share certain features with language – notably in its articulation of feelings and communication of ideas. Music communicates to audiences at a deeper level than language, but its expressive message appears to be more one of *evoking* responses in a listener (feelings of happiness, sadness, excitement, relaxation) than *possessing* intrinsic meaning. Musical sounds and patterns tap into neural networks in our brains that process and interpret sonic material. Schuppert et al. (2000, pp. 557–8) suggest that:

> music processing is based on widely distributed neural networks modulated by individual aspects of musicality and music experience.

Scientific and artistic, theoretical and experiential, objective and subjective processes are involved in our relationship with music.

Ann Kovalchick and Kara Dawson identify with Dewey in their assessment of the centrality of education to life – education that depends on practical engagement with phenomena, derived from lived experience:

> John Dewey was perhaps the greatest proponent of situated learning and learning by doing. Dewey reacted against the traditional educational framework of memorization and recitation and argued that 'education is not preparation for life, it is life itself.' (2004, p. 169)

Ernest Carroll Moore (1915, p. 138) echoed Dewey's assertion, identifying workshops, problems and examinations as 'efforts to provide an environment in which the student shall work out his own experience into more usable capitalized forms':

> According to this conception 'education is not for life, but it is life.' It cannot be a preparation for life without being life.

The knowledge we gain through practice – 'learning by doing', as Dewey advocated – is deep and meaningful. Education is diminished when it is viewed only as preparation for the world of work; music is misrepresented when its educational benefit is seen as having only extrinsic value, preparing an individual for something else or merely supporting learning in other areas of the curriculum. Of course, there is a functional dimension to education and music education, but that should not be its main or only purpose. We are transformed in the process of engaging with ideas, with the rich tapestry of sounds and patterns that constitute the diversity of our world's music. Mere exposure to music's power may affect us, like a beautiful sunset has an aesthetic appeal; deeper engagement with music through practical experience moves the listener from natural aesthetic appreciation to informed artistic knowledge. The transformational power of the arts contributes significantly to our human identity.

Education for Life...

> Knowledge comes, but wisdom lingers... (Tennyson 1842: *Locksley Hall*, line 141)

Education has its Latin roots in both 'educare' (to educate or train) and 'educere' (to bring or draw out). Knowing where to find information and how to use it is deemed more worthwhile to contemporary society than memorizing facts; acquiring subject knowledge is only one part of the educational process. If we are concerned to move beyond the simple 'I know what I like', we have to strive to educate the ear and eye beyond the merely familiar:

> [In] a world so focused on objectives and results, efficiency, effectiveness, and
> the rest, I would lay particular stress on what lies beyond the moment's grasp,
> on the uses of defamiliarizing the overly familiar (and thus invisible, inaudible)
> world. (Greene 2001, p. 206)

Education is crucial to our appreciation of and growth in artistic knowledge, to opening up new ways of seeing, hearing and imagining. Just as our perception of a piece of music or painting determines our response, so our view of education determines the level of our ability to uncover the riches of a work of art. What, then, is an appropriate music education for the individual and society that uncovers and engages with the intrinsic artistic knowledge of a composition or performance?

Whilst education has always had a practical purpose – namely, to equip an individual with necessary knowledge, understanding and skills for life – since the early 1980s, we have witnessed a shift from 'education for personal development' (the intrinsic value of education, of which Dewey wrote) to a more functional emphasis on 'education for work'. As a result, school music curricula have embraced a sociological agenda, where relevance to the 'real world' and breaking down perceived barriers between formal and informal education are assigned a central place in teaching and learning. In the UK, a review of what constitutes 'knowledge' coincided with the 'music for all' approach of the early 1970s. Almost 40 years after the publication of *Knowledge and Control* (Young 1971), Michael Young revisited the issue of knowledge in the formal and informal curriculum (Young 2008, p. 1), posing the question:

What is educationally worthwhile knowledge, and what are (and what should be) the significant differences between curriculum or school knowledge and the every-day, commonsense knowledge that people acquire at home, in the community and in the workplace?

Young recognized the need to identify distinctive forms of knowledge within different contexts, that some forms of knowledge are more 'worthwhile' than others. Almost 100 years earlier, Irving King (1915) anticipated the late twentieth-century interest in linking informal and formal education in his observation on 'the value of home and school associations in the development of a socially efficient education' (1915, p. 108):

> There is no better way to make the children feel that their school training is worth while. Such organization of a community about its educational interests will keep these interests in vital touch with life, and will go far toward making the work in the school not mere preparation for life, but real participation in life itself.

King echoed Dewey's perspective on education's intrinsic value and relationship to life, largely by advocating the relevance of formal education to the home and society. Today, the emphasis is more directly on bringing the informal world into the classroom than making education 'socially efficient' or organizing 'a community about its educational interests'. In his next chapter (7), King identifies *play* as preparation for life:

> It has been truly pointed out that play is, for instance, a preparation for adult life. (1915, p. 109)

Knowledge gained through role-play, games and imaginary activities helps the child relate to the external world. The arts in education have a central place in such preparation for adult life. For Vygotsky (1978), play was not so much an activity that gives pleasure as one that reflects a child's needs, where child development is considered to be more than theoretical or intellectual advancement. Vygotsky identified the need to play as a means of postponing immediate gratification, reflecting what he termed 'a zone of proximal development' (1978, p. 102) – an arena for linking the known with the unknown, development with learning:

> the preschool child enters an imaginary, illusory world in which the unrealizable desires can be realized, and this world is what we call play. Imagination is a new psychological process for the child; it is not present in the consciousness of the very young child, is totally absent in animals, and represents a specifically human form of conscious activity. Like all functions of consciousness, it originally arises from action. The old adage that child's play is imagination in action must be reversed: we can say that imagination in adolescents and school children is play without action. (1978, p. 93)

The period of formal education is now viewed as one part of lifelong learning, in which the student and experiential learning, rather than the teacher and subject knowledge, take centre stage. Alongside this change, educators have had to consider different forms of knowledge that are deemed appropriate for the different contexts in which individuals operate. Preparation for life is undoubtedly an important aspect of education – although 'life', as we have seen, is more than the world of work. Alison Kadlec's consideration of Dewey's critical pragmatism comments on the role that education plays in his philosophy of the social:

> Those who conceive of education as a process of 'preparation,' of 'unfolding,' or of 'formal discipline' all fail to see a fundamentally active and flexible component of the social function of education. (Kadlec 2007, p. 69)

Notwithstanding the benefits of relating formal and informal learning, there is a case for music education in schools to go beyond simply reinforcing what students experience outside school, to open their ears and eyes to musical experiences and artistic knowledge that are outside their everyday cultural encounter and which have the potential, therefore, to transform daily existence. Young's question, therefore, may be reframed as: 'What is educationally worthwhile *artistic* knowledge?' Imagination is an important motivational force in individual development (Stephens 1994) and a key aspect of such artistic knowledge. Indeed, our survival in a rapidly changing world is dependent on being able to find imaginative solutions to problems (Stephens 2000). Maxine Greene's advocacy for the arts in education highlighted the importance of imagination in transforming our worldview:

> Imagination is the capacity to posit alternative realities. (2001, p. 6)

Belief and Knowledge

> I had therefore to remove knowledge in order to make room for belief. (Kant 1787, preface)

In everyday life, belief is commonly portrayed as less reliable than knowledge; stated simply, what we know can be measured and objectively tested, whereas what we believe is a subjective matter. Whilst our beliefs are shaped by our knowledge, our knowledge is informed by our perception; we experience, describe and know a landscape differently depending on where we stand. In that regard, at least, knowledge may be just as reliable or unreliable as belief. Equally, belief need not imply uncertainty. On the basis of experience and trust, we believe that the sun will rise in the morning, that our money is safe in a bank, and that our marriage partner will remain with us until old age. At times, our knowledge and belief are found to be inadequate and our confidence misplaced: new knowledge challenges our certainties; financial institutions and partners let us down...

The relationship between knowledge and belief is complex, not least because there are many types of knowledge and belief. We know *that* something is true or false (propositional knowledge – Ryle 1949); we know *of* other people and places (acquaintance knowledge – Russell 1912); we know *about* things (theoretical knowledge – Dewey 1930; Aristotle 1955); and we know *how* to do something (procedural knowledge, technical expertise or 'know-how' – Ryle 1949). All four types of knowledge may be applied to the arts and our relationship with music as composers, performers and listeners. Knowing *how* to do something and knowing *that* something is true are, as Ryle (1949) observed, separate from belief – although it is easier to see a connection between belief and knowing *that* than belief and knowing *how*.

Plato (360 BC) identifies three stages of knowledge: knowledge as *perception* (where things are as they appear to the observer); knowledge as true *opinion* (that is, knowledge with discernment or judgement); and knowledge as justified true *belief* (where knowledge is supported by reasoning, definition or explanation). In a postmodern age, where truth is considered relative and one opinion as valid as another, Plato's first category of 'knowledge as perception' appears remarkably contemporary. And yet, it is clear that not all knowledge can be treated as relative – we need certain assurances in order to be able to plan our lives. We want our doctors and bank managers to deal in certainties! 'Knowledge as true opinion' is *informed* opinion, which requires the individual to make decisions based on reasoned investigation. Such knowledge is evident in the way a composer decides on the elements of a composition, or a performer on the interpretation of a composer's ideas. The perspective of 'knowledge as justified true belief' was generally accepted as higher-order knowledge until the mid twentieth century, when Gettier (1963, pp. 121–3) suggested that knowledge cannot be justified where one's *apparent* knowledge is coincidental (as in guessing the correct answer to an examination question, or assuming that a stopped clock is working, simply because it shows the correct time when one enters a room). Notwithstanding Gettier's observation, scientific knowledge based on reasoned analysis, definition and explanation, still dominates academia, while knowledge as perception and knowledge as true opinion are considered of lower significance.

Artistic knowledge includes the dimensions of perception, opinion and belief; it is propositional, experiential, theoretical and procedural; it is something to be shared with, rather than imposed on, others. A musical performance that is deemed *appropriate* represents one perception or interpretation of an unwritten musical tradition or of a notated musical score. However, the nature of artistic knowledge conveyed in a musical performance is more than 'knowledge as perception' – the insight of one musician (performer) into the intention of another (composer) for the delight of a third (listener). We expect our performers to demonstrate discernment ('true opinion') and conviction ('justified true belief') derived from a reasoned investigation of a musical score – to be able to support their interpretation by research into such aspects as composer intention, historical and social context, and appropriate performance practice. Effective musical performance is more than the perception of one person to entertain another; we may properly speak of informing or educating a listener through sharing artistic performance knowledge, of conveying something of musical substance beyond the surface pattern of sounds. Scientific and technical knowledge have a part to play in this process.

Truth and Knowledge

Kierkegaard (1846) linked truth and subjectivity in his *Concluding Unscientific Postscript* to the *Philosophical Fragments*. Truth may be seen as subjective, Kierkegaard argues, when it is based on a relationship rather than a set of impartial data. Within the context of religious faith, the believer holds certain objective propositions (such as historical facts and doctrines), but these become meaningful only if they are internalized – believed passionately and thus subjectively. A similar case could be made for artistic knowledge, that it is to do with internalized, subjective truths related to objective propositions about music or another art form. *Relationship* is at the heart of such knowing, just as it is in our most meaningful human encounters. And so, while we may not be able to quantify love in the way we can assess the value of our home, we *experience* love at a much deeper level than we can relate to the objective facts about the building in which we live – or even the person we love. Such experiential knowledge or truth is far more powerful in motivating behaviour and response than mere acquaintance with factual data. Locating truth within a subjective realm may jar with a rationalistic worldview; certainly Kierkegaard's perspective contrasts with Hegel's rational idealism (Dunning 1985, p. 39). However, the tension does serve to highlight the inadequacy of contemporary Western culture's emphasis on the objective and rational as a better, more reliable way of knowing truth; such objectivity lacks the richness of a deeper, subjective reality. Today, high status is afforded to scientific knowledge based on empirical evidence, so it is salutary to remember that there are limits to a scientific worldview, to seemingly objective ways of knowing. Artistic knowledge exists within a relationship – between the artist, the art and the audience; it requires a context for meaningfulness, an occasion for interaction. Jaensch's (1930) observation concerning human and artistic identity – where processes of logical thinking are common to child, artist and scientist – is pertinent to our present consideration of artistic knowledge that exists within relationships.

Kierkegaard's relational, subjective truth in artistic knowledge has much to commend it. Once again, the moral responsibility of the artist contained within the Greek concept of praxis suggests that artistic knowledge is not simply about pushing the technical boundaries of art, but balancing such necessary development with a need to relate art to life, with an artist's moral concern for an audience (Abhik and Starosta 2001, p. 7). In a world where commercially driven developments in scientific and technical knowledge have sometimes revealed a lack of due care for life and the environment, the moral and ethical dimensions of artistic knowledge provide a necessary corrective. Artistic knowledge, as a type of faith (belief related to knowledge) requires a personal and subjective relationship with art – and like religious faith, the relationship needs to be ongoing and vibrant to be meaningful. Knowledge that is more than factual information changes thinking and behaviour; it is responsive. Such knowledge requires active participation in doing, and in the process it is transformational. Kierkegaard's philosophy of subjective knowledge and truth – emphasizing the *manner* of our belief more than its content – resonates with contemporary thinking in curricula: knowing where to find information and how to use it appropriately is deemed more important than memorizing many facts.

Subjective and Objective Realities

The subjective–objective debate that shapes public opinion on the reliability of knowledge and belief continues to inform the school curriculum. As a result, subjects are graded in importance according to their objectivity (those that emphasize factual information) and their perceived relevance and 'value' to society (education's functional purpose). According to this measure, sciences are considered more important than arts because they are based on objective realities rather than subjective expression (on 'knowledge' more than 'belief'); moreover, science and technology are deemed useful to society, whereas the arts are considered decorative. It is interesting that subjective–objective perspectives still inform popular thinking about reliability and subject value in the curriculum. In the early twentieth century, Martin Heidegger proposed a more integrated interpretation where subjectivity and objectivity were considered part of a 'hermeneutic circle'[1]. Heidegger's hermeneutic approach (Heidegger 1927) involved a relationship between understanding ourselves and understanding our world, set within a phenomenological perspective.[2] For Heidegger, meaning was related to our lives as human beings (or 'Dasein' – our essential humanity or 'being' – rather than simply our existence, or presence, as Ludwig Feuerbach employed the term[3]).

In 1960, Gadamer (a student of Heidegger) published *Truth and Method*, in which the author suggested that it is impossible to be completely objective in our interpretation of events, but rather that we create meaning through subjective insight. Gadamer was unhappy with the growing emphasis on scientific method in the arts and humanities. He disagreed also with the view of Schleiermacher and Dilthey that correct interpretation depended on trying to reconstruct a work through the eyes of its creator (an interesting issue within the authentic musical

---

[1] Hermeneutics – the study of understanding or interpretation (its art, theory and practice).

[2] Phenomenology – the study of the structure of experience (the meaning and significance of 'phenomena') from a subjective / first-person perspective.

[3] 'To be here (Dasein) is the primary being, the primary determination' (Van Harvey 1995, p. 141).

performance debate). Understanding (according to Gadamer) is a result of our history and culture allied with a personal response to an object – what he termed 'interpretative understanding' (or 'verstehen'). This perspective allows the observer or listener to interpret a work of art in terms of the present, to discover its truth or artistic knowledge in a way that makes it meaningful to the individual. In this way, Gadamer related hermeneutics to aesthetics and historical understanding.

The issue of whether or not true objectivity is possible poses a challenge to the status of objective knowledge within the 'science versus arts' debate. Gadamer observes:

> We stand always in tradition and this is no objectifying process ... Tradition is always part of us, example or deterrent, a recognition of ourselves. (Gadamer 1975, p. 250)

According to Gadamer, understanding can never escape the historicity of tradition; knowledge always arises within the context of traditions, and the discernment of truth must answer to temporal positioning. Consequently, no final understanding of a phenomenon is possible, since analysts use subsequent interpretations to alter or supplant earlier ones (Abhik and Starosta 2001, p. 8). Our artistic knowledge, therefore, remains both partial and provisional.

Knowledge through Interaction

Gadamer's view of knowledge gained through interaction (conversation as 'discourse' – Misgeld 1977, p. 328) offers some interesting perspectives on our understanding of artistic knowledge – particularly in the area of music performance and improvisation. Gadamer's perspective places such interaction (with its attendant openness and possibility to change in the moment) above the more rationalistic perspective of Habermas (with its attendant emphasis on the 'rules' of discourse, which enable participants to be secure in their identity). Gadamer's use of metaphors of play resonates with a more open approach to knowledge and understanding beyond the more literal aspects of language. When it comes to communication through non-verbal language, as in music and visual art, metaphor provides a valuable means of extending our knowledge and understanding of a work, while the 'rules' of discourse and security in one's identity help set a framework for imaginative performance to take place. The uncertainties of performance (even where there is a high level of technical competence) are similar to the uncertainties of conversation (Gadamer 1975, p. 345), where we cannot be sure of every detail or know what will be said in advance – let alone how it will be received or interpreted. Beyond the ambiguities of language itself, meaning and understanding in verbal communication, like that of musical performance, are dependent on nuance, interaction and context – on the manner of delivery as well as the content.

Hermeneutics, in its broadest sense, is of particular interest to our present consideration of artistic knowledge – not least, because it provides an analytical lens for understanding artistic and scientific approaches to interpretation by asserting the principles involved in each interpretative act. Gadamer's perspective appears well suited to music performance, where appropriate knowledge has more to do with present, subjective application than historical, objective interpretation. Notwithstanding much valuable research that illuminates previous performance practice, the distance of time and lived experience means that we can, at best, only imagine what it must have been like to perform or hear a piece of music within its original cultural and historical context. The artistic knowledge we gain through such interaction with the past illuminates our understanding as much by providing an alternative way of hearing and experiencing music as by imagining what it must have sounded like to an original audience, unaffected by the sonic pollution and aural memory of a twenty-first-century soundscape.

Through the Eyes of a Musician

> Here is my secret. It's quite simple: One sees clearly only with the heart.
> Anything essential is invisible to the eyes. (Saint-Exupéry 1943, p. 63)

Whether or not Antoine de Saint-Exupéry considered the heart as the seat of the emotions or as the centre of one's thinking is uncertain. Understanding the nature of music, however, is not simply a matter of emotional response; it involves the mind and will. The 'eyes' of a musician are his ears; effective listening lies at the heart of all musical endeavour, although such listening is more than the physical hearing of patterns of sounds. In that sense, we might adapt Saint-Exupéry's observation, as 'anything essential is inaudible to the ears'. Music's intangible nature means the *essential* is 'invisible'; artistic knowledge and understanding lie at a deeper level than music's superficial appeal. Both our *anticipation* of a performance and what we bring to the listening experience (our metaphorical 'baggage', as well as knowledge and understanding) shape our response to the patterns of sounds and silences. Music's ambiguity is part of its universal appeal and power. Music education should take the student beyond the realm of the obvious.

At one level, the intention of a composer or performer may be considered central to meaning in music, and yet – as Gadamer observed:

> Meaning can be experienced, even when it is not actually intended. (1976, p. 30)

Artistic knowledge does not reside solely in a musical work or performance tradition, waiting to be released on a willing audience; the listener has a role also in constructing meaning. In *Musicking*, Small (1998, p. 2) goes further and dismisses attempts to define music's meaning and function as a definite phenomenon that resides in a musical 'work', stating:

> There is no such thing as music. Music is not a thing at all but an activity, something that people do.

Small's position is not dissimilar to that of Dewey or Gadamer, where knowledge arises through interaction, where music may be considered as a form of discourse rather than an object. The 'doing' of music in musical performance communicates artistic knowledge to an audience, but the communication is not one way only; the listener engages in the process of uncovering meaning or 'truth' through participating in the conversation. Just as some conversations are richer in vocabulary and concepts than others, so the level of reflective engagement and depth of participation by the performer and listener differs from one musical genre to another. To take the language metaphor further, I would suggest that when we listen to our spoken language, we focus less on the sounds than the understood meaning of the words; when we listen to an unfamiliar language, however, we are more likely to respond as we would to a piece of music, focusing on the sounds and the way musical parameters of pitch, duration, tempo, dynamics, articulation and timbre are portrayed. If we remain engaged, the sounds of unfamiliar words convey a type of musical meaning and identity – a knowledge that we experience but may not be able to comprehend or articulate. This uninformed, even involuntary, appreciation of unintelligible sounds could be considered *aesthetic* rather than *artistic* (Best 1982), for it relies on response rather than understanding. Such experiences help us consider musical meaning more as intention and response than as representation.

To further our consideration of artistic knowledge, it is instructive to consider the different ways musicians and music educators construct knowledge. In so doing, I do not wish to imply an artificial division between musical professions, or even simplify the argument to suggest a common approach exhibited by *all* musicians and music educators. Rather, my purpose is to consider the variety of ways we construct and communicate artistic knowledge in order to enrich our understanding of this important area.

The Composer

Notwithstanding Small's (1998) observation on music as activity rather than object, a work of art reveals something of the inner world of its creator (poet, composer, artist), as well as a perception of the external world. Within the Western classical music tradition, composers are at the heart of musical endeavour. Without *creation*, there would be no *re-creation* by performers, or *recreation* for audiences. Christopher Small (1977, p. 218) puts it this way:

> But the real power of art lies, not in listening to or looking at the finished work; it lies in the act of creation itself. In the process of artistic creation the creator engages his whole self; his reason and intuition, together with the most ruthless self-criticism and realistic assessment of a situation all come into play.

The creative process in music-making need not be limited to the composer, however; it should inform all aspects of the realization and reception of music by performer and listener. Elsewhere, Small (1998) locates music's meaning in the social, active realms of performing and listening, where performers are identified as 'creators of musical meaning' (p. 5). The singer-songwriters, the troubadours, the travelling musicians of previous ages demonstrated an artistic knowledge that was not compartmentalized into separate roles of composer–performer–listener that are a feature of much Western classical music. Instead, they combined the acts of improvisation/composition and performance in the creative and re-creative act. It is in this broad sense that the composer/creator may be considered to be at the heart of music-making across musical cultures and history.

The artistic knowledge that composers possess cover broad areas of musicianship, technique and craft; without imagination and creativity, however, none of these would be sufficiently persuasive. Originality is an important part of creative thinking and practice, but I would suggest it is not the main factor in uncovering a composer's special relationship with artistic knowledge. Pioneers, such as Henry Cowell, Alois Hába and John Cage may achieve certain notoriety for their exploits, but the innovator is not necessarily the most revered exponent of an art form. Johann Sebastian Bach was neglected for a generation, as the artistic knowledge he explored was out of step with changing musical fashion. Bach was more of a consolidator than an innovator, but he is now recognized as one of the most significant figures in music history because of the artistic and technical quality of his work, as well as an ability to communicate meaningfully across history and culture. Just as originality is not a determining factor in evaluating artistic knowledge, so novelty is no substitute for creative skill and imagination. An obsession with being 'contemporary' in order to be accepted as a serious artist becomes irrelevant after a generation; what matters is the artistic quality of a work – quality that is recognized within society and evaluated by those who are educated appropriately in the arts (and thus considered to be informed or credible witnesses). Interestingly, whilst classical music is recognized as having intrinsic artistic value, its appreciative audience is relatively small; popular appeal is not a significant factor in determining the quality of artistic knowledge in music.

Listening to the works of the 'great' classical composers, one is struck by the inner logic of their musical argument, the stylistic consistency that makes sense on its own terms. The artistic knowledge within a musical work is concerned with its integrity or 'truth'. Beethoven and Bartók construct their musical worlds differently, but each conveys artistic knowledge that demonstrates highly developed skill in devising musical patterns that 'work' in the ears of receptive listeners. Artistic knowledge for the composer involves a strong sense of inner conviction in the way sound patterns are organized. There is not one 'truth', an objective reality that a composer aspires to, but rather – like the infinite variety of snowflakes – multiple possibilities for patterning sound and silence. As each snowflake falls to the ground, a sense of unity, cohesion and wider consistency is evident – in the same way that a body of musical works represents the stylistic development of a composer, or typifies an historical period or culture, an unfolding artistic knowledge that is both individual and communal.

The Performer

Creative, artistic knowledge is not the exclusive territory of the composer. The 'best' performers demonstrate imagination and insight in the way they explore musical ideas, whether the music is a rendition of a composer's notated intentions, a jazz improvisation, or a performance of indigenous music. The human, interpretative factor in performance is an important part of the artistic knowledge conveyed, for whereas a computer may offer a precise rendition of many of the details of a score, the medium lacks the persuasiveness of personal communication. An important aspect of effective performance, therefore, is *conviction*. The level of commitment to the musical 'message' determines whether or not the listener experiences a heightened response to the music – the 'hairs rising on the back of the neck' sensation that may accompany a fine performance. An indifferent performance, even one that is technically accurate, is unlikely to touch the listener so deeply. Just like a declaration of love, the message is more than the words – the delivery has to be convincing!

Kierkegaard's distinction between objective and subjective truth (the 'what' and 'how' of thinking and understanding) raises some interesting issues for our consideration of artistic performance knowledge:

> The objective accent falls on WHAT is said, the subjective accent on HOW it is said. (1846, p. 181)

In musical performance, the 'how' is of particular importance. An effective and convincing performance is more than a dispassionate presentation of the content (the 'what') of a composition or musical genre; the process of interpreting a composer's wishes, or realizing an improvisation or presenting an example of indigenous music, requires the performer to convey the music *beyond* the notes. Artistic knowledge, therefore, is more than acquaintance, scholarship or technical skill. It is an ability to convey subjective 'truth' in a meaningful way to touch the lives of others; it exists as a relationship between the music, a performer and an audience.

Commenting on the way scientific method has influenced literary criticism, Richard Palmer observes how 'taking an object apart to see how it is made has become the prevailing model of the art of interpretation' (Palmer 1969, p. 6). In this approach, 'text is considered as object' (albeit an 'aesthetic object') and 'analysis as interpretation' (Palmer 1969, p. 6). At a simple level, a performer's attempts to 'interpret' the notated wishes of a composer may be seen as a return to Schleiermacher and Dilthey's view of interpretation as reconstruction – something that Stravinsky was keen to emphasize, when he substituted the word 'execution' for 'interpretation' (Small 1998, p. 6). Clearly, whilst integrity in performance is important, there are different views concerning how integrity may be realized in practice. Musical sensitivity to historical and cultural context or a composer's score may be considered an important part of a truthful performance; but if a performance is to be more than a strict execution of a composer's notated wishes, being true to oneself and one's audience are necessary factors also. Gadamer characterized this exchange as a type of conversation between a performer and a text, highlighting the importance of 'verstehen' (interpretive understanding) in conveying music's message (Vandevelde 2005). Jack Mendelson (1979, p. 53) comments as follows:

> Heidegger had shown that interpretation always begins with projections of meaning deriving from the interpreter's own situation and that understanding is the working-out of these 'fore-structures.' Gadamer argues that these anticipations are the conditions of the possibility of historical knowledge. Therefore, he attempts to rehabilitate the concept of 'prejudice.' Gadamer's claim is that all understanding inevitably involves some prejudices, i.e., never-fully-objectifiable fore-meanings. Historicism remains caught in an illusory rationalism to the extent that it sees prejudice as something entirely negative to be neutralized by scientific method. This attempt to 'deprive tradition of its power' is bound to fail since all historical knowledge requires prejudices. The facticity of the 'hermeneutical situation' is a given for the knower, something he finds himself in. It can never be dissolved by critical self-knowledge such that the prejudice structure could entirely disappear.

Gadamer (1960, p. 245) describes the relationship between an individual and history more poetically, observing that individual prejudices define us more than our judgements:

> History does not belong to us, but we belong to it. … The focus of subjectivity is a distorting mirror. The self-awareness of the individual is only a flickering in the closed circuits of historical life. That is why the prejudices of the individual, far more than his judgements, constitute the historical reality of his being.

And so, when we listen to an authoritative performance, we recognize a blending of composer's wishes, historical and cultural context, and the performer's insights (or 'prejudices') that relate the music to the present moment for an audience. Together, these elements convey the artistic knowledge of a musical work, a performance tradition or genre. Apart from a high level of technical skill and musicianship, the imaginative and creative blend of these elements illuminate a composition or musical form in a way that technical or historical accuracy alone cannot accomplish. The performer, then, becomes a translator of the artistic knowledge contained in the musical score, integrating personal insight with a work's historical and contemporary setting. When all come together in an appropriate synergy, the listener experiences 'the music beyond the notes',[4] not in a passive manner, but through actively engaging in the construction of meaning and artistic knowledge.

Composer and performer reflect different aspects of musical and personal identity and professional role; both are concerned with artistic knowledge within the patterning of sounds, created and interpreted. We turn now to a different sort of artistic knowledge – that demonstrated in the applied skills of music educators in schools and higher education.

Through the Eyes of a Music Educator

If we consider the curriculum to be a 'group composition' (a result of collective endeavour on the part of politicians and their education advisors), the teachers and lecturers are the 'performers', and the students the 'listeners'. Just as the musician's performance has to be true to the musical text of a composer or the integrity of a musical genre, so the teacher's performance has to reflect the intentions of the curriculum. However, unlike the concert hall where attendance is voluntary, the student audience is forced to 'listen to the music'. This in turn changes the nature of the performance, for just as a good performer responds to acoustic space and audience reaction, so a good teacher responds to a student audience and learning environment – only here, the response is more immediate, compelling and often improvisatory. In the concert hall, the listener may be physically passive; in the classroom, individuals become active listeners – engaging with the composition and the performance. In this way, the relationship between curriculum–teacher–student offers a model for positive interaction between composer–performer–listener in the construction, realization and appreciation of artistic knowledge in music. The model of applied artistic knowledge thus displayed may be considered closer to the art of the improviser than the 'performer', especially where the latter is reduced to executing a composer's wishes rather than engaging imaginatively with musical material and social context.

The Teacher

> Grown-ups never understand anything by themselves, and it is exhausting for children to have to provide explanations over and over again. (Saint-Exupéry 1943, p. 2)

Paradoxically, teachers are often the unsung heroes of education. Just as one may observe a hierarchical attitude to different musical professions (composer –

---

[4]   In the case of electroacoustic music, the composer and performer are often one and the same – the 'composer' acting as a performer in the diffusion of sound across multiple speakers. Whilst such performances may contain an interpretative dimension, the artistic knowledge in such a medium is of a different order to traditional performance.

performer – musicologist) that is dependent to some extent on the institutional context, musicians in general have higher status than music educators. And within the career profile, secondary teachers are respected more than primary teachers, who in turn are higher in the pecking order than nursery teachers. It is interesting that, across the world, status is based on subject *knowledge* more than subject *application*, and on the ages and stages of education – university being more important than secondary school, and secondary more important than primary. And yet the teacher's artistic knowledge at its best is among the most complex in the music profession. The teacher is required to possess adequate subject knowledge which, unlike the specialist university lecturer, has to encompass a diverse range of musical styles and musicianship, knowledge of curricular theory and practice, wider issues in education, philosophy, psychology and sociology, management techniques, and mixed-ability teaching and learning. The artistic knowledge of an effective teacher, therefore, is broadly located in subject knowledge, understanding and skill, and in professional application – in music as both phenomenon and craft. As the curriculum has expanded to include a wider range of musical and generic subjects, so the artistic and professional knowledge of the teacher has been stretched. Nevertheless, the *teacher*, as an embodiment of artistic knowledge, remains the greatest resource for learning.

A sociological approach, which relates formal and informal areas of education (Green 2008), has much to commend it – although, as we have seen, the relationship between society and school need not be one way. Some teachers may experience a degree of conflict between their desire to offer experiences that challenge students and extend their musical horizons, and the pressure to make everything socially relevant. In a crowded curriculum, it may be difficult to find time to go beyond superficial acquaintance and promote deeper artistic knowledge. Young's (2008, p. 1) question concerning 'educationally worthwhile knowledge' has the potential to cause controversy in the musical choices a curriculum espouses. In seeking to value all music as an expression of individual or cultural identity, we may be cautious to suggest that some forms of music contain and convey greater musical and technical substance than others. We are more comfortable to speak of *different* artistic knowledge rather than *richer* artistic knowledge when commenting, for example, on 'popular music' and 'classical music'. When it comes to indigenous music, the classroom – as an artificial environment – presents its own challenges to addressing music appropriately and with due attention to its original cultural context (Campbell 2004). There is a danger that the artistic knowledge conveyed may be deficient or distorted because of the time and resource constraints of formal education.

The Lecturer

The role of the lecturer differs in certain regards from that of the schoolteacher – notably in the nature of the 'composition' (or curriculum). Whilst contextualized within national curricular guidelines, there is often a greater degree of autonomy both within universities and among individual lecturers concerning what constitutes a curriculum and how learning should be constructed. Today, the role of the university lecturer in the UK and elsewhere emphasises research over teaching, with a consequent reduction in contact time between students and tutors. Furthermore, the music education curriculum has had to make space for a range of generic areas, covering such topics as inclusion, health and wellbeing, special education, social justice, behaviour management, curriculum and assessment, cross-curricular challenges, learning styles, professional partnerships, child protection, and literacy and numeracy across the curriculum. As a consequence, the lecturer's role has been redefined; there is less time to present the mechanics of how to *teach* music and an expectation for students to take greater responsibility for their own learning. Professional knowledge for lecturer and student teacher alike now involves a diverse range of contextual and generic aspects beyond that of subject knowledge and application. In the past, many of these aspects would have been taught within the context of the subject (for example, class management in music lessons); today's model tends to treat these areas as separate blocks of knowledge, to be applied to specific contexts by the student teacher. Interestingly, research undertaken in Australia (Ballantyne 2006) highlights a preference by early-career teachers for teacher preparation courses that focus on pedagogical and professional knowledge and skills, rather than general education and music knowledge and skills. It is salutary to consider whether or not the applied artistic knowledge of the contemporary music lecturer is able to support the learning requirements of students in the way they consider most useful. If musical meaning is constructed through the interaction of composer, performer and listener, do our present models of teacher education inhibit the flow of artistic knowledge construction by limiting vital areas of *practical* musical exchange between lecturer and student? The ancient apprenticeship model of master and pupil, exemplified in many indigenous musical traditions (whether one-to one, as in Indian sitar training, or individual and communal, as in Ghanaian Ewe drumming) offers an alternative and integrated model for the construction of musical and professional knowledge. The constraints of the school classroom or university lecture theatre, together with the subject compartmentalization of education into defined blocks of time, militate against a more interactive, practical musical exchange evidenced in many musical traditions in the 'real world'.

All Knowledge is Power...
(Bacon 1597, p. 131)

In George Orwell's *Animal Farm* (1945), the revolution did not bring liberation for the animals, but far worse exploitation than was experienced under human managers, as one animal group (the pigs) exploited their former fellow sufferers. Similarly, Francis Bacon's famous slogan regarding the power of knowledge has become corrupted from its original altruistic meaning to something more self-centred. With due acknowledgement to *Animal Farm:*

> All knowledge is power, but some knowledge is more powerful than others...

For Bacon, the power of a God-given knowledge was to be used for the good of others, not as an end in itself. And it is this more altruistic, applied knowledge that I propose should characterize a contemporary model of artistic knowledge – one where the artist serves both the art and the audience, not primarily for personal, political or financial gain, but to enrich the lives of others. An ideal educational environment, therefore, would involve composer and performer, teacher and student, working together in exploring musical meaning and constructing relevant artistic knowledge. Security in one's artistic and professional identity is essential to an ability to appreciate and value other identities. It is as 'artist-teacher' (Stephens 1995) that we are able to engage others in appreciating and understanding the arts – the application of subject knowledge and skill within a creative, ethical framework of learning.

Artistic knowledge is reflective of human identity – it is imaginative and creative, down-to-earth and meaningful, relational and synthetic. Artistic knowledge is practical, responsive knowledge – conversational more than declarative, subjective more than objective, deeply persuasive rather than merely informative. It involves perception, opinion and belief; it is propositional, experiential, theoretical and procedural. Artistic knowledge is dependent on personal insight, on historical, cultural and situational understanding; it is something to be shared with, rather than imposed on, others. Like the identity of the artist, it is not about 'numbering and counting, but ripening like a tree' (Rilke 1903, p. 24), where growth and maturity are evidenced in the quality of the experience, in beauty rather than function. Artistic knowledge in practice is transformative, moral and ethical – thoughtful and sensitive to the art, the artist and the audience.

> The arts will not resolve the fearful social problems facing us today; they will not lessen the evils, and the brutalities afflicting the modern world. But they will provide a sense of alternatives to those of us who can see and hear; they will enhance the consciousness of possibility if we learn how to attend. (Greene 2001, p. 47)

For one twentieth-century composer, the compelling drive to compose music was balanced with a desire for his art to communicate with a world in need of consolation, reconciliation and inspiration. The integrity of the relationship between art, artist and audience was fundamental to a vision of artistic knowledge that, for Michael Tippett, was imaginative, practical and caring:

> Whether society has felt music valuable or needful I have gone on writing because I must. And I know that my true function within a society which embraces

all of us, is to continue an age-old tradition, fundamental to our civilisation, which goes back into pre-history and will go forward into the unknown future. This tradition is to create images from the depths of the imagination and to give them form whether visual, intellectual or musical. For it is only through images that the inner world communicates at all. Images of the past, shapes of the future. Images of vigour for a decadent period, images of calm for one too violent. Images of reconciliation for worlds torn by division. And in an age of mediocrity and shattered dreams, images of abounding, generous, exuberant beauty. (Tippett 1974, pp. 155–6)

Questions for Reflection

1. How might our relationship with music be enriched through exploring artistic processes of knowledge construction?
2. What are the specific forms of artistic knowledge within different musical traditions and genres?
3. Given that artistic knowledge is more than factual information, how should our music curricula be structured and delivered to provide appropriate, valuable and transformational learning opportunities for students?

References

Abhik, Roy and Starosta, William J. (2001). Hans-Georg Gadamer, Language, and Intercultural Communication, *Language and Intercultural Communication*, 1(1), 6–20.

Andrews, Molly; Squire, Corinne; and Tambokou, Maria (eds) (2008). *Doing Narrative Research*. London: Sage.

Aristotle. *The Nicomachean Ethics* (1955), trans. J. A. K. Thomson. London: Penguin.

Bacon, Francis (1597). *Meditationes Sacræ [Sacred Meditations]. De Hæresibus [Of Heresies]*. 'Knowledge is power' ['Nam et ipsa scientia potestas est']. In Steven Matthews (2008). *Theology and science in the thought of Francis Bacon*. Aldershot: Ashgate.

Ballantyne, Julie (2006). Reconceptualising Preservice Teacher Education Courses for Music Teachers: The Importance of Pedagogical Content Knowledge and Skills and Professional Knowledge and Skills. *Research Studies in Music Education*, 26(1), 37–50.

Beijaard, Douwe; Meijer, Paulien C.; and Verloop, Nico (2004). Reconsidering Research on Teachers' Professional Identity. *Teaching and Teacher Education*, 20, 107–128.

Best, David (1982). The Aesthetic and the Artistic. *Philosophy*, 57, 357–72.

Buber, Martin (1970). *I and Thou*, trans. Walter Kauffman. New York: Charles Scribner's Sons.

Campbell, Patricia Shehan (2004). *Teaching Music Globally: Experiencing Music, Expressing Culture*. New York: Oxford University Press.

Chase, Susan E. (2005). Narrative Inquiry: Multiple Lenses, Approaches, Voices. In Norman K. Denzin and Yvonna S. Lincoln (eds), *The SAGE Handbook of Qualitative Research* (3rd edition). Thousand Oaks, CA: Sage, 651–79.

Chen, Kuan-Hsing (1987). Beyond Truth and Method: On Misreading Gadamer's Praxical Hermeneutics. *Quarterly Journal of Speech*, 73(2), 183–99.

Cooper, Karyn and Olson, Margaret R. (1996). The Multiple 'I's' of Teacher Identity. In Michael Kompf, W. Richard Bond, Don Dworet and R. Terrance Boak (eds), *Changing Research and Practice: Teachers' Professionalism, Identities and Knowledge*. London: The Falmer Press, 78–89.

Dewey, John (1930). *An Introduction to the Philosophy of Education*. New York: Macmillan.

— (1934). *Art as Experience*. New York: Minton, Balch & Company.

Dolloff, Lori (1999). Imagining Ourselves as Teachers: The Development of Teacher Identity in Music Teacher Education. *Music Education Research*, 1(2), 197–207.

— (2007). 'All the Things We Are': Balancing our Multiple Identities in Music Teaching. *Action, Criticism, and Theory for Music Education*, 6(2). Retrieved from http://act.maydaygroup.org/articles/Dolloff6_2.pdf

Dunning, Stephen N. (1985). *Kierkegaard's Dialectic of Inwardness: A Structural Analysis of the Theory of Stages*. Princeton, NJ: Princeton University Press.

Fulwiler, Toby (1997). Telling Stories and Writing Truths. In Joseph F. Trimmer (ed.), *Narration as Knowledge: Tales of the Teaching Life*. Portsmouth, NH: Heinemann, 84–97.

Gadamer, Hans-Georg (1960). *Truth and Method*. Second revised edition, trans. Joel Weinsheimer and Donald G. Marshall (1989). New York: Crossroad (London: Sheed and Ward).

— (1975). Hermeneutics and Social Science. *Cultural Hermeneutics*, 2, 307–316.

— (1976). *Philosophical Hermeneutics*, trans. and ed. David E. Linge. Berkeley: University of California Press.

Gettier, Edmund (1963). Is Justified True Belief Knowledge?" *Analysis*, 23, 121–3.

Gotshalk, Dilman Walter (1967). Form and Expression in Kant's Aesthetics, *British Journal of Aesthetics*, 7(3), 250–60.

Graham, Gordon (1997). *Philosophy of the Arts: An Introduction to Aesthetics*. London: Routledge.

Green, Lucy (2008). *Music, Informal Learning and the School: A New Classroom Pedagogy*. London: Ashgate.

Greene, Maxine (2001). *Variations on a Blue Guitar: The Lincoln Center Institute Lectures on Aesthetic Education*. New York: Teachers College Press, Columbia University.

Heidegger, Martin (1927). *Being and Time*, trans. John Macquarrie and Edward Robinson (1962). New York: Harper & Row.

Hinchman, Lewis P. and Hinchman, Sandra K. (1997). *Memory, Identity, Community: The Idea of Narrative in the Human Sciences*. Albany, NY: SUNY Press.

Jaensch, Erich Rudolf (1930). *Eidetic Imagery and Typological Methods of Investigation*. London: Routledge and Kegan Paul.

Kadlec, Alison (2007). *Dewey's Critical Pragmatism*. Plymouth: Lexington Books.

Kant, Immanuel (1787). *Critique of Pure Reason*. (Preface to second edition, 1966.) New York: Doubleday.

Kierkegaard, Soren (1846). *Concluding Unscientific Postscript to the 'Philosophical Fragments'* [published under his pseudonym, Johannes Climacus], trans. David Swenson and Walter Lowrie (1974). Third edition, Princeton: Princeton University Press.

King, Irving (1915). *Education for Social Efficiency: A Study in the Social Relations of Education*. New York: D. Appleton and Company.

Kovalchick, Ann and Dawson, Kara (eds) (2004). *Education and Technology: An Encyclopedia*. Vol. 1. Santa Barbara, CA: ABC-CLIO.

Maslow, Abraham H. (1962). *Toward a Psychology of Being*. Princeton, NJ: D. Van Nostrand.

Mendelson, Jack (1979). The Habermas-Gadamer Debate. *New German Critique*, 18, 44–73.

Misgeld, Dieter (1977). Discourse and Conversation: The Theory of Communicative Competence and Hermeneutics in the Light of the Debate Between Habermas and Gadamer. *Philosophy & Social Criticism*, 4, 321–34.

Moore, Ernest Carroll (1915). *What is Education?* Boston: Ginn and Company.

Orwell, George (1945). *Animal Farm*. London: Secker and Warburg.

Palmer, Richard E. (1969). *Hermeneutics*. Northwestern University Studies in Phenomenology and Existential Philosophy. Evanston, IL: Northwestern University Press.

Plato (360 BC). *Theætetus*, trans. Benjamin Jowett (2008). Charleston, SC: BiblioBazaar Reproduction Series.

Rilke, Rainer Maria (1903). *Letters to a Young Poet*, trans. Stephen Mitchell (2001). London: Random House.

Roberts, Brian (1991). *Musician: A Process of Labelling*. St John's: Memorial University of Newfoundland.

Rogers, Carl (1951). *Client-Centered Therapy: Its Current Practice, Implications and Theory*. London: Constable.

Russell, Bertrand (1912). *The Problems of Philosophy*. London: Home University Library of Modern Knowledge, Williams & Norgate. London: Oxford University Press (1959).

Ryle, Gilbert (1949). *The Concept of Mind*. New York: Barnes & Noble.

Saint-Exupéry, Antoine de (1943). *The Little Prince*, trans. Richard Howard (2000). Orlando, FL: Harcourt.

Schuppert, Maria; Münte, Thomas F.; Wieringa, Bernardina M. and Altenmüller, Eckart (2000). Receptive Amusia: Evidence for Cross-Hemispheric Neural Networks Underlying Music Processing Strategies. *Brain*, 123, 546–59.

Small, Christopher (1977). *Music, Society, Education.* London: John Calder.

—(1998). *Musicking: The Meanings of Performing and Listening.* Middletown, CT: Wesleyan University Press.

Stephens, Jonathan (1994). Metamorphosis: Creative and Integrated Teaching Methods in European Music Education. *British Journal of Music Education*, 11(3), 239–48.

— (1995). Artist or Teacher? *International Journal of Music Education*, 25, 3–15.

— (2000). Shades of Meaning: A Consideration of Aspects of Peer Learning and Peer Assessment in Music and the Arts. In *Proceedings of the International Conference on Peer Learning and Peer Assessment in Music and Cognate Disciplines* (Resource Pack, Part 2). Belfast: University of Ulster, 49–55.

— (2003). Imagination in Education: Strategies and Models in the Teaching and Assessment of Composition. In Maud Hickey (ed.), *Why and How to Teach Music Composition: A New Horizon for Music Education.* Reston, VA: MENC.

Stravinsky, Igor (1975). *An Autobiography.* London: Calder and Boyars.

Tennyson, Alfred Lord (1842). *Poems. Locksley Hall.* Boston: W. D. Ticknor. London: Macmillan, 1891.

Tippett, Michael (1974). *Moving into Aquarius.* St Albans: Paladin.

Vandevelde, Pol (2005). *The Task of the Interpreter: Text, Meaning, and Negotiation.* [Chapter 2: Interpretation as Event: A Critique of Gadamer's Critical Pluralism.] Pittsburgh, PA: University of Pittsburgh Press.

Van Harvey, A. (1995). *Feuerbach and the Interpretation of Religion.* Cambridge: Cambridge University Press.

Vygotsky, Lev (1978). The Role of Play in Development. In *Mind and Society*, trans. Michael Cole. Cambridge, MA: Harvard University Press, 92–104.

Winkler, Gisela (2003). Ethical Issues in Narrative Research. *Educational Action Research*, 11(3), 389–402.

Young, Michael (ed.) (1971). *Knowledge and Control: New Directions for the Sociology of Education.* London: Collier Macmillan.

— (2008). From Constructivism to Realism in the Sociology of the Curriculum. *Review of Research in Education*, 32(1), 1–28.

Chapter 5

Problematizing what Counts as Knowledge and the Production of Knowledges in Music

Pamela Burnard

In this chapter, I want to do two things. First, I wish to problematize what counts as teacher knowledges in music, to acknowledge what *kind* of musical knowledge is held and why that knowledge is important in the particular contexts in which teachers teach. Second, I will acknowledge the increased attention being given to the role of culture (and cultural learning) in teacher knowledge and the growing understanding of the influence culture has at the heart of learning (Cultural Learning Alliance 2011). I am aiming to reinstate the issue of knowledge creation as being integral to music and music teacher education; that is, what precisely do new teachers need to know and what is the knowledge that can be gained from music classroom environments that address what Invaldi and O'Neill (2008) call the 'resonance gap', which is a gulf between student interest and the school music curriculum?

Theme 1: Why do Conceptions of Music *Knowledges* need to be Broadened?

The Western approach to defining what constitutes musical knowledge has been to compartmentalize, or to look at, one type of music; for example, concentrating on European/Western classical 'art' tradition, in isolation from popular music and non-Western cultures. We see this, for example, in the distinction between high and low art which, as Cook in *Music: A Very Short Introduction* (1998) argues, 'still persists in the standard format of music history or appreciation textbooks'. This approach tells the story of Western 'art' music, focused at first on Europe and then expanding in the nineteenth century to North America. And then, after the story is basically finished, they add a chapter or two on popular music (possibly tracing its history before the twentieth century, but concentrating on jazz – which has been transformed since the Second World War into a kind of alternative 'art' tradition – and rock) (p. 44).

By compartmentalizing and privileging one type of music over another we delude ourselves into thinking that we are seeing the whole picture. We see this, for example, when Elliott (1991, p. 37) describes musical performing as 'both a form of knowledge and a source of knowledge' – that there is a presumption that the epistemological importance of musical performances of Western classical and jazz, which are the examples given, is what lies at the core rather than at the limits and across the boundaries of *all* musics.

More fundamentally, children in the early childhood years do not think and work in a compartmentalized way. For them, experience is interconnected, as argued by Manins (1994, p. 39) where 'language, drama, movement, art and music can be inextricably bound together in an enjoyable experience that both stimulates the imagination and stands by itself as an aesthetic entity'. It is time for *musical knowledges* to be broadened out from historically and culturally singular and specific cases, defined by both a mainstream and a core of accepted texts, methods and presumptions. Indeed, the history of subject knowledge in school music needs to be replaced by a pluralistic perspective on music knowledges. It is as much about the distinction between informal learning involving context-specific cultural knowledge as about formal learning of high-order codified knowledge.

According to Wilson and Demetriou (2007, p. 215), teacher knowledge can be interpreted and classified into two categories (Table 5.1). First, *codified knowledge*, which underpins formal learning, is based on the idea that learning is primarily a cognitive 'of the mind' or an accumulation of propositional knowledge that can be transferred to practice through a variety of contextual situations. Codified knowledge is embedded in texts, cultural practices, scholarship and research and takes the form of organization-specific information such as textbooks, records, correspondence and manuals. Codified knowledge is related to intellectual development and progresses through a hierarchy leading to greater levels of sense-making and meaning, of abstraction and a deeper understanding. Second, *context-specific knowledge*, which is acquired informally and underpins informal learning, is practical, context specific and known variously as cultural knowledge (Eraut 2004) or horizontal knowledge (Bernstein 1999).

Table 5.1   Types of teacher knowledge (according to Wilson and Demetriou 2007)

Codified knowledge		
Formal learning	Declarative knowledge	Intellectual development
	Propositional knowledge	Greater levels of abstraction
	Vertical knowledge	Understanding universal ideas
		Making meaning
		Progress through a hierarchy of knowledge and skills
Context-specific knowledge		
Informal learning	Practical knowledge	Experiential
	Cultural knowledge	Problem-solving
	Horizontal knowledge	Processes
		Making informed judgements

For Bernstein, knowledge structures differ in two ways. The first is in terms of what may be called *verticality*. Verticality is concerned with how theory develops. Horizontal knowledge structures, on the other hand, are plural, consisting of series of parallel incommensurable languages. The stronger the grammar of a language, the more stably it is able to generate empirical correlates and the more unambiguous because it further restricts the field of referents. In Bernstein's terms, the organization of knowledge is, most significantly, a device for the regulation of consciousness, thus promoting a fundamental change from *what is known* (and how) to *who knows it*. In other words, the knower's structures in music can vary depending on whether the knower possess a privileged 'gaze' – that is, a particular mode of recognizing and realigning what counts as an music or how 'knower-grammar' (or social relations) is framed and illustrated by notions of 'natural talent', 'genius', 'trained' or 'cultivated', which refers to the strengths of classification and the framing of privileged knowers and their dispositions. To admit that music knowledges are but perspectives – points of view on the world – like paradigms – is to acknowledge *received conceptions of musical knowledge* and their relation to power, so that the political investments of *all* musical knowledges and discourses, as well as their content, become objects of analysis and contestation (see Lamont and Maton 2008, for an exploratory study in the low uptake of music as a school curriculum subject using a Bernsteinian classification of the formation of music knowledge as a school curriculum subject). This opens up a multiplicity of postmodern vantage points about rethinking what constitutes music knowledges produced at specific times and places, where their genesis is reconsidered central to the music they produce. Postmodern and critical realist approaches to conceptions of musical knowledge share claims for music's powerful relationship between language and discourse, leading to a standpoint on the authenticity of the voice (or knower) and experience. As Kramer highlights, from the perspective of postmodern musicology:

> As the polarization of music and language erodes, and the participation of music in the communicative economy gains recognition, the distinction between music in itself and an external conceptual or narrative 'substrate' becomes increasingly arbitrary … narrative elements in music represent, not forces of structure, but forces of meaning. (Kramer 1995, p. 67)

The result, in terms of the privileged musical knower, where knowledge is defined by the 'knower' (and knower group), is in the organization and positioning of certain knowledges to education. A major reason for our interest in the changing nature of music teacher knowledges is to inform the professional formation and development of teachers so that they in turn can help to rethink and recontextualize what kind of music knowledges they hold and why that knowledge is important in the particular contexts in which they will teach (see Maton and Moore 2010). What if the processes of music knowledges and their production were acknowledged as produced outside of history, capable of being assessed and re-evaluated independently of the space and time of its production? We cannot assume that ideas about music teacher knowledge that apply in one setting have universal application.

Theme 2: What kind of Musical Knowledges are held, and Why are they Important in the Particular Context in which Music Teachers Teach?

One feature of a knowledge economy is a political requirement to audit and serve providers in order to establish a cost–benefit analysis for expenditure in particular areas. Teachers' music knowledge *for* teaching has not been immune from this societal preoccupation from auditing (Woodford 2011). And it is not that these issues are unimportant, but that how they are dealt with depends on prior attention to the question of knowledge and the type of knowledges that can be *acquired* and *produced* at school, college or university and on the common-sense or *practical knowledge* that we acquire in our everyday lives. The discontinuity between *curriculum music knowledge* and everyday musical experience is just one of the challenges facing teacher education. There are presumptions about knowledge production and assessment, the criteria by which knowledges are produced and how such knowledges are judged to be of value and/or true.

What do music teachers need to 'know about' and experience as practical knowledge? Or is it the experience of 'not knowing' a highly productive moment where uncertainty is generated in which the cultural dimension of pedagogical content knowledge and the practice of teaching come together in a different way from when the construct of pedagogical content knowledge was introduced? As Shulman himself noted about the teaching effectiveness studies which were popular when he proposed the idea of pedagogical content knowledge, 'to conduct a piece of research, scholars must necessarily narrow their scope, focus their view, and formulate a question far less complex than the form in which the world presents itself in practice' (Shulman 1986, p. 6). Shulman focused on specific school subjects at secondary school level and studied teachers in California. But can the observations of teachers in one US state produce a construct that has the same meaning throughout the world? For example, Shulman asked about the knowledge needed by a teacher when presented with 'flawed or muddled textbook chapters', and what 'analogies, metaphors, examples, demonstrations, and rephrasings' the teacher can use to explain, represent or clarify ideas (Shulman 1986, p. 8). Yet the cultural embedding of music knowledge for and in teaching in the national cultural discourses in which music teaching and learning are represented in this book consider music teacher knowledge as a social construction that is shaped by the particular national educational system wherein it functions. The problem here is what manifests as the singular use of *received* music *knowledge* rather than the constitution of and competing obligations of teaching and developing music knowledges *for* teaching in diverse 'knowledge economy' cultures and cultural settings.

By acknowledging the cultural dimension of teachers' musical knowledges we increase attention of the role of culture in music teacher knowledge. For teachers to possess such competing knowledges of musics from the margins and the spaces between music disciplines (such as composition in video gaming, film music, digital livecoding, DJing and Mcing, etc.) brings both practical experience and theoretical research to bear on the spaces of exclusion between music disciplines and systems of contemporary music knowledges. How would they be judged?

From a global perspective, one of the fundamental principles of the way we are educating our children looks at *how and what count as knowledges are defined, construed and constructed* within and outside of formal classrooms. As Green (2000) and hooks (1994) have stated, there remains a dissonance between what teachers (and schools) must do and what parents and children understand education to be. Greene insists that to 'understand education we must consider the various contexts that affect it' (p. 219). These principles are shifting and redefining the way musical skills and knowledge are perpetuated and for the formal organization of music learning and teaching in relation to music and education. What was described once as *music education* is being revised to focus on *world music in education* with global perspectives on learning and teaching *music cultures in education* denoting the diversity and multiplicity of musics and musical environments, cultures and communities, encounters and experiences, musical identities and knowledges. New music invites new practices (Burnard 2012).

Swanwick, in his seminal text *Musical Knowledge: Intuition, Analysis and Music Education* (Routledge 1994) argues for a *form of musical knowledge* for distinguishing curriculum knowledge from the knowledge we acquire in the course of our everyday lives. The critique here concerns the notion of tying musical knowledge to a singular or compartmentalized form rather than as multiple forms to particular fields of production, and of recognition of the cultural need for a sub-based curriculum which does not exclude all voices except those of the Western tradition or academic elite. The multiple forms of music knowledges – which are all products of fluid rather than fixed *social practices* and which recognize interrelations between the individual, school context, home cultures and the wider community, as well as the integrative process of diverse fields of production – need to be acknowledged *and* valued.

Many practising musicians work as teachers of music in education. These professionals are particularly skilled at representing types and distinct conceptions of music knowledges that are transmitted and acquired at school, college or university. The common-sense or practical knowledge that they construct and construe in their everyday informal encounters and musical experiences – as commonly coined 'enculturated' (Smith 2013) – are often fundamental aspects that are not explored in precise and detailed ways nor present or promoted in in-service training programmes. The potentialities of drawing upon and within their musical worlds are given less emphasis than on a *body of knowledge* to be *learned* rather than *renewed* through multi-modal forms (such as achieved through the body's sensorimotor capacities operating as bodily engagement with acoustic, kinesthetic, tactile/gestural and visual modes). Teachers' self-images or identities as musicians are invested with sedimentations of professional and personal and communal histories and futures that exemplify and articulate musical knowledges rather than those which recognize a distinction between the type of musical knowledge that can be acquired at school, college, or university and the common-sense or practical knowledge that we acquire in our everyday lives. To put it another way, music curriculum knowledge remains discontinuous, not continuous with every musical experience, especially in terms of the *possibility of knowledges and their construction*. As Grosz (1995, p. 37) asserts:

> Knowledges are not purely conceptual nor merely intellectual; they are not governed by a love of truth or a will to comprehension. The images of knowledges have always been, and remain today, bereft of an understanding of their own (textual) corporeality. Knowledge is an activity; it is a *practice* and not a contemplative reflection. It *does things*. As product or thing, it denies its historicity and asserts its indifference to questions of politics in such a way that it functions as a tool directed to any particular purposes its user chooses. Knowledges are effects of a drive for mastery, a visceral force or impulse to appropriate and subdue, a will to power.

Within the institutional theories of music, which dominate contemporary discourses in the field of music education, there is an increasing awareness about the way that musical knowledges are being expressed (and transmitted) and the need for socio-cultural considerations of the nature of music knowledges in teaching. Student teachers are encouraged to think about the significance of theory and practice in the characterization, assessment and development of teachers' musical content knowledges but they are also advised to approach the cultural 'given's, typically unseen and unquestioned, by seeing possibilities beyond familiar ways of being and doing and looking to practice in cultures other than their own. In this way they are invited to engage critically with the way their music teaching may be being corralled into a process which can be antithetical to its goals and to self-consciously position their making within these structures as they are played out within the field of music education. Likewise, a significant numbers of musicians/music educators today work in ways that may be described as *socially engaged*, for example where they work musically with a community to represent and explore social justice (see for example, Gould et al. 2009) or foreground the significance of music in the construction of identities and ethnicities and re-vision ways to teach music as social practice (O'Neill 2009).

Theme 3: So what Constitutes Professional Knowledge for Music Teachers?

Just as the riding of a bicycle denotes or connotes meaning(s) grounded in embodied, practical knowledge, Polanyi (1967) calls 'tacit' knowledge that which eludes modes of abstract thought. By tacit knowledge he means something like the bodily ability to act in relation to things such as the many instances and localities within the contingencies of everyday experience of listening to – or participation in and comprehension of – music, which puts into play a whole host of assumptions and presumptions about what constitutes professional knowledge and knowledge creation for music teachers. Tacit or enculturated knowledge is the precondition for most social and cultural practices of music in that 'we can know more than we can tell' (p. 4). It follows that not all musical practices are representable through language nor can they necessarily be taught through linguistic means. There are many instances and localities outside the contingencies of everyday life (those of religion, ritual, culture, the Internet) where people have attended to the needs of their musical interests in highly specialized ways; music is one of the most concentrated, intended, individuated in thought/action, and embodied of socio-culturally produced activities, practices or things that contribute to knowledge and the meaning potentials in the pedagogic field of arts education.

Within the three ways of referencing the field of music education, music in education and education in music, these different ways of conceptualizing the relationship between education and music point to the plurality of music knowledges that characterize everyday experience. The latter two remove the adjectival status of music (e.g. music education) in schooling, teaching and learning, and assign music equal status to education. Those advocating this perspective on music and education see this linking process as setting a tone that encourages learners and teachers to be co-constructors and shapers of knowledge rather than recipients of knowledge shaped primarily by forces external to them. Moreover, there is little problem in recognizing the legitimacy of musical practices as a form of knowledge production, but this puts into play a whole host of assumptions and presumptions about what constitutes professional knowledge – that is, the knowledge of those whose livelihoods depend on employment in settings where such experiences and knowledges are created, such as artists and audiences, students and/or community members. The experiences that inform and are informed by music and the creative practices they potentially nurture become paramount. In this way, the construction of musical knowledge is predicated on understanding the cultural and social contexts that shape and sustain new practices, musical art forms and interactions, the products that emerge from them, and the sense of self, possibility and learning that is experienced in and through music. However, in the disjunction between the different imperatives of institutional pedagogies, music teacher education and arts educational research, diverse forms and manifestations of arts-based knowledges and knowledge creation are often deemed inappropriate. Presumably, this non-recognition relates to the way in which such practices, although they may be educational in themselves, do not explicitly investigate, analyse or evaluate artistic/musical practices as educational processes: they do not represent the process because they are the process. But these processes are forms of knowledge embodied through action on and with musical materials designed for and within specific physical and cultural environments.

Although forms of knowledge are increasingly recognized within the musings of academe as embodied, social, constructed and multimodal (Addison 2003), researchers within the field often follow mono-modal, abstract procedures when enquiring into educational phenomena such as the knowledge of specialized subjects in order to produce mathematicians or musicians, or that each teacher, through his or her specialism, contributes to 'the total enterprise' that 'develops the mind' through the 'medium' of the disciplines (Addison 2003, pp. 61–2). The limitations of language-based analysis and evaluation tend to overlook other forms of knowledge production such as different *fields of knowledge production* where discourses are redefined and changed (Moore and Maton 2010). In claiming this I do not wish to belittle the central position of written language as a significant form of knowledge, particularly in relation to professional knowledge with the field of music teacher education, but to question the way it is privileged. The hierarchical mono-modality that underpins this emphasis has been critiqued from a number of quarters; notably by Addison (2003), who notes the rupture between the everyday practices of an increasingly digitally literate population and educationalists. This hierarchy is particularly felt in music education by music educators whose habitus, dispositions (here I am referring to the tendencies toward different patterns of behaviour and professional skills) and professional practices gravitate towards modalities other than words and numbers. What follows is an attempt to open up, state and discover what constitutes, notably, my own reservations about my music teacher training course, the ennobling interchange between one's own practices, research, theory and policy, and daring to think differently about music teacher education in sensitive and expansive ways.

Theme 4: The Significance of Knowledge Creation for Renewal in Music Teacher Education

What specialized knowledge of music does a music teacher need to have in order to go into a class or studio to teach children, young people and adults, in schools, organizations and other communities? Beauchamp (2010, p. 305) reported on a five-year study that examined primary school student teachers' knowledge of the musical elements as they entered their teacher training (the one-year Post Graduate Certificate in Education (PGCE) course in one institution). The results suggest that particular musical elements 'as defined by relevant national curricula (duration, pace, pitch and silence) need refreshment' while student teachers' knowledge of timbre, texture, dynamics and structure 'need significant development in schools and in training courses' (p. 305). He concludes that 'knowledge does not guarantee effective teaching' (p. 317).

The dilemma for professionals is that there continue to be mixed messages from policy-makers and agencies which support policy implementation about what is of real value within education and learning in both school and higher education environments. Increasingly, calls for enhanced awareness of the uniqueness of knowledge developed through the arts suggest that students learn to innovate and think creatively and are provided with opportunities for the exploration and formation of values and an opportunity to develop social skills that do not occur as naturally in other arts. While the arts are certainly not the only creative domain, they are decidedly creative arenas where the application of knowledge and skills in new ways to achieve a valued goal is characterized. Within higher education and workplace learning discourse, artists' knowledge has been characterized as practitioner knowledge or know-how valued in the art-making process. Within the rapid changes of the knowledge society, creating new knowledge and making knowledge accessible from outside the bounds of formal institutions and learning are becoming explicit goals in schools.

The construction of knowledge within a particular environment is a notion that was pioneered by Dewey (1980, p. 79): 'I believe that the school must represent present life – life as real and vital to the child as that which he carries on in the home, in the neighbourhood, or on the playground.' These ideas resonate with the idea that learning is 'situated'; it does not occur in a vacuum but rather through one's environment and lived experiences. The concept of musical knowledges and how they are constructed within communities is the intentional activity of individuals who, as members of a community, make use of and produce representations using a collaborative attempt to better understand and transform their shared world. In this way, knowledge creation becomes the production of knowledge as collaborative knowledge-building – whether by teachers in classrooms or researchers working with teachers to investigate the ways students enquire into their musical worlds and their musical learning. In these and other interactions, musical knowledges and knowledge creation require us to unpack assumptions about what constitutes musical reality and relevance for students and is as critical as the content of our teaching. Similarly important is uncovering the process by which emerging and practising music educators come to know what they know about the content and nature of musical cultures and experiences, and the students, families, and communities whom they support.

Concluding Thoughts

Trainee teachers need alternative approaches to those which rest on assumptions that emphasize the *differences* rather than the *continuity* between types of knowledge – and specifically the differences between theoretical (i.e. between types of knowledge that are a mere reflection of traditions established and canons from earlier times) and everyday or common-sense musical knowledge which has *epistemological* and *pedagogical* significance. In other words, they relate in fundamental ways to how young people learn and how they produce and acquire new musical knowledges.

Music teacher educators need to seek new opportunities to become producers of research knowledge rather than simply its users, so they will improve their practice in the light of evidence of which they have ownership. Young people are remarkably insightful in discussing their commitments to and experiences of learning. If we are genuinely interested in supporting what musically and creatively matters to pupils, then we need not only to gain a deeper understanding of how these changes occur but also to ask what music education should look like and what it ought to be. As music educators we can respond to these challenges by taking our agenda for change, at least in part, from both children and young people's accounts of the ways in which they come to know music throughout the world. We need to become professionally and personally engaged in raising questions about children and young people's musical experience – their observations about the role music plays in their lives; what they use music for in their daily lives; what the shifts in young people's engagement in music are; what characterizes school music cultures and whether they are appropriate.

If we are to open new musical realms for children and young people as musically creative learners who delight in pleasure and choice, then we need to create new possibilities for experiencing music diversity. We need to continue to redefine school music and its relevance to young people. We need to continue to build bridges between the diverse musical realities of young people and the musical reality of the school from within the formal curriculum and complementary educational sites. One step is to listen to pupils not just in the evaluation and planning of pedagogic practices which foreground creative learning in music. They need to explicitly have our respect for what they have to say about – and what they do creatively in –music. Another step is through school-based educational research and development where music teachers receive grants to support teacher-led research. We also need to share teacher-led research (along with practice) via networked learning communities, which can play a critical role in providing opportunities for the exploration and implementation of alternative forms and view of what constitutes musical knowledges.

Questions for Reflection

1 How should the division of types of teacher knowledges – into useful practical knowledge, theoretical educational research knowledge, codified and context-specific knowledge – be balanced in the training of music teachers?
2. Express the values you consider important for rethinking the role of practising music teachers and music teacher educators in the creation, application and dissemination of professional knowledge about what works in schools and classrooms.
3 Why is becoming a teacher considered to be a socially constructed and dynamic process involving interpretive interactions with new contexts?

References

Addison, Nicholas (2003). Productive Tensions: Residencies in Research. In Nicholas Addison and Lesley Burgess (eds), *Issues in Art and Design Teaching*. London: Routledge Falmer.

Beauchamp, Gary (2010). Musical Elements and Subject Knowledge in Primary School Student Teachers: Lessons from a Five-Year Longitudinal Study. *British Journal of Music Education*, 27(3), 305–318.

Bernstein, Basil (1999). Vertical and Horizontal Discourse: An Essay. *British Journal of Sociology of Education*, 20(2), 157–73.

Burnard, Pamela (2012). *Musical Creativities in Practice*. Oxford: Oxford University Press.

Cook, Nicholas (1998). *Music: A Very Short Introduction*. Oxford: Oxford University Press.

Cultural Learning Alliance (2011). *Key Research Findings: The Case for Cultural Learning*. London: Cultural Learning Alliance.

Dewey, John (1980). *Art as Experience*. New York: Perigee Books.

Elliott, D.J. (1991). Music as Knowledge. *Journal of Aesthetic Education*, 25(3), 21–40.

Eraut, Michael (2004). Informal Learning in the Workplace. *Studies in Continuing Education*, 26, 247–73.

Gould, Elizabeth; Countryman, June; Morton, Charlene and Rose, Leslie Stewart (eds) (2009). *Exploring Social Justice: How Music Education Might Matter.* Volume 4 of the Biennial Series *Research to Practice*, Series Editor Lee R. Bartel. Toronto: Canadian Music Educators' Association.

Green, Maxine (2000). *Releasing the Imagination: Essays on Education, the Arts and Social Change*. San Francisco: Jossey-Bass.

Grosz, Elizabeth (1995). *Space, Time and Perversion: Essays on the Politics of Bodies*. London: Routledge.

hooks, bell (1994). *Teaching to Transgress: Education as the Practice of Freedom*. London: Routledge.

Ivaldi, Antonia and O'Neill, Susan A. (2008). Adolescents' Musical Role Models: Whom do They Admire and Why? *Psychology of Music*, 36(4), 395–415.

Kramer, Lawrence (1995). *Classical Music and Postmodern Knowledge*. Berkeley and Los Angeles: University of California Press.

Lamont, Alexandra and Maton, Karl (2008). Choosing Music: Exploratory Studies into the Low Uptake of Music GCSE. *British Journal of Music Education*, 25(3), 267–82.

Manins, Stuart (1994). Bridge Building in Early-Childhood Music. *Music Educators Journal*, 80(5), 37–41.

Moore, Rob and Maton, Karl (2010). *Social Realism, Knowledge and the Sociology of Education*. London: Continuum.

O'Neill, Susan A. (2009). Revisioning Musical Understandings through a Cultural Diversity Theory of Difference. In Elizabeth Gould, June Countryman,

Charlene Morton and Leslie Stewart Rose (eds), *Exploring Social Justice: How Music Education Might Matter.* Volume 4 of the Biennial Series *Research to Practice*, Series Editor Lee R. Bartel. Toronto: Canadian Music Educators' Association, 70–90.

Polanyi, Michael (1967). *The Tacit Dimension.* London: Routledge.

Shulman, Lee (1986). Those who Understand: Knowledge Growth in Teaching. *Educational Research*, 15(2), 4–14.

Smith, Gareth Dylan (2013). *I Drum, Therefore I Am: Being and Becoming a Drummer*. Farnham: Ashgate.

Swanwick, K. (1994) *Musical Knowledge: Intuition, Analysis and Music Education*. London and New York: Routledge.

Wilson, Elaine and Demetriou, Helen (2007). New Teacher Learning: Substantive Knowledge and Contextual Factors. *Curriculum Journal*, 18(3), 213–29.

Woodford, Paul G. (ed.) (2011). Re-Thinking Standards for the Twenty-First Century: New Realities, New Challenges, New Propositions. *Studies in Music from The University of Western Ontario*, 23, 1–149.

PART II
Professional and Pedagogical Practice

Chapter 6

Constructing Professional Paths in a School-Embedded Methods Course

Suzanne L. Burton

It is 7:00 a.m.. The pre-service music teachers embark upon their first teaching experience at the middle-school general music practicum site. They arrive early, leaving enough time to prepare materials for their lessons and to participate in the school's daily ritual of the Pledge of Allegiance, announcements, trivia question and a moment of silence. Dressed in their finest teacher-clothes, they are excited, nervous, and concerned. Now serving in the role of 'music teacher', they wonder: Will the students like us? Will they be interested in our lessons? How can we engage and excite them about making music? The morning bell rings and twenty-eight middle-school students filter into the classroom. Taking their seats, they eye the new teachers in the room and are curious as to what they have in store for them. They speculate: Will we like music class as taught by these new teachers? Will we *have* to participate in their activities? Will class be fun or boring? In these first silent moments of student–teacher interaction, the pre-service music teachers' semester-long experience of teaching in an authentic context begins. (Pre-service music teachers' first day at Shipley School)

Introduction

The observation of music teaching and learning is not enough for pre-service music teachers to develop the expertise necessary to succeed in the early years of a career. 'Only when [teacher] preparation programs become deeply engaged with schools will their clinical preparation become truly robust and will they be able to support the development of candidates' urgently needed skills and learn what schools really need' (NCATE 2010, p. 3). Through school–university partnerships, pre-service music teachers become socialized into the profession, particularly when such partnerships are based on dialogue among the triad of pre-service music teacher, in-service music teacher and university professor (Conkling and Henry 1999; Burton and Greher 2010; Abrahams 2011). Situated learning (such as in a school setting) provides a vehicle for pre-service music teachers' development of expertise and specialized knowledge about music teaching and learning (Shulman 1986; Alexander 2003). For pre-service music teachers, the practicum setting offers an *approximate* authentic context for the development of knowledge (Schön 1987).

Contextual learning contributes to pre-service music teachers' growth as professionals, providing the milieu to 'put on' the role of music teacher.

Authentic Contexts for Learning

'When someone learns a practice, he is initiated into the traditions of a community of practitioners and the practice world they inhabit' (Schön 1987, p. 36). Teaching experiences in authentic contexts are fertile ground to nurture the capacity of pre-service music teachers to plan effectively for instruction, become acculturated to the nature of schooling, make connections between theory and practice, and have a greater understanding of the musical competence of school students (Schön 1987; Conkling and Henry 1999; Conkling 2004, 2007; Burton and Greher 2007, 2010, 2011). Campbell and Thompson suggested that the development of professional knowledge occurs in terms of a progression in which the pre-service music teacher advances from task concerns to self-concerns, eventually to impact concerns (as cited in Campbell, Thompson and Barrett 2010). Over time, a shift occurs in which pre-service music teachers move towards a greater focus on school students as learners. Direct encounters with school students in authentic contexts may help facilitate pre-service music teachers' acquisition of professional knowledge as they concentrate on music teaching in light of student learning.

Firsthand experience working with the underlying knowledge and skills necessary for teaching music are critical to pre-service music teachers' success in the music classroom. Opportunities to plan for student learning based upon a long view of curriculum construction and implementation may facilitate pre-service music teachers' selection of instructional goals by being active decision-makers and curriculum implementers. Assessment of student learning and analytical reflection holds the possibility for pre-service music teachers to gauge their own effectiveness in the classroom. Through this type of work – authentic work in authentic contexts – they may become more student-oriented, allowing for the diversification of the musical landscape to support music learning with relevant purposes for different students (Thiessen and Barrett 2002; Hammerness et al. 2005; NCATE 2010).

Bransford, Darling-Hammond and LePage (2005, p. 11) stated that professional practice within a democratic society is formed from teachers having deep knowledge of (a) their learners and their development in social contexts; (b) subject matter and curriculum goals; and (c) teaching. In kind, methods courses should be created to address these aspects in order to facilitate and support pre-service music teachers' understanding of how students learn and the corresponding implications for the skills and knowledge they must acquire. Therefore, the formation of professional knowledge must not only incorporate how pre-service music teachers gain pedagogical content knowledge, but also an operative understanding of 'what *students* need for their teachers to know' (Bransford, Darling-Hammond and LePage 2005, p. 21).

Constructivism as a Basis for School-Embedded Learning

Developing the professional knowledge and competencies of pre-service music teachers through school-embedded learning is recommended by researchers who study learning how to teach (for example, see Berliner 1985; Schön 1987; Zeichner 2007, 2010; Darling-Hammond 2009). Methods courses structured with a combination of school-embedded practice and laboratory-type experiences, along with related coursework, appear to help pre-service music teachers develop both the knowledge base and skills of professional practice. Yet, within the United States, teacher education researchers consistently acknowledge 'the disconnect between what students are taught in campus courses and their opportunities for learning to enact these practices in their school placements' (Zeichner 2010). With this disassociation in mind, I contemplated how a university methods course with such features as school-embedded learning might facilitate and support the growth of professional knowledge within pre-service music teachers. Just as Dewey (1998) argued, the justification for a curriculum resides in how it relates to the experiences and responsibilities a student is likely to have upon finishing school. Looking to constructivism as the underpinning for the school-embedded design, I created the course *Teaching Secondary General Music* with the aim of blending course material with a significant amount of practical teaching experience in the context of a middle school (grades 6–8, approximately ages 11–14).

Constructivist-Based Pedagogy

Constructivism is a theory of knowledge which forms a philosophical basis for the formation of a number of learning theories. Taken together, these theories inform constructivist pedagogy, in which education is grounded in real life experience (Dewey 1963), with understanding formed cognitively from one logical structure after another through assimilation and accommodation (Piaget 1950). It is an interactive, social process (Vygotsky 1978) where new ideas or concepts are acquired based on students' current knowledge (Bruner 1960). An intertwined process of teaching and learning, knowledge and meaning are generated through human interactions and experiences (McMahon 1997; Fosnot 2005). Not to be confused with *constructionism* (Papert and Harel 1991), a derivative of constructivism, which asserts that learning occurs when people are makers of tangible products, constructivist theory places the responsibility of learning upon the student, enabled through constructivist-based pedagogy. In the enactment of this pedagogy, the instructor is the creator of an environment designed to foster the making of meaning within each learner, functioning as a facilitator in the interconnected process of teaching and learning (Dewey 1998; Brownstein 2001; Fosnot 2005). With constant interchange through guided questioning and provocation, the facilitator assists the learner in moving from a passive role to that of an active participant. The learner becomes increasingly capable of engaging in metacognition through experience and guidance (Israel 2005). Over time, the learner is assisted through the zone of proximal development, increasing his or her practical and conceptual knowledge with less and less dependence on the facilitator to scaffold learning (Vygotsky 1978).

School-Embedded Teacher Education

In a school-embedded methods course, pre-service music teachers negotiate many disparate elements within an educational setting: school students, in-service teachers and administrators, the school environment, their pre-service peers, and university course instructor. Constructivist-based pedagogy, by design, should enable the acquisition of professional knowledge due to its very features of learning while doing, and the participation of pre-service music teachers in critical reflection and discourse while working in a challenging, contextualized environment.

From the very beginning of the *Teaching Secondary General Music* course, I deliberately viewed the cohort of six, third-year pre-service music teachers as young professionals, charging them to take on the role of 'middle school general music teacher', giving them the task of constructing, implementing and assessing the curriculum that they would put into place at the practicum school. Throughout the semester, the pre-service music teachers became a professional learning community (PLC). They worked collaboratively on course and practicum assignments, furthering the PLC concept, which features the cooperation of practitioners towards continuous enquiry and improvement for the betterment of their students. This approach to the methods course displaced me from the comfort zone of 'university professor, curriculum overseer' to the position of 'coach' on the sidelines, allowing the university course design to emerge, based on the pre-service music teachers' and school students' needs.

Scholarship of Teaching and Learning

Shulman asserted that participating in the 'Scholarship of teaching and learning supports our individual and professional roles, our practical responsibilities to our students and our institutions, and our social and political obligations to those that support and take responsibility for higher education' (Shulman 2000, p. 53). Engaging in the scholarship of teaching and learning was crucial to understanding my students' experiences within the course. Therefore, it was natural for me to participate in practitioner research: 'instead of research *on* teacher education *by* an outside party, it is research *by* teacher educators *about* their practice' (Borko, Whitcomb and Byrnes 2008, p. 1029). As a practitioner-researcher, I wanted to understand the realities created by the pre-service music teachers. I was concerned how the school-embedded design of the methods course functioned, and foremost whether professional knowledge was constructed as they made pedagogical decisions through observation, enquiry, education and experience (Stake 2010). Taking part in the scholarship of teaching and learning as a practitioner-researcher allowed for an approach through which I could evaluate the methods course and learn more about the knowledge and skills the students' gained, or the pitfalls they encountered throughout the semester (Robbins 1993; Patton 2002).

Course Context

The practicum was held at Shipley School, a middle school serving students in grades 6–8. In this setting, the school administration gave permission to the in-service teachers to step aside and allow the pre-service music teachers to take ownership of their classes. The school is racially, socially and economically diverse as compared to the six pre-service music teachers, who were white, from middle- to upper-class families. Often, the school students do not choose to be in general music class, but find that it is has been placed on their schedules due to lack of sufficient electives, thus many of the students do not want to be there. Over the 15-week semester, pre-service music teachers' time in the course was divided between 15 practicum visits to Shipley School and 15 class sessions at the university. The pre-service music teachers taught three general music classes per visit, teaching in dyads for the first five classes of the semester, progressing to solo teaching for the remaining ten classes of the semester.

Course Evaluation

To study the effectiveness of this approach to the methods course and its influence on the formation of the pre-service music teachers' professional knowledge, I sought multiple perspectives primarily through assignments that encouraged reflective practice. Within 24 hours after each school visit, the pre-service music teachers submitted reflective journals by email. 'Journals are a useful way to capture and record evolving learning and thinking ... journals kept over time produce ideas that go beyond the surface, exposing what is both familiar but forgotten, as well as uncovering what is new' (Robbins 1993, p. 47). The journals were a means for the pre-service music teachers to debrief and interpret their teaching experiences. As another mode of reflection, pre-service music teachers were videotaped as they taught and subsequently wrote pre-and post-video observation reports. Detailed fieldnotes (which often doubled as feedback memos to the pre-service music teachers), curriculum outlines and lesson plans, the course syllabus, notes from classes held at the university, and the results of an open-ended, questionnaire through which the pre-service music teachers were to provide advice to the 'next generation' of secondary general music students provided additional vantage points from which to evaluate the functionality of the course.

I deliberated over the pre-service music teachers' journal entries, videotapes and papers, as well as fieldnotes sampled from the beginning, middle and end of the semester, to create a formative representation of the pre-service music teachers' construction of professional knowledge. I also re-familiarized myself with the additional course documents. From this analysis, three broad themes emerged: (a) Relational Music Education, (b) Instructional Enlightenment, and (c) Becoming Real. The themes elucidate the professional knowledge created (or left by the wayside) by the pre-service music teachers over 15 weeks' time.

Professional Knowledge: Under Construction

As the pre-service music teachers progressed through the school-embedded methods course, their acquisition of professional knowledge was clearly under construction. Following are accounts that illuminate what pre-service teachers learned about middle-school students, the creation and implementation of curriculum, and their perspectives on their development as music educators.

Relational Music Education

> I was pleasantly surprised after my first day at Shipley School. Given the profile of the school, I was anticipating a lot of behavioural issues and didn't have high expectations for the music classes we were going to work with. What I found out was that the students at Shipley are really quite open to learning music. Some of the students weren't as willing to participate, but I think that in time, we will be able to have the whole class engaged in our lessons. (Tania)

Like Tania, the pre-service music teachers began their practicum experience with a concern for engaging the middle-school students in music. Though they were nervous and anxious about the first few classes, they wanted to build relationships with the students and have a positive impact on them, even amidst challenges of relating to diverse students with diverse musical tastes and backgrounds. At the beginning of their practicum, they primarily had 'book knowledge' regarding adolescent learners and were concerned with what the students knew and were able to do musically.

As the pre-service music teachers grew to know the students as people rather than students whom they were practising to teach, the more self-confidence they displayed in the classroom, and the more confidence the school students had in themselves, resulting in a positive effect on their class participation. Over time, the pre-service music teachers took ownership of the students under their charge. Later in the semester, Marcus, Cindy and Melanie expressed a sense of pride for 'their' students and what they were accomplishing musically. As one pre-service music teacher pointed out, 'Teaching is HARD. Moreover, you get thrilled with every step your students make, making it all worthwhile.'

Relevant, Relatable Curriculum

As the pre-service music teachers implemented their initial lesson plans it was clear that they were not meeting the musical needs of their students. After a passionate discussion on the merits and disadvantages of using popular music, they determined that its use would be a positive vehicle for student learning. They realized that their curriculum should be relatable to their students and its implementation adaptable and flexible in order to meet their students' interests. The pre-service music teachers discovered that the students at Shipley became the most interested and involved in music class when relevant music was used, and the students learned how to play the electric drums, guitar and keyboard, with beat-boxing effects. They realized how powerful active music-making is in the lives of adolescents. On behalf of the cohort, Belinda described the new direction of their curriculum in an email to me after their third class: 'We are planning to introduce the different parts of the drumset tomorrow so that we can start progressing to our final goal. By the end of our time we would like to teach them simple improvisation (I and V) to a popular song and hopefully include one person on the electric drumset and maybe keyboard [and guitar] if we can get that far and hopefully create a "class band" which will unify the class and give them something to be proud of.' The culminating goal of forming a class band became the driving force of the curriculum that was created, furthering a focus for their lesson planning and class preparation.

At first, the students at Shipley were challenging, making classroom management of paramount concern to the pre-service music teachers. However, the new curricular direction inspired the Shipley students to participate musically. Toward the end of the semester I was coaching the students less on classroom management strategies. They felt that they had commanded a 'different kind of attention and respect' from what they had experienced at the beginning of the semester. A bond was created with the students through music, even with the most difficult class that they had taught. 'It is funny to think back to the beginning of the semester when we first taught this class and how we weren't very fond of them. They quickly became my favourite class to teach ... The select few who were troublemakers in the beginning were fully participating and even helping out their classmates. I am definitely going to miss teaching this class!' (Bethany)

Instructional Enlightenment

> Music teaching and learning is a never-ending process, always evolving and always being edited. (Belinda)

Theory into Practice

During classes at the university, various learning theories were discussed along with their practical application. The fruit of these discussions became apparent in the pre-service music teachers' instruction. Understanding adolescent development was critical as the pre-service music teachers discussed various ways of enacting the curriculum in the PLC meetings. Methods derived from music learning theory (Gordon 2007) influenced curricular sequencing and planning for instruction. Scaffolding (Vygotsky 1978) was observed in their planning and instruction, as were principles of social learning theory (Bandura 1977; Haston 2007).

Constructivism also found its place in their curriculum as they gained comfort to afford the Shipley students opportunities to learn on their own or with peers. Having theoretical knowledge about adolescents and ways to instructionally maximize their learning created space for pre-service music teachers to reflect on their practice and how it impacted the Shipley students.

Turning on a Dime

At the beginning of the semester, intensive lesson planning dominated the pre-service music teachers' curricular focus – they were dependent on their memorized plans. As they became more at ease with the Shipley students, they began to take instructional risks. Marcus related, '[Spontaneously] we decided to split the class up into smaller groups. This turned out to be a very good idea as smaller groups provided opportunities to work more closely with each student.' Melanie learned how to 'think and learn on the fly'. Cindy contended that preparation was key to good teaching: 'I make sure I am prepared, and then I feel ready to teach. Improvising has also become an important part of my teaching. I feel like this is a great attribute to have, especially because a teacher can only plan so much, and the real-world scenarios like fire drills, questions, and a plan not unfolding accordingly always arises.'

Though the pre-service music teachers became more flexible with their teaching, pacing and time management posed to be challenges throughout the semester. Some lessons went uncompleted ('I was going to add in movement, but we didn't get to it'), or the students felt they could have 'move[d] at a faster pace to keep everyone excited and moving [along]'. A sense of relief was expressed by Marcus when class time was utilized as planned: 'it was also supremely gratifying to not only get through the classes, but to succeed in accomplishing the objectives of our lessons.' The pre-service music teachers understood the need for time management and the pacing of their lessons to keep the students' interests, but were still developing these skills at the end of the semester.

Techniques for Teaching

The use of observation, imitation and modelling were effective means for teaching keyboard, electric drums, guitar, and beat-boxing. The pre-service music teachers' would *show* students how to form a good hand position on the keyboard, *demonstrate* how to hold and strum a guitar, or be a *visual example* for playing a simple backbeat on the electric drums along with a pop song. While teaching keyboard, Cindy used modelling to teach improvisation over the chord functions of Bob Marley's song 'One Love' so that students would have an example to work from: 'I explained what the word improvisation was, and then modelled a bassline [using the roots of the I and V chords] with improvised rhythmic patterns ... I allowed them to play their patterns several times ... when it was time to put the whole thing together [playing the bassline and singing the song] the students did really well, and performed very musically.'

Modelling was taken a step further when they employed peer teaching with the school students. When teaching a lesson on guitar, Melanie noted, 'In this lesson I faced a diversity in ability because some students already knew how to play the guitar. Brandon knew all of the chords I was teaching so I had him show me the chord first and that was beneficial because he acted as another visual model for his peers.' Marcus inadvertently found that peer teaching was a means for encouraging the participation of students who were reluctant to try playing the instruments, whereas Bethany 'noticed that some students who had more experience on the guitar or the keyboard were taking the initiative to help their peers'. Here, the pre-service music teachers witnessed the school students helping each other through the zone of proximal development (Vygotsky 1978), seeing constructivism at work firsthand. The school students were eager to assist each other in meeting the aims of creating a garage band for their final class with the pre-service music teachers. The school students led the pre-service music teachers in a natural progression from teacher-based instruction to more of a constructivist approach.

Managing Content
Early on, I suggested that the pre-service music teachers make visual organizers for school students to manage all that they were being taught. Though I tried to help them realize the instructional importance of creating a diagram of the keyboard for students to label the names of the keys or the parts of the guitar or drumset, providing students with chord charts, or creating a word wall to remind students of musical vocabulary, the pre-service music teachers did not take hold of this idea very quickly. They would forget to bring materials, or would hastily create materials at the school site. Melanie wrote in her journal that there was 'dead space' due to the need to write notation on the board and that she should 'have had it prepared before her students came into the classroom'. In time they realized that there was value in making such preparations, but not until they approached the final days of teaching, as mentioned by Belinda in reference to the final class: 'As the students were leaving we handed them three worksheets: one was a strumming pattern, one was the notation to the song 'One Love', and one was a list of guitar resources.' The pre-service music teachers slowly understood the need for teaching in ways that would assist students' learning by meeting a variety of learning styles.

Assessment was routinely addressed during classes at the university and in the pre-service music teachers' lesson plans. At the start of the semester, most assessments were whole-group-oriented; this persisted into the middle of the semester. Becoming better acquainted with their learners and viewing students as individuals rather than as a collective group contributed to the development and use of appropriate assessments. Eventually, student self-assessments, paper and pencil quizzes, questionnaires, and observation checklists were used to gauge what students learned. Towards the end of the semester, the pre-service music teachers began to use assessment results as a way to evaluate their instruction.

The backward design principle for curriculum creation provided a framework to sequence instruction towards a final goal. In practice, the pre-service music teachers moved from teaching *to* the class to a more interactive approach. This involved determining the readiness of the students to learn new material by breaking down concepts and skills in a logical and clear manner. Melanie's comments illustrate the growth that had occurred within the pre-service music teachers during the semester: 'Instead of hearing what I want to hear, I now listen for their readiness for the next part of the lesson ... This is so important in making the lessons sequential and increasingly difficult. If they are struggling with something simple, they cannot move on to something more difficult until they have a full understanding.'

Realizing Students' Potential

Belinda observed that the students were at different ability levels when learning how to play the keyboard. She created additional activities to differentiate her instruction and to help advanced students make progress: 'in the future I will be able to give them exercises to challenge them at the same time the other students are learning the basics.' Marcus echoed a shared sentiment: '[They were] more capable than we realized. All students can achieve when they are reached, you just have to find out how to reach them.' Importantly, they discovered that middle-school students would meet high expectations and were taken aback by what the students had accomplished. As pointed out by one pre-service music teacher at the end of semester, '[I was] humbled at the abilities of my practicum students. Kids are smart. Respect that and they will respect you. And always be humbled by the fact you are changing their lives and school experiences for the better by being there and giving your all.'

Becoming Real

> I really felt like a teacher today. I think I am finally starting to reach them and they are realizing that they are learning! (Melanie)

Newfound Skills

Participating in a school-embedded course provided numerous occasions for the pre-service music teachers to try out their recently acquired skills in 'real time'. For example, the teachers remarked about learning how to play and teach drumset, keyboard and guitar within a very brief period of time. Marcus felt 'stretched learning the basics of playing [the] instruments' but became quite proficient over the semester so that 'he felt comfortable teaching them'.

In the practicum setting, the pre-service music teachers planned together, shared ideas, critiqued each other's teaching, and endeavoured to make each lesson an improvement from the last for the benefit of the Shipley School students. Through this PLC, they were enlightened as to what it meant to be a middle-school general music teacher and actively supported each other's professional growth.

They felt 'challenged by the level of excellence of their peers' and shared that their 'teaching had improved with the feedback that [they] received throughout the practicum from each other, [their] university professor, and the graduate assistant'.

Finding the Teacher Voice Within
As the semester neared its end, all of the pre-service music teachers were well on their way to discovering their unique 'teacher voice'. Belinda asserted: '[I have] discovered my teaching style, my strengths and weaknesses, likes and dislikes, and a better sense of how I will be as a music teacher.' Tania concluded, 'In this class I learned about real classroom experiences, planned and taught lessons, and saw what it is really like to be a teacher.' Noting the pre-service music teachers' progression over the semester, Cindy shared, 'It's amazing to see that I and the other teachers in our class are becoming exactly that ... teachers! It is very exciting to think of how much we improved as educators.'

At the end of the course, five of the six pre-service music teachers had determined that middle-school general music was a viable career option. However, Bethany relayed, 'This past semester has been an extremely valuable experience. Before going to Shipley, I wasn't sure which grades I was interested in teaching. After these past couple of months, I've realized that I am not really interested in teaching middle school. As much fun as it was, I just don't think it is a good match for me.' The school-embedded course *Teaching Secondary General Music* was a platform for the pre-service music teachers to learn about themselves as teachers, their role in the classroom, and where they saw themselves as future professionals.

Conclusion

Schön (1987) advocated for combined in-class work at the university with situated learning experiences, in which 'reflection in and reflection on' (p. 311) is central for college students to 'live through the initial shocks of confusion and mystery, unlearn initial expectations, and learn to master the practice of the practicum' (p. 311). Whereas some researchers have indicated that on-campus courses and off-campus practicums are often disconnected (Eisenhart, Behm and Romagnano 1991; Zeichner and Conklin 2008; Abrahams 2009), the *compelling situation* of the course brought together the 'careful balance of challenge and opportunity' (Ewell 1997, p. 9). Because the Shipley students were under their charge, pre-service music teachers had *the need to know*, and over time made meaningful connections between theory and praxis. The school-embedded course supported metacognitive practice in lesson planning and instructional execution. It provided a foundation for the pre-service music teachers to construct professional knowledge about adolescent growth, the musical needs of adolescents, the development of pedagogical music skills, the creation of a relevant, relationship-based, action-oriented curriculum, and the discovery of what it is that music teachers 'do'. The course configuration facilitated their understanding of curriculum in academic and practical terms (Castle, Fox and Souder 2006; Murray 2008). The pre-service music teachers' professional interactions as a PLC and with the school students enabled their journey from entering the course as music education majors to their eventual self-construction as music teachers.

Experienced teachers perform differently from novice teachers; likewise, novice teachers perform differently from pre-service teachers (Berliner 1988). As Berliner (1992) emphasized, 'What looks to be so easy for the expert and so clumsy for the novice is the result of thousands of hours of reflected-on experience' (as cited in Cochran-Smth, Feiman-Nemser and McIntyre 2008, p. 814). The school-embedded course advanced pre-service music teachers' acquisition of professional knowledge. Participation in a semester-long school embedded course did not provide enough time to achieve the many teaching competencies that lead to the earned title of 'expert teacher'. However, a school-embedded course design, with a constructivist-based pedagogical focus such as *Teaching Secondary General Music*, may accelerate the progression from pre-service to novice music teacher (Ridley, Hurwitz, Hackett and Miller 2005) through the construction of pedagogical competence and professional knowledge, thereby leading novice music teachers to enjoy more success in their first years of teaching.

Questions for Reflection

1 How does this US method's course design compare with those found in the preparation of music teachers in other countries?
2. What did the pre-service music teachers learn about themselves as burgeoning music teachers in the school-embedded course? Pinpoint several ways that the course may have facilitated their self-understanding.
3 Consider the professional knowledge that these pre-service music teachers constructed in the school-embedded course. What implications might exist for those pre-service music teachers who may not have such experiences?

References

Abrahams, Frank (2009). Examining the Pre-Service Practicum Experience of Undergraduate Music Education Majors – Exploring Connections and Dispositions through Multiple Perspectives: A Critical Grounded Theory. *Journal of Music Teacher Education*, 19(80). doi:10.1177/1057083709344044.
— (2011). Nurturing Pre-Service Music Teacher Dispositions: Collaborating to Connect Practice, Theory, and Policy. *Arts Education Policy Review*, 112(3), 108–114.
Alexander, Patricia A. (2003). The Development of Expertise: The Journey from Acclimation to Proficiency. *Educational Researcher*, 32(8), 10–14.
Bandura, Albert (1977). *Social Learning Theory.* New York: General Learning Press.

Berliner, David C. (1985). Laboratory Settings and the Study of Teacher Education. *Journal of Teacher Education*, 36, 2–8.

— (1988). *The Development of Expertise in Pedagogy*. Washington, DC: American Association of Colleges for Teacher Education.

— (1992). The Nature of Expertise in Teaching. In Fritz K. Oser, Andreas Dick and Jean-Luc Patry (eds), *Effective and Responsible Teaching: The New Synthesis*. San Francisco, CA: Jossey-Bass, 227–48.

Borko, Hilda; Whitcomb, Jennifer A. and Byrnes, Kathryn (2008), Genres of Research in Teacher Education. In Marilyn Cochran-Smith, Sharon Feiman-Nemser and John D. McIntyre (eds), *Handbook of Research on Teacher Education*, third edition, New York: Routledge, 1017–49.

Bransford, John; Darling-Hammond, Linda and LePage, Pamela (2005). Introduction. In Linda Darling-Hammond and John Bransford (eds), *Preparing Teachers for a Changing World: What Teachers Should Learn and Be Able to Do*. San Francisco, CA: John Wiley & Sons, 1–39.

Brownstein, Bonnie (2001). Collaboration: The Foundation of Learning in the Future, *Education*, 122(2), 240–247.

Bruner, Jerome (1960). *The Process of Education*. Cambridge, MA: Harvard University Press.

Burton, Suzanne L. and Greher, Gena. R. (2007). School-University Partnerships. What Do We Know and Why Do They Matter? *Arts Education Policy Review*, 109(1), 13–24.

— (2010). Research Meets Reality in School-University Partnerships: An Analysis of Two Diverse School-University Collaborations. In Margaret Schmidt (ed.), *Collaborative Action for Change*. Lanham, MD: Rowman & Littlefield, 155–81.

— (2011). Foreword, *Arts Education Policy Review*, 112(3), 105–107.

Campbell, Mark. R.; Thompson, Linda. K. and Barrett, Janet. R. (2010). *Constructing a Personal Orientation to Music Teaching*. New York: Routledge.

Castle, Sharon; Fox, Rebecca and Souder, Kathleen (2006). Do Professional Development Schools (PDS) Make a Difference? A Comparative Study of PDS and non-PDS Teacher Candidates. *Journal of Teacher Education*, 57(1), 65–80.

Cochran-Smith, Marilyn; Feiman-Nemser, Sharon; and McIntyre, John D. (eds) (2008), *Handbook of Research on Teacher Education*, third edition), New York: Routledge.

Conkling, Susan (2004). Music Teacher Practice and Edentity in Professional Development Partnerships. Paper presented at the *Third Symposium on A Sociology of Music Education*. Denton: University of North Texas.

— (2007). The Possibilities of Situated Learning for Teacher Preparation: The Professional Development Partnership. *Music Educators Journal*, 93(3), 44–8.

Conkling, Susan and Henry, Warren (1999). Professional Development Partnerships: A New Model for Music Teacher Preparation. *Arts Education Policy Review*, (100)4, 19–23.

Darling-Hammond, Linda (2009). *Teacher Education and the American Future.* Charles W. Hunt Lecture. Presented at the annual meeting of the American Association of Colleges for Teacher Education. Chicago, IL.

Dewey, John (1963). *Experience and Education.* New York: Macmillan [1938].

— (1998). *How We Think.* Boston: Houghton Mifflin [1938].

Eisenhart Margaret; Behm, Stephanie, L.; and Romagnano, Lew (1991). Learning to Teach: Developing Expertise or Rite of Passage? *Journal of Education for Teaching,* 17, 51–71.

Ewell, Peter T. (1997). *Organizing for Learning: A Point of Entry.* Draft prepared for discussion at the 1997 AAHE Summer Academy at Snowbird. National Center for Higher Education Management Systems. Retrieved from www.intime.uni.edu/model/learning/learn_summary.html, accessed on 14 September 2012.

Fosnot, Catherine T. (2005). Constructivism Revisited: Implications and Reflections. *The Constructivist,* 16(1), 1–17.

Gordon, Edwin E. (2007). *Learning Sequences in Music: A Contemporary Music Learning Theory.* Chicago, IL: GIA Publications.

Hammerness, Karen; Darling-Hammond, Linda; Bransford, John; Berliner, David; Cochran-Smith, Marilyn; McDonald, Morva; and Zeichner, Kenneth (2005). How Teachers Learn and Develop. In Linda Darling-Hammond and John Bransford (eds), *Preparing Teachers for a Changing World: What Teachers Should Learn and Be Able to Do.* San Francisco, CA: John Wiley & Sons, 358–89.

Haston, Warren (2007). Teacher Modeling as an Effective Teaching Strategy, *Music Educators Journal,* 93, 26–30.

Israel, Susan (2005). *Metacognition in Literacy Learning.* Mahwah, NJ: Erlbaum.

McMahon, Mark (1997). *Social Constructivism and the World Wide Web: A Paradigm for Learning.* Paper presented at the ASCILITE conference. Perth, Australia.

Murray, Frank (2008). The Role of Teacher Education Courses in Teaching by Second Nature. In Marilyn Cochran-Smith, Sharon Feiman-Nemser and John D. McIntyre (eds), *Handbook of Research on Teacher Education,* third edition, New York: Routledge, 1228–46.

NCATE (National Council for Accreditation of Teacher Education) (2010). *Transforming Teacher Education through Clinical Practice: A National Strategy to Prepare Effective Teachers.* Washington, DC: Author.

Papert, Seymour and Harel, Idit (1991). *Constructionism,* New York: Ablex Publishing Corp.

Patton, Michael Q. (2002). *Qualitative Research and Evaluation Methods,* Thousand Oaks, CA: Sage.

Piaget, Jean (1950). *The Psychology of Entelligence.* New York: Routledge.

Ridley, D. Scott; Hurwitz, Sally; Hackett, Mary R.; and Miller, K. Kari (2005). Comparing PDS and Campus-Based Pre-Service Teacher Preparation: Is PDS-Based Preparation Really Better? *Journal of Teacher Education,* 56(1), 46–56.

Robbins, Janet (1993). Preparing Students to Think like Teachers: Relocating our Teacher Education Perspective, *The Quarterly,* 4(1), 45–51. Retrieved from www-usr.rider.edu/%7Evrme/v16n1/volume4/visions/spring7, accessed on 14 September 2012.

Schön, Donald A. (1987). *Educating the Reflective Practitioner: Toward a New Design for Teaching and Learning in the Professions.* San Francisco, CA: Jossey-Bass.

Shulman, Lee (1986). Those Who Understand: Knowledge Growth in Teaching, *Educational Researcher*, 15(2), 4–14.

— (2000). From Minsk to Pinsk: Why a Scholarship of Teaching and Learning? *Journal of the Scholarship of Teaching and Learning*, 1(1), 43–53.

Stake, Robert. E. (2010). *Qualitative Research: Studying How Things Work.* New York: Guilford Press.

Thiessen, Dennis and Barrett, Janet (2002). Reform-Minded Teachers. In Richard Colwell and Carol Richardson (eds), *The New Handbook of Music Teaching and Learning*, New York: Oxford, 759–85.

Vygotsky, Lev (1978). *Mind and Society: The Development of Higher Mental Processes*, Cambridge, MA: Harvard University Press.

Zeichner, Kenneth (2007). Professional Development Schools in a Culture of Evidence and Accountability, *School-University Partnerships*, 1(1), 9–17.

— (2010). Rethinking the Connections between Campus Courses and Field Experiences in College- and University-Based Teacher Education, *Journal of Teacher Education*, 61, 89–99. doi:1177/0022487109347671.

Zeichner, Kenneth and Conklin, Hilary. G. (2008). Teacher Education Programs as Sites for Teacher Preparation. In Marilyn Cochran-Smith, Sharon Feiman-Nemser and John D. McIntyre (eds), *Handbook of Research on Teacher Education*, third edition, New York: Routledge, 269–89.

Chapter 7

Artistic Knowledge Among Music Education Students in Germany: Being Trained to be Exactly What?

Andreas Lehmann-Wermser

Without doubt, being a proficient instrumentalist is one important facet of being a music teacher. Higher music education programmes, in various ways and different domains, assist students in acquiring the necessary artistic knowledge. However, while they seem to follow the logic of professionalization characteristic of all teacher programmes, music education programmes are marked by some unique phenomena:

- The family background of music education students has a deep influence on their motivation to become a music teacher (Bailer 1999, 2002).[1]
- Music education students decide earlier than other teachers to major in music in order to pass the audition (Pfeiffer 1994; Bailer 1999, p. 26; Madsen and Kelly 2002; Isbell 2010).
- They have spent much of their leisure time learning how to play an instrument and have had intense emotional experiences by the time they enter higher education (Bastian 1987, 1995; Bailer 2002).
- Consequently they feel deeper bonds with their subject compared to other students in higher education (Weiß and Kiel 2010).

Bailer quotes from an interview with a student whom she regards as typical of the biographical pattern in music education:

> I come from a family of musicians; my father is a musician, my brothers and sisters went to music school; somehow this was preprogrammed. Only because I did less performing but wanted to teach more and had more pedagogical skills I came across music education. My pathway began at home. (Bailer 2002, p. 71)[2]

---

[1]   This seems to be a stronger influence in German than in English speaking countries (cf. Isbell 2010).

[2]   As this chapter deals primarily with higher education in German-speaking countries many of the references are German. They are translated by the author if not indicated differently.

Any student entering a music programme with a high level of instrumental proficiency has, for a long time, been so deeply involved in making music that biographical questions of personality – or, to be more precise, identity – are an important factor in the programme. The question is: how is this reflected in music programmes?

Competing Principles of 'Doing School'

Two basic and competing principles of 'doing education' (and consequently 'teaching music' and training future music teachers) seem to exist in industrialized countries. Large-scale assessments like the OECS's PISA (Programme for International Student Assessment) or the IEA's TIMSS (Trends in International Mathematics and Science Study) have documented deficits in educational outcomes during the late 1990s. The educational goals, described in general terms and more dedicated to establishing a philosophical basis for individual development than a psychologically valid understanding of learning, were, in part, held responsible for the shortcomings. Ever since then there has been a heated debate on how the school system, administration and teaching should develop. In this debate we find a mix of economic, pedagogical and political arguments. However, regardless of national traditions, one may say that the lines of debate are often reduced to two positions.

In the first of these it is maintained that education needs to be highly structured (and has to take into consideration requirements of the labour market). Consequently standards are outlined and assessment is highly valued; qualifications and competences are key terms within this tradition. As Baumert and Kunter put it:

> School educates in the first place by the intellectual challenges of its programme, by the changes between explorative phases of learning and problem-solving and settings of achievement where mandatory standards are enforced. (Baumert and Kunter 2006, p. 473, author translation)

Without doubt this principle has some advantages. Based on the demands made of schooling and teaching one can describe necessary (or desirable) competencies, design study programmes and assess individual proficiency levels.

Alternatively, in the second position, education is regarded as holistic personal development within society. Supporters of this position often subscribe to the idea of *Bildung* as outlined by Wilhelm von Humboldt, German reformer of the school system in the beginning of the nineteenth century. Generally speaking, and without regard to changing concepts in the past, *Bildung* rests upon the foundations of *general* education (in the sense of it being open to all) of voluntary learning and the formation of personal identity, which is a value in itself and independent of the use the labour market may make of it.[3] Thus, *Bildung* aims at properties and goals

---

[3]   There is no room here to discuss this further. An overall history of the concept can be found in Bruford (2009), an encompassing account of the connections between school

that are impossible to assess, but the holistic approach corresponds much better with principles of free individuals developing in a democratic society.[4]

Georgii-Hemming (this volume, p. 19) has characterized the conflicting principles as setting priorities in 'efficiency and measurability', on the one hand, or in learners as 'seekers of meaning', on the other.

The discourse outlined above can be observed in various settings. Its most prominent place is the public debate over the state of education and general guidelines for schooling and teaching. However, the same conflicting lines can be observed in debates on music education where these principles are stated to be basically incompatible.[5]

On yet another level these differing principles also determine music teacher training, as can be seen in the nature of instrumental training in higher education. And although the study presented here refers to conditions in Germany the underlying problem seems to be of an international nature. Traditionally students who have passed the audition – until about 15 years ago this was possible only in 'classical music' – receive four more years of training in universities or academies. This is provided by artists who also teach performing musicians and focus almost exclusively on the interpretation of great works of art. As these artists are not familiar with the demands of teaching in schools the instruction does not follow – and does not *want* to follow – concepts of qualifying musically for teaching.[6] However, this is not regarded as derogatory as the power of *Bildung* is thought to integrate instrumental proficiency (as a form of knowledge) and experience. Ever since this high-quality instruction became part of teacher training in music in Germany in the late 1920s (and thus legitimized higher esteem and better payment for music teachers) it was the unquestioned basis that didn't even need explicit justification: it is, indeed, difficult to find contemporary documents or papers legitimizing this structure.[7]

---

system and concept in Tenorth (2000), and more detailed reflections with respect to music education in Kaiser (1995) and in Varkøy (2010).

[4] Critique of the concept of professionalization and standardization comes from conservatives and radical reformers alike, as documented in *Action, Criticism, and Theory* (volume 10, issue 1). Kaiser (2010) has suggested that we consider Marx's term *Arbeit* (work) to bridge the gap between 'theory' and 'practice' and include aspects of morality in society.

[5] One can take a condensed look at the international debate by studying the proceedings of the ISAME (Brophy and Albert 2008; Brophy 2010; for Germany cf. the special edition of *Zeitschrift für Kritische Musikpädagogik* (2008 – www.zfkm.org).

[6] Various conflicts arise from this setup, one being that music education students are forced to meet higher standards, ones they cannot match. And while the high-quality training is certainly an advantage, personal conflicts in time management and identity arise that can lead to psychosomatic disorders commonly observed among music students. Isbell (2010) has described this as conflicting powers in the formation of identity.

[7] Hofmann has cited German publications from the early 1920s that emphasize the power of music teachers who direct and lead ('lenken und führen') young students by means

A contrasting paradigm has gained ground in recent years. Relying on psychological theories and turning to concepts of professionalization, features of the 'good teacher' are defined. Instead of a holistic concept of teacher personality and good teaching, elements of cognitive knowledge and beliefs on the nature of education, subjects and attitudes are described that can be subject to empirical research. Lee Shulman's writings were most influential in conceptualizing teachers' competence and teacher training (Shulman 1986). The German Secretaries of Education Standing Conference (KMK), for instance, has described teachers' competencies. It states that teachers '*are experts for teaching and learning ... are aware that the task of educating* in school is closely related to lessons and school life, ... *assess* ... in a competent, just and responsible manner ..., *develop their competencies permanently ... and engage in the development of schools*' (KMK 2010, p. 5f., original italics; see also KMK 2004).

Breaking down the general description of competencies to the level of subjects, the KMK's paper states that: music education graduates 'have multifaceted practical skills and artistic and aesthetic competencies which enable them to support students in school in building up musical proficiency, to stimulate their perception of music, musical inventions and compositions, and to support talking about music and by that end aesthetic judgement' (KMK 2010, p. 32). Most obviously this paradigm differs considerably from a concept of *Bildung* as it relates skills and competencies to the necessities of the school. However, it is not a new concept. Taebel (1992) introduced similar concepts in the evaluation of music teachers, but the change of paradigms has gained relevance as the political context and its implications for schools has changed (see also Fautley 2010).

Summing this up, radical positions concerning instrumental instruction in higher education would favour *either* training covering only what could be applied in school lessons *or* experiencing art music without consideration of what teachers need as part of developing a rich personality.[8]

Beyond the Lines

There are good reasons to question the bipolar and competing nature of these principles. The history of the Prussian school system in the first half of the nineteenth century shows that *Bildung* as an end in itself never worked, as society

---

of a strong and convincing personality as musician. He therefore speaks of the 'paradigm of personality' (2011, p. 95).

[8]   This is changing somewhat as students with a strong background in popular music enter the college programme. And although their family background is similar (Bailer 2002) their musical, and especially instrumental, socialization differs considerably. Detailed studies are lacking but it is likely that their identity as teachers and musicians is differently structured. However, it will be argued that the basic problem in music teacher training remains untouched by this.

quickly set mechanisms of allocating positions and success in professional life and thus guaranteed what *Bildung* could not (Tenorth 2000). Bourgeois society foiled the idea of general *Bildung* for *all* people as the sole principle of education and secured its exclusive character by highly qualifying some and leaving others with remnants of schooling. So it seems necessary to discuss the idea with regard to society's conditions and the political context of professions.

On the other hand, the concept of professionalization cannot be reduced to a narrow-minded qualification apt only for the job market and its demands. For the German discourse, at least, Klieme, Avenarius and Blum (2003) have pointed out that the key term 'competency' as developed by German educational researchers Roth and Weinert does not follow a narrow understanding of qualifying solely for the sake of being able to work; other aspects have to be included.[9] And while authors have suggested a dichotomy of 'knowledge' on one side, and 'beliefs', 'attitudes' and 'conceptions' on the other (Thompson 2003; Müller, Felbrich and Blömeke 2008), recent and more complex concepts of being a professional teacher go beyond content knowledge, pedagogical, and pedagogical content knowledge (Shulman 1986; Hofmann 2011). Following these studies other dimensions, such as general and subject-related beliefs, have to be acquired (Müller, Felbrich and Blömeke 2008; Felbrich, Schmotz and Kaiser 2010). The findings of the study reported here suggest the existence of yet another problem.

How German Music Education Students Perceive their Artistic Competences

In order to gain a better understanding a study was conducted among music education graduate students at Bremen University. The state programme in teacher education calls for a first music education class in the first MA term and the preparation of a four-week teaching assignment.[10] It was assumed that by that time students would have developed a clear concept of their own artistic capacities and of the meaning of the programme. Regarding the role of their instrumental instruction it was furthermore assumed that a majority of the students would not tend to see this instruction as either solely serving everyday school teaching or as an end in itself. Rather, we assumed that motivations and perceptions would mix.

---

[9]   The history of education suggests that the principles have to be discussed and balanced in a political process; for the implications in music see Knigge (2011).

[10]   Until 2011 the study programme following state regulations asked for polyvalent BA grades opening up other fields besides school. This implied that music education classes were reserved for the MA programme while instrumental and ensemble training as well as music theory and musicology were part of the BA programme. However, very few students drop out after their BA as there is no employment market on this level, so the revised programme asks for early music education classes and teaching experiences.

Most importantly, we figured that this mixture would change before and, even more, during the teaching experience.

During three subsequent years complete classes were included, with 39 students taking part. Data collection consisted of transcripts of group discussions in the preparation phase, essays on the students' own musical biography, a comment on the appropriateness of their instrumental capacities for school life and an interview with their mentoring music teacher (both to be compiled during the assignment). Those parts of the interviews considered to be relevant were transcribed. The corpus gathered consisted of about 16,000 words. Computer-aided analyses were conducted using Mayring's (2002) approach of 'qualitative Inhaltsanalyse'.[11]

Analyses show that the sample displays features similar to earlier studies. These students, too, are early starters in music, highly motivated, with a strong commitment to education. As with other music education students they find it hard to meet standards set by their instrumental teachers (Bastian 1995). But some findings are highly puzzling to music educators responsible for structuring a programme.

Students in their texts often refer to very personal experiences:

> To make music is very important to me. Besides talking, it is another way to express myself and communicate content, emotions, and moods. (Male student, age 23)
>
> Most important in playing or singing is to express my own emotions. (Female student, age 23)
>
> If I had not had this training and was watching friends making music I would certainly lack something. (Female student, age 24)

Many of the texts report progress in instrumental proficiency not only on a technical level but also in terms of understanding music:

> An important stimulus was my weekly voice training and singing lesson. It opened up doors (with hopefully much more to come) because I hadn't sung with joy since I was a child, when my grandmother used to sing with me. (Male student, age 27)
>
> Since I play the recorder I am used to people who smile at a 'recorder major'. Apart from that, I feel as an artist and love making music. ... Playing music is very important to me. (Female student, age 23)

Apparently studying music education gives the students a good opportunity to develop, both personally and as professional musicians; it fosters their 'identity

---

[11] This may be translated as *qualitative content analysis*, but the German term is firmly established and refers to set routines of coding and validating understandings of codes and categories.

as musicians' (Isbell 2010).[12] And it serves as an important personal experience in the sense of *Bildung*:

> It's difficult to judge whether my main instrument, the saxophone, will do me any good in school. It's nice to get lessons and it's fun to advance on my instrument. However, I get the impression that it is all about me myself and my self-esteem. (Male student, age 25)

What is so puzzling is the fact that their artistic identity is often disconnected from their experiences in schools:

> It is important to mention that I had almost no opportunity to gather experiences in the arts during my teaching assignment due to a lack of time. There was no chance to bring in my own musical proficiency, which I had gained at the university, especially during my last term.[13] (Female student, age 22)

Many texts construct a contrast between their arts-oriented instrumental training and the courses directed at everyday school teaching by, for instance, accompanying classes ('schulpraktisches Klavierspiel'):

> Standards … are totally different from my previous instrumental training. Shaping music and building up an expression were very important; now it is about learning how to accompany a group of children who want to perform, say, a pop song. (Female student, age 24)

Another student does emphasize the difference, but in his statement artistic proficiency becomes merely a motivational vehicle:

> Good instrumental proficiency can motivate children, as I found out myself. If you accompany a pop song with normal harmonies [i.e. triads] and a simple rhythmic pattern the kids will sing. But if you spice up chords and rhythms kids will be highly motivated and start moving. (Male student, age 28)

It seems that the dichotomy outlined above is not merely about concepts of teacher training but is rather *lived* and *experienced* by the students. However, in most cases they cannot relate the two areas: to see what proficiency is good for, but also that it has value in its own right. There was also no change during the assignment

---

[12] cf. Perkins and Triantafyllaki in this volume.

[13] Music classes in high schools bear the character of general music education all the way through to graduation. Often music theory and history constitute a good part of the time – although this is slowly changing with teachers seeking more practical experience in either popular or in classical music.

(contrary to our expectations). The texts did not refer to any development or *new* perspectives.

The next quotation is an exception showing that there are some students who succeed in establishing the connection:

> To sum it up I would say: instrumental proficiency is a prerequisite and a trailblazer for communicating about music in school. I would like to draw the conclusion that the better a teacher can play the better he can help students to improve musically. (Male student, age 26)

From Academy to School

An important factor in student teacher education is the experienced teachers the students are assigned to. Unfortunately there is little support for a balanced identity as artist *and* teacher:

> Talking to teachers, a basic attitude towards their own instrumental training became clear. You don't need these skills in school and they are not noticed and valued by students. The teacher feels over-qualified and, more so, he has given up in terms of handing down some of his skills and knowledge. (Male student, age 26)
>
> In [general music classes] they sang a lot, but apart from that no further musical activity took place, since this 'leads nowhere and is a lot of fuss' [according to the teacher]. There was little reflecting, i.e. they didn't work on the singing or apply new knowledge or experiences. (Female student in elementary school, age 23)

Although these quotes may be dismissed as bad examples that can be found in any school system the underlying conflict the students experience seems to perpetuate itself in everyday school life. Other quotations report similar beliefs even for 'high-quality' teachers. It seems, therefore, that good role models in schools are scarce. The combination of a structural conflict in the study programme and the lack of convincing mentors poses a serious problem.

There is not much in the way of hard data on dropout or burnout among music teachers in Germany. Hildebrandt, Spahn and Seidenglanz (2002) reported that 45 per cent of all music students need help due to medical problems while studying. The low esteem of music teachers was identified as a serious health problem by Bastian (1995, p. 122). Moreover, Pfeiffer (1994) pointed out other potential risks for music teachers in their professional careers.[14] Considering the findings that indicate a lack in the integration of different aspects of knowledge and a failed

---

[14]   For the USA, with its different legal status of teachers and different working conditions, see Kim and Barg (2010). In comparison it becomes obvious that an

development of a balanced identity there may well be a connecting line between this phenomenon and the state of health of music teachers. For higher education in the music teacher programme this also implies that in the field of instrumental proficiency it is necessary to obtain a broad understanding of instrumental competency, its relevance for teaching in schools and its meaning for personal development, which goes far beyond simply 'useful' skills but keeps complex everyday school life in focus.

Outlook

How does this relate to the concepts of knowledge acquisition? We started out this chapter by characterizing what we call the 'competing principles' of schooling. In the light of this study the 'critical incidents' the students deal with cannot be interpreted as a problem of theory and practice – in other words, a problem that arises when theoretically well planned phenomena are confronted with everyday life. Although that is popular rhetoric it does not fit well the complexity of phenomena: neither is there theory without practice or vice versa.[15] The 'competing principles' are not alternatives but rather necessary supplements. Certainly, arts-oriented instrumental training that aims at individual development and experiences and that has value in itself and is independent of everyday teaching is an essential element of teacher training and appropriate to the nature of art. At the same time competencies that enable future teachers to struggle successfully with the requirements of music classes in heterogeneous schools are indispensable. Support for this understanding of supplementary facets also comes from the large international study COAKTIV. In this study teachers who could cross-link different aspects of knowledge were successful (cf. Baumert and Kunter 2006, p. 495). It is a challenge to structure the study programmes in higher education so as to meet both ends.

Questions for Reflection

1. If you think about the discourse in public and in the scientific music education community) is it more marked by the ideas and the ideals of *Bildung* or of 'competencies'? Do you go along with the majority?
2. Beginning with your own experiences, how would you describe the relation between identity as a musician and identity as a teacher?
3. If you were to write guidelines for instrumental teaching staff in higher education what would they state about the phenomena in question?

---

understanding of the processes of knowledge acquisition can only be gained with respect to the political constraints and the conditions of society.

[15]   cf. Lehmann-Wermser and Niessen 2004.

References

Action, Criticism, and Theory for Music Education (2011). 10(1).

Bailer, Noraldine (1999). *Musikerziehung als Beruf? Eine Befragung.* Vienna: Universal-Edition.

— (2002). *Musik lernen und vermitteln: Das Studium der Musikerziehung und seine Absolventen*, Vienna: Institut für Musikpädagogik.

Bastian, Hans-Günther (1987). Schulmusiker werden – nein danke! Ein Berufsbild in der kritischen Bewertung instrumentaler Talente, *Musik und Bildung* 10, 735–41.

— (1995). Studien- und Berufsmotivation von Musiklehrerstudentinnen und -studenten: Ergebnisse einer Befragung in den alten und neuen Bundesländern. In Niels Knolle and Thomas Ott (eds), *Zur Professionalisierung von Musiklehrern*. Mainz and London: Schott, 91–154.

Baumert, Jürgen and Kunter, Mareike (2006). Stichwort: Professionelle Kompetenz von Lehrkräften. *Zeitschrift für Erziehungswissenschaft* 9(4), 469–520.

Brophy, Timothy S. (ed.) (2010). The Practice of Assessment in Music Education: Framework, Models, and Designs. In *Proceedings of the 2009 Florida Symposium on Assessment in Music Education*. Chicago: GIA.

Brophy, Timothy S. and Albert, Kirsten (eds) (2008). Assessment in Music Education: Integrating Currulum and Practice. In *Florida Symposium on Assessment in Music Education*. Chicago: GIA.

Bruford, Walter Horace (2009). *The German Tradition of Self-Cultivation: 'Bildung' from Humboldt to Thomas Mann*. Cambridge: Cambridge University Press.

Fautley, Martin (2010). *Assessment in Music Education*. Oxford and New York: Oxford University Press.

Felbrich, Anja; Schmotz, Christiane; and Kaiser, Gabriele (2010). Überzeugungen angehender Primarstufenlehrkräfte im internationalen Vergleich. In Sigrid Blömeke (ed.), *TEDS-M 2008: Professionelle Kompetenz und Lerngelegenheiten angehender Primarstufenlehrkräfte im internationalen Vergleich*. Münster: Waxmann, 297–325.

Hildebrandt, Horst; Spahn, Claudia; and Seidenglanz, Karin (2002). Wirksamkeit eines Lehrangebotes zur Prävention von Spiel- und Gesundheitsproblemen bei Musikern. *dissonanz/disonance* (73), 35–37.

Hofmann, Bernhard (2011). Experten für Musiklehre: Auf der Suche nach der 'guten' Musiklehrkraft. In Martin D. Loritz, Andreas Becker, Daniel Mark Eberhard and Rudolf-Dieter Kraemer (eds), *Musik – Pädagogisch – Gedacht: Reflexionen, Forschungs- und Praxisfelder*. Augsburg: Wißner, 95–103.

Isbell, Daniel S. (2010). Understanding Socialization and Occupational Identity Among Undergraduate Music Teachers. In Margaret Schmidt (ed.), *Collaborative Action for Change*. Lanham, MD, New York and Toronto, ON: Rowman & Littlefield Education, 87–104.

Kaiser, Hermann Josef (1995). Die Bedeutung von Musik und Musikalischer Bildung. *musikForum* (83), 17–26.

— (2010). Verständige Musikpraxis: Eine Antwort auf Legitimationsdefizite des Klassenmusizierens. *Zeitschrift für Kritische Musikpädagogik*, 46–68. Retrieved from http://zfkm.org/10-kaiser.pdf, accessed on 17 September 2012.

Kim, Sung Eun and Barg, David (2010). Reducing Music Teacher Turnover and its Consequences. *Music Education Policy Beliefs*, 2, 1–7. Retrieved from www.bu.edu/muedpolicyproject/brief2.pdf.

Klieme, Eckhard; Avenarius, Hermann; and Blum, Werner (2003). Zur Entwicklung nationaler Bildungsstandards: Eine Expertise. Retrieved from www.bmbf. de/pub/zur_entwicklung_nationaler_bildungsstandards.pdf, accessed on 17 September 2012.

KMK (Sekretariat der Ständigen Konferenz der Kultusminister der Länder in der Bundesrepublik Deutschland) (2004). *Standards für die Lehrerbildung. Bildungswissenschaften.* Retrieved from www.kmk.org/ fileadmin/veroeffentlichungen_beschluesse/2004/2004_12_16-Standards-Lehrerbildung.pdf, accessed on 17 September 2012.

— (2010). *Ländergemeinsame inhaltliche Anforderungen für die Fachwissenschaften und Fachdidaktiken in der Lehrerbildung.* Retrieved from www.kmk.org/ fileadmin/veroeffentlichungen_beschluesse/2008/2008_10_16-Fachprofile-Lehrerbildung.pdf, accessed on 17 September 2012.

Knigge, Jens (2011). *Modellbasierte Entwicklung und Analyse von Testaufgaben zur Erfassung der Kompetenz 'Musikwahrnehmen und Kontextualisieren'*, Münster: LIT Verlag.

Lehmann-Wermser, Andreas and Niessen, Anne (2004). Die Gegenüberstellung von Theorie und Praxis als irreführende Perspektive in der (Musik-)pädagogik. In Hermann Josef Kaiser (ed.), *Musikpädagogische Forschung in Deutschland: Dimensionen und Strategien.* Essen: Die Blaue Eule, 131–62.

Madsen, Clifford and Kelly, Steven (2002). First Remembrances of Wanting to Become a Music Teacher. *Journal of Research in Music Education*, 50(4), 323–32.

Mayring, Philipp (2002). *Einführung in die qualitative Sozialforschung*, fifth edition, Weinheim: Beltz.

Müller, Christiane; Felbrich, Anja; and Blömeke, Sigrid (2008). Überzeugungen zum Lehren und Lernen von Mathematik. In Sigrid Blömeke, Gabriele Kaiser and Rainer Lehmann (eds), *Professionelle Kompetenz angehender Lehrerinnen und Lehrer. Wissen, Überzeugungen und Lerngelegenheiten deutscher Mathematikstudierender und -referendare. Erste Ergebnisse zur Wirksamkeit der Lehrerausbildung.* Münster: Waxmann, 247–76.

Pfeiffer, Wolfgang (1994). *Musiklehrer: Biographie, Alltag und berufliche Zufriedenheit von Musiklehrern an bayerischen Gymnasien; eine theoretische und empirische Analyse*, Essen: Die Blaue Eule.

Shulman, Lee S. (1986). Those who Understand: Knowledge Growth in Teaching, *Educational Researcher*, 15(2), 4–14.

Taebel, Donald K. (1992). The Evaluation of Music Teachers and Teaching. In Richard Colwell (ed.), *Handbook of Research on Music Teaching and Learning*. New York: Schirmer Books, 310–29.

Tenorth, Heinz-Elmar (2000). *Geschichte der Erziehung: Einführung in die Grundzüge ihrer neuzeitlichen Entwicklung*. Munich: Juventa.

Thompson, Alba Gonzalez (2003). Teachers' Beliefs and Conceptions. In D. A. Grouws (ed.), *Handbook of Research on Mathematics Teaching and Learning: A Project of the National Council of Teachers of Mathematics*. New York: Macmillan, 127–46.

Varkøy, Øivind (2010). The concept of 'Bildung'. *Philosophy of Music Education Review*, 18(1), 85–96.

Weiß, Sabine and Kiel, Ewald (2010). Berufswunsch Musiklehrer/in: Motive und Selbstbild. *Bulletin of Empirical Music Education Research*, 1(2), Retrieved from www.b-em.info/index.php?journal=ojs&page=article&op=view&path%5B%5D=38&path%5B%5D=83, accessed on 17 September 2012.

Chapter 8

Astonishing Practices: A Teaching Strategy in Music Teacher Education

Kirsten Fink-Jensen

Introduction

'What constitutes experience in teaching?' 'How can we educate music teachers in a way that prepares them to deal with pedagogical problems and at the same time further develops their teaching?' These questions are important for all educators at universities, colleges of education, schools and music schools. Very often new teachers at primary and secondary schools are critical of the educational programme that should have prepared them for the job. Some of the critical remarks deal with the relation between theory and practice in the programme. 'Teacher education is too theoretical', they say, or 'The theory we were taught has nothing to do with the practical problems we are experiencing!' There may be many explanations for such feelings, related not only to the structure and content of the educational programme, but also to the specific teaching methods used.

I intend to discuss the two initial questions (above) in terms of how theory can contribute to the development of practice and how the relationship between theory and practice in music teacher training can be addressed. My answer to these questions is based on an understanding of the teacher as a certain kind of researcher. So the 'music teacher as researcher' is the issue of this chapter. This issue is treated in different ways in the literature. A well-known example is Peter Jarvis' book *The Practitioner-Researcher* (Jarvis 1999). In my work I was inspired by Brian Roberts' article 'Music Teachers as Researchers' (Roberts 1994). He points out that research in music education can be qualified by the use of the music teacher's inside information and that teachers ought to be involved in the research process. I argue that this point is a challenge both to research in music education and to the education of music teachers. Further, I argue that this point poses a challenge for the teacher educator to pursue two objectives:

- Music teacher students have to be trained in observation techniques.
- Music teacher students have to be trained in the use of theory in practice.

I propose the implementation of a teaching strategy, 'astonishing practices', which I, over a period of eight years, have used and developed in a university course. A teaching 'strategy' is not the same as a teaching 'method'. 'Method' is a concept that tells the teacher of possible concrete ways of teaching which might be used in different educational situations. 'Teaching strategies' are overall principles for a procedure that is implemented in the course and that has to be followed by the students. When following a teaching strategy, music teacher students may use different methods depending on the educational problem they are dealing with.

The teaching strategy of 'astonishing practices' was introduced as an exercise in a course in the study programme of master in music education. Participants in this course were music teacher students with different qualifications. Some students were enrolled in the study programme of musicology, others were trained as music teachers (bachelors), and others had graduated from music conservatories as instrumentalists or music teachers. Thus, the music teacher students were aiming at professional careers at different levels of the educational system.

Preconditions of the strategy are that theory *can* contribute to, and *ought to be* used in relation to, practice (Kvernbekk 2001) and that theoretical knowledge is necessary for the development of practice. Therefore, the object of the strategy was to develop the students' understanding of how theory can inform teachers' considerations in and of practice.

Examples presenting two students' different ways of using this strategy are included to describe and discuss how the student's level of familiarity with the field influences the process. The empirical study of how the strategy works is based on project reports, interviews, project diaries and evaluation surveys completed by the participants after the course.

The Idea of 'Astonishing Practices'

The point of departure of the strategy is a problem, selected by the teacher student, which becomes apparent to the student observer in a situation in a music education practice. The first challenge for the teacher student is to be able to 'see' a problem. The observed situation may be complex, with many different factors influencing what happens. Problems may arise from musical issues, but the relation between pupils and the teacher, and between the teacher and the musical subject, also has great influence. Furthermore, each teaching situation is a part of an institutional context conditioned by laws, economics, traditions and so on. It is necessary to know something about all of these conditions to understand the background of a problem that appears in an observed situation. The teacher has to reflect pedagogically and psychologically on how to plan the teaching and respond to different events in the classroom. But the ability to respond in a professional way in specific situations calls for both professional knowledge and a capacity to be present in an open, sensuous way. So, even though the teaching strategy of 'astonishing practices' encompasses introductions to pedagogical and psychological theories, the central point of departure is a problem that has become apparent in a specific practical situation. What does the student see? Does he or she wonder why something happens? To stress this part of the strategy,

I introduce the concept of 'astonishment', inspired by anthropological research. As a consequence the music teacher students have to be present as participant observers in the selected situation of music education.

Astonishment

In cultural anthropology it is believed that astonishment is a universal feeling. The anthropologist encounters cultural differences with feelings of surprise, curiosity, excitement, enthusiasm or sympathy, while others may respond with horror, outrage, condescension or lack of interest (Shweder 1991). 'Astonishment' is a phenomenon – a feeling – that may arise in an encounter with something or somebody in a specific situation. The feeling of astonishment lies in the break with one's expectations, which are developed on the basis of previous lived experiences, habits and acquired knowledge. To experience this feeling, the teacher has to be present with the same open-mindedness as an anthropological researcher. Such open-mindedness also requires that all forms of private or professional theory must be put into 'brackets' – for example, pre-understandings, well-known peda-gogical or psychological theories or actual discourses about the phenomenon in focus (Zahavi 2001; 2003, p. 21).

A core question in this exercise is how to understand the practice of observation in this context. I shall discuss this problem of 'seeing' below.

The Problem of 'Seeing'

Observations are based on perception. For a participant observer, 'seeing' does not mean just using one's visual competences, but using all senses. In psychology the question of how knowledge occurs is central. From an empiricist's point of view 'simple seeing' refers to the sensuous process, which, for instance, characterizes vision: the fact that light enters through the pupil and casts an image on the photosensitive region at the rear of the eye. A perceiver supplements these sensations by means of associations that result from learning (Gleitman, Fridlund and Reisberg 1999, p. 252). In contrast, nativists argue that the perceiver plays a more important role in perception. Perception cannot occur without interpretation, so they conclude that the mechanisms used in perception are innate. Further discussions among psychologists have resulted in the conclusion that the achievements of perception are neither purely learned nor purely innate (Gleitman, Fridlund and Reisberg 1999, p. 252).

Observation and seeing are essential, not only to researchers, but also to teachers. To reflect and act upon a problem in teaching, the teacher has to be able to 'see' the problem. As we shall see later, familiarity with the field may be a problem as well as an advantage in this matter.

Perception is the keyword in participant observation. What, then, is the role of theoretical knowledge? Tone Kvernbekk argues that:

theoretical knowledge greatly enhances our capacity to see in practice, primarily because of its vital role in indirect cognitive perceptions. (Kvernbekk 2000, p. 357)

Kvernbekk distinguishes between 'seeing', 'seeing as' and 'seeing that'. I find this distinction very fruitful in a discussion of how theory can contribute to practice with knowledge. According to Kvernbekk, the notion of 'seeing' designates a simple process, which does not involve the utilization of professional knowledge in the formation of a belief about what is seen. We simply see things when we look around. We may see a creature flying in the wood, without knowing anything about this creature. 'Seeing as', on the other hand, expresses relationships between seeing and knowing. 'Seeing as' refers to the fact that the observer carries with her associations, images, understandings and actions from earlier similar situations. For example, a flying creature in the wood may look like a snowflake (seeing as) but we may know from previous experiences and from school that it is a kind of insect (seeing that). The images, understandings and earlier actions are always part of the observer's perspective and affect her way of seeing in the situation. From a phenomenological point of view our perception is always based on a first-person perspective. Therefore, a phenomenologist would argue that perception is not simply seeing but at least 'seeing as'. Nevertheless, the phenomenologist aims at 'seeing' using the technique of epoché, which is the process of trying to put the personal perspective into brackets.

The notion of 'seeing that' expresses the relationship between seeing and knowing. 'Seeing that' enables us to see facts and not only objects. It is a kind of indirect cognitive perception (Kvernbekk 2000). There may be a difference between our common sense and the knowledge we have gained from theories (e.g. based on research or philosophical issues from our professional education and training). This is expressed in the model shown in Figure 8.1. The model represents an understanding of both the notion of theory and the relation between theory and practice.

A Model of the Relation Between Theory and Practice

Theory may be placed at different levels in relation to practice. An example of a model that reflects the relation between theory and practice has been made by Erich Weniger (Weniger in Imsen 1997).

Theories are generalizations of knowledge. When a teacher gains experience from a long period of teaching she develops certain general assumptions of what it is appropriate to do along with normative opinions about educational problems. One of the points of the model in Figure 8.1 is that a professional teacher must be able to use theory on all three levels. But there is a need to distinguish between different concepts of theory. The teacher already has a theoretical perspective when she enters the classroom (T1 in the figure). Some of these theories are hidden

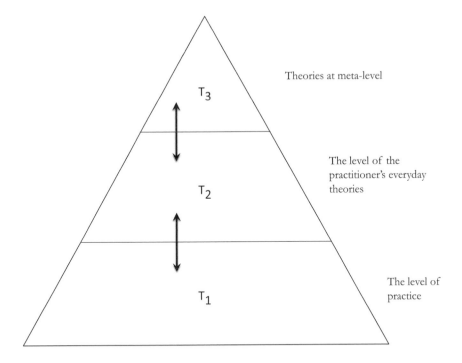

Figure 8.1   Erich Weniger's model of theories in different levels

from her own knowledge; they are a part of her lived body, tacit knowledge from previous experiences and studies. On the level of practice, the teacher must react to what is going on. In her actions she may draw upon her 'seeing that' from common sense or from a research-based theory. Some theoretical positions may occur in verbal discussions with colleagues before or after the lesson (level T2). These theories may be a result of experiences of what 'works' in the music lessons, or they may stem from earlier studies and actual discourses of what is important in music education. We shall call the knowledge on levels T1 and T2 'everyday knowledge'.

Theories on levels T1 and T2 are all more or less personal theories, which are developed as a result of experiences or a mingling of experience with an everyday understanding of questions that may concern music education. These theories are somewhat concrete, because they are connected to specific situations or a specific context. That is not the case with theory on the third level. Theories on level T3 are abstract, developed as general claims about psychological, philosophical or pedagogical matters. They are based on careful argumentation and/or empirically based results. These theories are tools for reflection on pedagogical questions that arise in the teaching situation; theories that make it possible for the teacher to develop her teaching. Over time the new theories may be incorporated and become part of the teacher's everyday knowledge. The ability to reflect on this level is the objective of working with the strategy of 'astonishing practices'.

'Theory' is not a precise concept. There are many different theoretical models in education. Kvernbekk describes two overall conceptions of theory: a logical positivistic one, which is termed syntactical, and a semantic one (Kvernbekk 2005). The syntactical conception is based on a hypothesis, which is confirmed scientifically; the semantic one takes its point of departure from a problem or phenomenon that occurs in an educational context. Following the semantic position, theories are constructed by abstracting from observed phenomena.

The strategy of astonishing practices is based on a semantic theoretical model. The formation of a new theory takes place in two steps or, more specifically, two processes of abstraction. The first process of abstraction is a written description of the phenomenon in focus, emphasizing the most interesting traits in a common-sense reflection. The second process of abstraction is based on an analysis from a relevant theoretical perspective (T3). How this may happen is described in the example below.

> A group of first graders are going to play a rhythmic piece of music together. They are playing different instruments. One girl, Anne, is playing conga. The teacher shows the children how to play, and the children try to follow the teacher. Anne does not play at once, but keeps looking at the teacher. Next, she looks at the other pupils' hands. Finally, she looks at her own hands and starts playing. The playing works well for everybody except Anne. The other children feel the beat of the music and play synchronically, while Anne does not succeed in following the rhythmic movement.

From a common-sense point of view the pedagogical problem in this case concerns Anne's participation in the musical activity. General questions may relate to children's rhythmic competences at the age of seven and how the teacher can react when a child has difficulties feeling the beat in a piece of music. One possibility is to study theories of children's rhythmic competences taken from psychological literature about children's' musical development (Hargreaves 1986). A teacher's thoughts on how to relate to the problem may be elucidated in different theories of didactics and/or *Bildung* (Nielsen 1998).

In other words, the analytical process consists of two steps: First, it is necessary to reduce the phenomenon to a focused question. The teacher needs analytical tools to make this abstraction. First of all the teacher must ask: 'What does it mean that Anne cannot feel the beat?' Several different explanations are possible: maybe she got off to a bad start that morning and is having difficulties concentrating (a question of mood). Or she may have trouble moving her hands (a question of developing motor skills). Or she cannot perceive the rhythmic structure of the music (a question of developing rhythmic perception).

There are other possible explanations. When the teacher selects one of them she makes an abstraction from a number of other facts.

Second, the analytical process must be continued by taking other perspectives and relating them to the primary abstraction. This process is a movement to the next step, which involves constructing a theory on the basis of documented claims and, in certain forms of research, more overriding laws. The final part of this process is based on the contribution of theories at level 3 (T3).

These two processes are a part of the analytical phase in the exercise of astonishing practices.

The result of my reflections on the relation between theory and practice and how to implement this in music teacher education is the development of the model described below.

The Model of Astonishing Practices

The practical part of the teaching strategy consists of five phases, which are common to various forms of research that use qualitative methods (Haavind 2000; Rønholt, Holgersen, Fink-Jensen and Nielsen 2003). The model is an example of how to use participant observation in education, drawing on research for inspiration. Descriptions of the five phases follow.

1. A Preparing Phase

Contact and pre-understanding are keywords in this phase. The student makes contact with a practitioner or chooses a situation from her own practice. In both cases she considers her pre-understanding of the selected practice and writes it down before the observation takes place. In this phase video recording is not relevant.

2. An Observing Phase

The student is present with a video camera in the selected practice. She may participate in two different ways: as an external observer or as a teacher. As an external observer she records a film or makes notes about important observations *during* the situation; as a teacher she makes notes *after* the situation. The notes may be supported by descriptions of the physical framework, premises and participants. It is relevant to put some questions to the teacher before the observation takes place. Questions may be:

- What is the subject? What music activities? What kind of music?
- What is the objective of the teaching?
- Why are the students going to learn about this subject?
- How should they be taught? What methods might be useful?
- What materials should be used?

- Why is this the right moment to teach this subject given the students' qualifications?
- What are the characteristics of the institution in which the teaching takes place?

During or after the observation the students make notes of feelings, sensations and astonishing experiences. Making notes is just one of the techniques used in participant observation. Interviews with the participants are a relevant supplement to the observations. A video recording of this phase is important; this becomes evident in the examples below.

3. A Data-Generating Phase

The student writes descriptions on the basis of observations, interviews and notes, focusing on what surprised her in relation to her pre-understanding. The descriptions are a result of the first common-sense analysis. In the first description, the student has to be very open and make the behaviour of the participants clear to the reader. Video recording offers the student the possibility of comparing observations with logbook notes. Additional recordings may be made and the exercise may be completed using the technique of 'stimulated recall', which includes a presentation of the video recordings to selected participants. The comments from these participants may then provide important information in the analysing process. Later on the student has to show her video recordings to other students to find out how they understand the situation. The student must do so without revealing her own understanding of the situation.

4. An Analysing Phase

In this phase the student may draw on a variety of information and theoretical perspectives to reflect on the observed phenomena. In this process the video recordings are an important input for a closer study and analysis of the details of the situation. After studying the video recordings the student chooses the central phenomenon and decides which theories are able to shed light on this. The decision may be discussed with other people – other students, or the observed participants themselves. This phase is the groundwork for a product (a text) to be used in the next phase.

5. A Presenting Phase

This phase is concerned with the report and oral examination. The student presents her project in written and verbal form as a topic for discussion. The final presentation takes place when the student takes an examination, which is partly oral, partly written. She makes a 25-page report, which is the starting point of a discussion between the student and the examiner.

These five phases are not quite chronological. The first three steps have to be carried out one after the other. But in the analytical phase the student moves back and forth between data material and different theoretical perspectives, as in a hermeneutic spiral (Fink-Jensen 2007).

The point of departure is not a study of theory or previous research, followed up by a research question to guide the project. In this way this strategy differs from other common teacher strategies. Even though the objective of the strategy is to gain insight into how theory can contribute to the development of practice, the point of departure is empirical. The procedure may be reminiscent of 'grounded theory' yet the approach is different. The first step of the analytical process is based on a phenomenological method. The difference is that, from the very beginning, the first-person perspective always has to be reflected on. This position is based on the realization that the teacher or researcher always has prior experiences, expectations, feelings and interests that influence her way of seeing and the theory of practice that is at play in a given situation.

In the next paragraph I shall present the way in which the strategy was implemented in the course. The implementation revealed some problems. Students' ability to have an open attitude as a participant observer seemed to depend on their degree of experience as music teachers. I shall introduce this problem in two cases with two different students.

The Implementation of Astonishing Practices

The teaching of the music teacher students was marked by the fact that they had to work with a case based on empirical studies. The observations were made in a primary, secondary or upper secondary school, or in a university, conservatory or music school.

The student worked together with the music teacher who had agreed to take part in the student's project. Alternatively, the student could make observations of her own practice, which, in turn, had other implications and provided a particular challenge.

Before starting the project every student had to write down her own expectations related to the place and the participants. To understand her own personal perspective she also had to write down her own preconditions and pre-understandings. In what kind of music education did she participate in school, leisure time and so on? Was she aware of having any pedagogical or musical preferences? There might be a tendency to forget these expectations and preferences after having made the observations.

In order to prepare the students for the empirical work, selected research methods were introduced and discussed. The course included, in particular, an introduction of how to make a case study, the method and questions related to 'participant observation', the use of different techniques such as video recordings and stimulated recall, and an introduction to the analysis of the empirical material. For the analysis the student had to find relevant theories. For this purpose, the course introduced different kinds of basic psychological and educational theories. Working with their individual projects the students very often had to supplement these with other theories to shed light on the chosen phenomenon.

In implementing the strategy of astonishing practices, several problems occurred which are common to other research methods. However, in what follows I shall emphasize only one particular problem encountered by the music teacher students.

In the introduction, I referred to Brian Roberts' point that the music teacher's insider information was an advantage in music education research. The music teacher student also has a kind of familiarity with the situations she observes. Familiarity has to do with personal perspectives. In research based on a phenomenological point of view the personal perspective always has to be considered. Familiarity, then, is a strength but also a problem. In the two examples below I shall show how familiarity was a problem for two different music teacher students working with 'astonishing practices'.

Familiarity: A Key Issue in the Use of the Strategy

The use of 'astonishing practices' was new to the students, and it was difficult for them to abandon a theoretical approach to the project from the very beginning. However, this was necessary, because astonishment is contingent on the student's ability to be present in an open sensuous way, leaving behind both established and personal theoretical presumptions.

This leads us to the fact that the students had to develop techniques for reflecting on their personal perspective. This need became especially evident in my study when the teacher was very experienced. An experienced teacher has the benefit of a wealth of ideas of what to do and knowledge about what works. She has developed a normative position, so that her personal perspective dominates in a way that may prevent her from seeing in an open sensuous way. She develops a certain kind of blindness. 'Dinah's astonishment' (below) is an example of how that occurred in my study at the university.

Dinah was one of the most experienced teachers in the group of students. However, everyone had some level of familiarity with the field of observation. This familiarity originated from participation as learners or teachers in music lessons at school, music school, university or other musical contexts. Even though familiarity may enable the observer to understand several academic and practical activities, it may hinder them in seeing educational problems. Familiarity is part of the everyday knowledge that may influence sensuous impressions in the observing situation. Therefore, I had to consider the question of how a student's familiarity with the observed field might influence his or her ability to be present with an open sensuous attitude. What does the strategy of astonishing practices offer to solve this problem for students with very different levels of experience in teaching? To illustrate and discuss this problem I shall describe the astonishment of two students which became apparent in their descriptions of their observations of music lessons at a public school and at a high school.

Michael's Astonishment

Michael, a student, was in his twenties with only limited teaching experience. He studied musicology at the University of Copenhagen and had never before attended a course in music didactics.

Michael and three other students contacted a teacher at an upper secondary school and arranged to make a video recording of a music lesson. On the arranged day the teacher was absent due to illness. So Michael agreed to teach the class, while the other students participated, sitting in the room with a video camera. Michael did not know the students in the class beforehand and, because of his own previous experiences of being a secondary school student, he did not have great expectations of them.

> The lesson is about singing in a choir
> First, Michael asks the students to stand in a semicircle. Then he asks the sopranos to stand to the right and the altos to stand to the left. Immediately a girl asks: 'What am I?' Michael says: 'Those who have a high voice go to the right, and those who have low voices go the left!' The girls discuss the matter. A girl says: 'Sopranos are the low voices, aren't they?' Two girls go to the right. A girl says: 'Could you please sing the tones you want us to sing?' First, Michael plays a high tone on the piano. Second, he sings the tone in falsetto. The girls burst out laughing, and then all the girls in the soprano group move to the alto group.

In spite of his low expectations, Michael was astonished by the students' lack of knowledge of musical terms. Michael used an academic vocabulary that he assumed was common language, but this appeared not to be the case. Not until very late in the process he did understand that.

Michael's astonishment is about the students' academic competences. He does not know them and this causes communication problems. His approach to music education is 'trial and error' because of his lack of training. The advantage of 'trial and error' as a teaching strategy is its openness: the teacher knows that it may not work. He is ready to try a new method. In the communication with the girls this is very obvious. The challenge is to explain what the words alto and soprano mean. He can play a tone, sing a tone or use language, talking about high and low voices. His knowledge of these different methods is based on his musical education and previous experience. He is very familiar with musical vocabulary and he is also able to use this knowledge. He has professional competences in the subject of music but he is untrained in teaching.

In the teaching process Michael had pedagogical problems because of his inexperience, but on the other hand his 'seeing' was not influenced by normative pedagogical considerations developed over years of teaching practice. In his analysis he looked at the problem in an open way by discussing it from the perspective of 'didactic irritation' and the question of the teacher's competences relating to the ability to act in the situation (Rønholt 2003). 'Didactic irritation' is a phenomenon on the phenomenal level (observed reality), which manifests itself through bodily and verbal expressions and actions and is of crucial importance for processes of education and learning. A didactic irritation offers the possibility of a 'pedagogical moment' (an unforeseen opportunity for pedagogical action).

Dinah's Astonishment

The student Dinah is in her forties and has a great deal of experience in teaching music in different schools and to different grades. She is currently teaching music to recreation centre teachers and she is studying music didactics at the Danish School of Education. Thus she has the prerequisites for being able to reflect on didactic problems on level T3.

Dinah observed a lesson with children in second grade at a public school. The music activity was a singing game with movements. Dinah describes the situation like this:

> The children are standing in a circle. They are going to rehearse a new song. The text has many words and neither the text nor the tune is easy to remember. The teacher introduces the children to the song, talking about a 'new dance' and at the same time showing the choreography. The children are aware of the movements. Imitating the teacher's movements, they 'forget' about singing.

After the observation Dinah studies the video recording and writes about her feelings and her observations on a common-sense level (the italic type shows her didactic reflections; the non-italics show her observations):

> In the video I saw that the children were very engaged in a singing activity. But I also saw that it was very difficult for them to learn a new melody, a new text and choreography at the same time. *I think that it might have been a better idea to teach the three parts of the song activity separately. Maybe the children would have been better able to sing the song.* I also noticed that the song is without accompaniment and in a low key. *I think that an accompaniment would help the children to sing in tune. I also believe that it would be easier for the children to sing it in a higher key.* I noticed that the children primarily were concerned with the choreography. *I wonder if it is possible for children of this age to do so many things at the same time and also have an aesthetic realization.* Later on I saw that the singing part of the activity was supporting the being together in music. *These observations make me want to write about the singing activity because I think that for this age group it is a fundamental discipline in music education.*

In her reflections she cannot help using her knowledge of this kind of activity. Her special interest in singing is very evident. Her astonishment is expressed in this sentence: *I wonder if it is possible for children of this age to do so many things at the same time and also have an aesthetic realization.* Furthermore, Dinah was astonished that the children's singing voices were not pedagogically supported and that no attention was paid to singing in a key that is appropriate and natural for the children's vocal chords. From Dinah's normative perspective this was a problem. One conclusion is that her astonishment was chiefly about what the teacher did not do! Therefore she asked the teacher about her educational intentions with this activity. The teacher answered that the beat was the focus and the intentions were to create a sense of musical community and to make an orchestra of voices without instruments. The objectives of the singing activity were:

- that the children have fun taking part in the activity
- that the children indirectly gain new knowledge of music
- that movement and singing can go together
- that the children gain knowledge of different musical forms of expression, in this case the combination of movement and song.

The teacher's everyday theory was that the combination of movement and song may be transferred to everyday situations. She presumed that the ability to combine and coordinate different expressions is important for the development of the brain and general education. The teacher thinks that many grown-ups today are unable to coordinate singing and movement, and that the integration of movements in a singing activity is easier for children. Generally speaking, it is important for children to move, because movement strengthens the general ability to learn, and at the same time it makes the children more relaxed.

Thus, this everyday knowledge gave the teacher good reason to implement the activity. Dinah's astonishment pointed to a dilemma between the teacher's intentions and the children's ability to do several things at the same time. Dinah, with her special interest in singing, noticed that it did not work, but she was only able to study a short part of the process. Maybe Dinah's knowledge of children's singing voices was more developed than the teacher's. The fact is that Dinah's astonishment was a kind of didactic irritation connected to a question: 'Why does the teacher fail to see the possibility of teaching singing?' (This was important to Dinah, but not to the teacher.) Dinah admitted that in this situation she places herself in the teacher's position and thinks of how she, herself, would act.

This highlights the question of the theoretical perspectives she brought into the classroom. Dinah's way of dealing with the exercise was characterized by her normative position. The theories she had developed in her own practice dominated her reflections, and it was very difficult for her to look at her own position from a meta-perspective. The advantage of this position is her knowledge of 'what is possible' in a situation like this and her knowledge of the voice. The danger of her position is that, without a self-reflecting attitude, she may choose theories in the analysis that stress her own preferences instead of trying to challenge her own pre-understanding. Instead of taking up the issue of the importance of singing, she should be open in the first analytical abstraction from her observation and ask about the terms of the activity: Did the teacher reach the objective of this activity? If not, what problems occurred? It is also possible to deal with a problem concerning the musical knowledge of the participating teacher by means of a more general question: what musical competences are required for the teacher to implement this kind of musical activity? This is a question that is much more open to detailed discussion than Dinah's wish to write about the importance of the singing activity. There is a danger that writing about the importance of the singing would not challenge, but only confirm her position.

Familiarity: Problem or Advantage?

These examples seem to indicate that it is easier for inexperienced teachers to have an open attitude. Michael has not yet developed a normative position; each reaction from the students is a challenge to him. Because of his theoretical background it is easy for him to analyse the phenomenon, but still he needs some training to be able to act upon the result of his reflections in practice. In Michael's case he experiences the educational problems directly. This also has something to do with music as a subject. In many musical activities there is a requirement to perform, and the student becomes very visible to the teacher, who is then able to observe the result of his initiatives.

Astonishing practices do not replace the training in practice that Michael needs. But the exercise provides an opportunity for him to train his analytical abilities in a concrete episode from practice. To do this he needs theoretical knowledge from pedagogical and psychological sources.

Dinah is very experienced at teaching music. She is familiar with the activities she observes, and she knows what is best! This creates serious problems in the analytical phase. The main problem is how she can learn to 'see' her own normative considerations (Field and Latta 2001). The strategy of astonishing practices is based on the need to reflect on one's own position. This happens in the confrontation with other students' perspectives while looking at the video recording. By repeating the study of the video recording she will see something that was not visible during the first observation. These steps are ways of creating a distance from oneself; seeing oneself as a part of the situation. Optimally, this can result in an important self-awareness that can enhance her seeing by raising new questions instead of using traditional explanations. A central question is: is it possible to understand this phenomenon in a new way? Dinah 'sees that' immediately. But the basis of her 'seeing that' is previous experiences and the preferences she has developed concerning singing in music education. It does not give her new ideas. That should have been possible if she had been open to the teacher's intentions. However, her professional knowledge of singing is strong and makes it possible for her to criticize the professional knowledge of the teacher in this matter.

The conclusion is that video recording is of great importance in the strategy – for example, in Michael's position as both a teacher and a researcher. By looking at the video recordings it was possible for him to reflect on his own participation and to discuss the situation with the three students present. My study of the implementation of the strategy of astonishing practice in my teaching has shown that the process of writing down the pre-understanding, combined with video observation, is an important way for the student to develop her self-awareness to a greater extent. The pre-understanding gives the student partial access to her tacit knowledge and stresses her expectations. These expectations may be provoked in the situation and raise her normative pedagogical considerations. This process is reinforced by looking at the video recordings and by the presentation of the video recordings to other persons – for example, in an interview using the technique of stimulated recall (Lyle 2003) in a dialogue with the observed teacher. In that process her everyday theory will be challenged by other theories at all levels. Some students needed extensive support from me in that process, and many years of familiarity with the field did not necessarily seem to be an advantage. Generally, the video recordings provided a great deal of information to all students, and, by looking at them several times, they experienced a breakthrough in their understanding.

Conclusion

At the very beginning of the chapter I asked: 'What constitutes experience in teaching?' 'How can we educate new music teachers in a way that prepares them to deal with pedagogical problems and at the same time further develops their teaching?' The implementation of the teacher strategy 'astonishing practices' provides an opportunity for students to see and deal with problems in music education. Following this strategy it is necessary for the students to get first-hand experience of a music teaching practice. But being present in the situation is not sufficient. The students need knowledge of research methods – in particular of participant observation – and, in the analysis, some knowledge of relevant pedagogical and psychological theories.

Brian Roberts' argument about the importance of the music teacher's insider information was discussed in the examples of Dinah and Michael. Familiarity with the situation is at the same time an advantage and a challenge. Normative attitudes are closely linked to familiarity. In the course of time, theories and experiences from practice are mingled together in a kind of 'embodiment' and may result in normative ideas. The challenge is then to remain able to adopt an open attitude.

Experience in teaching is not just experience in practice but also experience of using theory in practice. These experiences must be based on a high degree of openness to new understandings of how to deal with well-known problems.

Questions for Reflection

1. How do you understand the concept of astonishment in this chapter, and why is it important?
2. How can the teacher prepare herself to be present in an open-sensuous way in the teaching situations?
3. How can theoretical knowledge contribute to development of practice?

References

Field, James C. and Latta, Margaret A. Macintyre (2001). What Constitutes Becoming Experienced in Teaching and Learning? *Faculty Publications: Department of Teaching, Learning and Teacher Education.* Retrieved from http://digitalcommons.unl.edu/teachlearnfacpub/5, accessed on 17 September 2012.

Fink-Jensen, Kirsten (2007). Attunement and Bodily Dialogues in Music Education, *Philosophy of Music Education Review*, 15(1), 53–68.

Gleitman, Henry; Fridlund, Alan J.; and Reisberg, Daniel (1999). *Psychology*, fifth edition, New York: W.W. Norton.

Haavind, Hanne (ed.) (2000). *Kjønn og fortolkende metode: Metodiske muligheter i kvalitativ forskning.* Oslo: Gyldendal Akademisk.

Hargreaves, David J. (1986). *The Developmental Psychology of Music.* Cambridge: Cambridge University Press.

Imsen, Gunn (1997). *Lærerens verden: Innføring i generell didaktik.* Oslo: Tano Aschehoug.

Jarvis, Peter (1999). *The Practitioner-Researcher: Developing Theory from Practice.* San Francisco, CA: Jossey-Bass.

Kvernbekk, Tone (2000). Seeing in Practice: A Conceptual Analysis, *Scandinavian Journal of Educational Research*, 44(4), 358–70.

— (2001). Teorityper og bruk av teori. In Frede V. Nielsen and Harald Jørgensen (eds), *Nordisk Musikkpedagogisk Forskning årbok 5.* Oslo: NMH-publikasjoner, Norges Musikkhøgskole, 25–42.

— (2005). *Pedagogisk teoridannelse: Insidere, teoriformer og praksis*, Bergen: Fagbokforlaget.

Lyle, John (2003). Stimulated Recall: A Report in Its Use in Naturalistic Research, *British Educational Research Journal*, 29(6), 861–78.

Nielsen, Frede V. (1998). *Almen musikdidaktik*, second revised edition, Copenhagen: Akademisk Forlag.

Roberts, Brian (1994). Music Teachers as Researchers, *International Journal of Music Education*, 23(1), 24–33.

Rønholt, Helle (2003). Didaktiske irritationer. In Helle Rønholt, Sven-Erik Holgersen, Kirsten Fink-Jensen and Anne Maj Nielsen (eds), *Video i pædagogisk forskning: Krop og udtryk i bevægelse,* Copenhagen: Forlaget Hovedland, 106–153.

Rønholt, Helle; Holgersen, Sven-Erik; Fink-Jensen, Kirsten; and Nielsen, Anne Maj (2003). *Video i pædagogisk forskning: Krop og udtryk i bevægelse,* Copenhagen: Forlaget Hovedland.

Shweder, R.A. (1991). *Thinking through Cultures: Expeditions in Cultural Psychology,* Cambridge, MA: Harvard University Press.

Zahavi, Dan (2001). Beyond Empathy: Phenomenological Approaches to Intersubjectivity, *Journal of Consciousness Studies,* 8(5–7), 151–67.

— (2003). *Fænomenologi,* Copenhagen: Roskilde Universitetsforlag.

Chapter 9

The Cultural Dimensions of Music Teachers' Professional Knowledge

Teresa Mateiro and Maria Westvall

Introduction

Music teachers' professional knowledge is influenced by the cultural contexts from which it springs and the social contexts in which it is displayed, internalized and enacted. In a common search for improved practices, there are, however, few discussions on how cultural conditions and social representations of music and music education in our societies affect the ways in which we think and act in relation to the teaching of music. It is not unusual among scholars to approach the field of professional knowledge in music education as if everything was agreed and undisputed.

The contemporary international music education debate addresses questions about what music education should encompass, and which forms will promote students' musical growth and sustainable musical development through life, whether through formal or informal practices. As there are few studies on how cultural meanings and understandings in a society shape music education and music teachers' opinions on music education, the international debate on this topic is rather low in intensity. We believe that this issue merits wider discussion.

When we teach music we tend to approach and understand this task through the lens of values and beliefs that we are accustomed to. We have obtained those values by participating in our own social and cultural environment, and the experiences so acquired are accumulated in our personal 'depots' of social and cultural understandings (Stålhammar 1995; Westvall 2007). Consequently, there is an inherent cross-cultural diversity in the ways in which music education is carried out and understood. Therefore, music teacher education needs to address the importance of reflecting on one's own practices through the lens of another.

The development of student music teachers' understanding of cultural diversity in music education is vital in order to reflect and meet their social and cultural reality. A critical examination of the student teachers' own beliefs and attitudes, together with exposure to new and different perspectives on music teaching, should be an essential part of their development of professional knowledge in music teacher education (Froelich 2007; Westvall 2007).

This chapter explores how a group of student music teachers in Sweden were exposed to a familiar activity – music education – with an unfamiliar agenda in a different cultural and educational context. During a music pedagogy class, the students watched a 25-minute video of a music lesson that took place in a Canadian Grade 1 class with 6–7-year-old children. The aspects of the lesson that the student teachers found compelling included the way in which the teacher structured and carried out the lesson, the student–teacher relationship and the teacher's choice of lesson content. These aspects of a music teacher's professional knowledge, identified by the student music teachers, lead us to consider how a teacher's social and cultural contexts influence his or her perceptions of what will be counted as logical and satisfactory professional ways of conducting a music class.

Music Teachers, Professional Knowledge and Cultural Influences

We can assume that a teacher's values and actions are shaped by opinions and methods that are familiar and, therefore, claimed to be 'normal', within his or her educational context. Thus, professional knowledge in music education is determined by the social norms and values that are central in the cultural environment in which it is situated (Froelich 2007; Westvall 2007).

One of the ways of acquiring insights into – or broadening – our understanding of music education is to examine customs and traditions in social and cultural environments that are different from those we are accustomed to. When we look at the practices of others through a critical, comparative lens, we may acquire insights into our own customs and traditions.

In the field of cross-cultural research in education, Spindler and Spindler (2000) were pioneers. They analysed the responses by teachers in Germany and the USA to a film of an American classroom. Since their analysis the interest in comparative perspectives, practices, attitudes and assumptions has increased, and publication of research findings in this area have contributed to the broadening of our understanding of social and cultural differences and commonalities. A key challenge to consider in comparative research, however, is that the compared factors need to be compatible to avoid simplification and inappropriate generalizations (Tate 2001).

In an attempt to meet global quality requirements such as efficiency, excellence, competence and productivity, along with promoting values associated with the concepts of equality, citizenship, ethics, justice and the right to education, studies of teacher education are constantly being intensified. In framing these essential educational concerns, Kushner's question (2008, p. 239), 'How can we then establish the quality debate and decision making in education worldwide?', is crucial.

Today, the exchange of ideas between teachers, scholars and students is a frequent part of internationalization and globalization processes. This is also the case in the world of music education 'in order to find a better way of teaching music' (Kertz-Welzel 2008, p. 439). A recent example of looking at cultural similarities and differences in music education is a study by Burnard, Dillon, Rusinek and

Sæther (2008). They highlight a number of assumptions that supported their decision for conducting a comparative study:

> we can't possibly understand our own classrooms until we've looked at those of others. Second, we share the view that a comparative study has the potential to uncover the hidden assumptions that underpin what we do (and do well) in our classrooms. Third, it offers alternatives to the ways in which we have always done things. (Burnard et al. 2008, p. 111)

Burnard et al. compared music teachers' pedagogical choices in Great Britain, Spain, Australia and Sweden. The researchers' intention was to describe and compare the pedagogical work of four music teachers, with an emphasis on social inclusion.

Knowledge in Teaching

Essential knowledge for the profession of teaching is usually associated with the content of the curriculum of teacher education courses in higher education. Curriculum studies, studies of professional knowledge, and studies of teacher knowledge have been central themes in research for decades.

Shulman's work (1986, 1987) on the knowledge of teaching and the epistemology of professional practice (Schön 1983, for example) laid the basis for many later studies of practical knowledge, professional knowledge, competence and expertise acquired through professional education, professional learning, professional knowledge and professional status.

Shulman (1987) established seven categories that provide a useful way of thinking about the knowledge base for teaching: content knowledge, general pedagogical knowledge, curriculum knowledge, pedagogical content knowledge, knowledge of learners, knowledge of educational contexts and knowledge of educational ends. Among these categories, pedagogical content knowledge is the category that distinguishes the teaching profession from other professions. According to Shulman, 'the teacher can transform understanding, performance skills, or desired attitudes or values into pedagogical representations and actions' (p. 7).

Furthermore, Shulman (1986) suggested three forms for representing that teacher knowledge: propositional knowledge, case knowledge and strategic knowledge. For propositional knowledge he argued that there are fundamentally three types: principles, maxims and norms. The last one 'reflects the norms, values, ideological or philosophical commitments of justice, fairness, equity, and the like, that we wish teachers and those learning to teach to incorporate and employ' (p. 11). He emphasized that this kind of knowledge is based on what is considered morally and ethically correct, which means that it is an aspect of normative knowledge and not an aspect of theoretical and practical knowledge.

Studies of different areas of knowledge have increasingly focused more on researching the type of knowledge needed for teaching than on the ways of representing that knowledge. The study presented in this chapter addresses selected elements of Shulman's (1986, 1987) construct of pedagogical content knowledge and elements of propositional knowledge in the context of teaching-in-action.

Familiar Conventions and Contrasting Principles

We are inclined to become aware of our own musical practices when we are exposed to different musical approaches and practices (Swanwick 1999). O'Flynn (2005) argues that 'musical activities and ways of thinking about music relate to the wider beliefs and values of the society concerned' (p. 195). Ethnomusicologists Lundberg, Malm and Ronström (2000) agree:

> Music is our 'keyhole', our portal into studies of society's cultural fields of tension. By studying music we can gain knowledge about peoples' lives on a large scale, knowledge which can be difficult to get in any other way. (Lundberg, Malm and Ronström 2000, p. 17)

The student music teachers in the present study were exposed to – what was for them – a 'different' kind of music education context as they watched a video film of the Canadian teacher and her students. The differences ranged from the elements of the music curriculum, the language used (including different forms of expression) and the age group taught, to the power relations between the teacher and her students. Because early childhood music education is not typically emphasized in music teacher education in Sweden, nor in the current music curriculum, one interesting aspect of this study was the responses of Swedish student music teachers to a lesson with a class of 6–7-year-old Canadian children.

The main focus in Sweden is on music education for 'young people', defined as 13 and up, and the relationship between 'their music' within and outside school (Stålhammar 1995, 2006; Olsson 2001; Georgii-Hemming and Westvall 2010a, 2010b). The focus on this age group has been a significant feature of music education in Sweden since the 1970s and is explicitly formulated in the music curriculum (Skolverket 2000) and the national evaluations of music as a subject in general education (Skolverket 1994/2006), as well as in music teacher education.

After their viewing, the Swedish student music teachers – individually and in group discussions – compared and contrasted what they had just watched to their own 'familiar' music education context. The intention was that this task would encourage the student music teachers to put on different cultural 'lenses' which would contribute to their development of a broader cultural competence within the area of music education. This, in turn, is a crucial factor in their development as future music teachers within a global society, as well as for the development of new knowledge, ideas, methods and a generally broadened repertoire within the area of music education.

The Context of (Music) Education in Sweden

> The task of the school is to encourage all pupils to discover their own uniqueness
> as individuals and thereby actively participate in social life by giving of their
> best in responsible freedom. (Skolverket 1994/2006, p. 3)

This quotation from the Swedish curriculum of general education draws our
attention to the fact that an overarching goal within all subjects in general
education, including music, rests on the basis of democratic actions, equality and
active citizenship (SOU 2000, p. 1).

Democratic principles have a long and strong tradition in the Swedish
education system. Accordingly, the aim is to encourage and prepare the citizens
to be responsible and seek out new paths within their society. Critical thinking
is promoted from an early age and, for this reason, students are encouraged to
be critical of authorities in schools (such as teachers), lesson plans, methods and
traditions. According to the Democracy report (SOU 2000) Sweden is one of
the least authority-bound countries in the world and, in Sweden, the individual's
prospects for self-development are generally highly valued.

In relation to music education, the general curriculum for compulsory
education in Sweden (ages 7–16) states that students should 'develop and use their
knowledge and experience in as many different forms of expression as possible
covering language, pictures, music, drama and dance' (Skolverket 1994/2006, p.
10). The goals of the music curriculum are intended to encourage the students'
development of musical knowledge and confidence. This includes, for instance,
their ability to sing and play music individually and in groups, listening to music,
creating their own music and communicating their (musical) thinking.

Thorsén (2002) suggests that there are two key foundations for music in
general education. One relates to the developmental aspects of the child where
music supports other skills, such as the development of motor, emotional and
cognitive abilities. In this case music, for its own sake, plays a subsidiary role.
The second foundation focuses on social and communicative aspects of the
child's development and encompasses the children's musical socialization and
construction of identity.

In the early years of compulsory school in Sweden, music is featured as
an integrated part of a holistic curriculum. At a fairly young age, students are
encouraged to bring 'their own music' to the music lesson. Important musical
events in many schools in Sweden are the end-of-term gatherings for the whole
school. On these occasions classes or groups perform for each other (often in
choirs, solo or in 'sing-alongs') and draw considerable attention from the other
students and faculty at the schools.

Along with the philosophy of the general curriculum (Skolverket 1994/2006),
music education is promoted to be conducted in a child-centred or – even more
so – youth-centred way. This includes consideration of the students' musical
preferences as well as students' input regarding how the music class will be

organized and carried out. Since the end of the 1960s 'teenage music' has been formally promoted as an accepted part of music education in Sweden (Sandberg 2006; Georgii-Hemming and Westvall 2010b). An informal approach in a formal setting, such as forming pop bands with fellow students during a music class, has been an important attribute of general music education, along with encouraging each student's development of musical self-expression. The curriculum suggests that each school should value the students' right to 'develop their own individual way of learning' as well as to 'develop confidence in their own [musical] ability' (Skolverket 1994/2006, p. 9). Consequently, the task of a music teacher in Sweden today is to consider each individual student's needs, ideas and previous experiences, and allow students to develop 'their ability to express themselves creatively and become more interested in participating in the range of cultural activities that society has to offer' (Skolverket 1994/2006, p. 10).

The idea of promoting young people's music is, however, not a recent idea in music education in Sweden. It dates back to the 1930s, when musician and music teacher Knut Brodin challenged the established ways of carrying out music education at the time, and suggested that the use of 'hit songs' of the era was an excellent way for students to develop their singing as well as expressing themselves emotionally through music (Sundin 1988; Ryner 2004). Brodin's ideas were profoundly criticized by his peers, but, in increasingly democratized schools towards the end of the 1960s, his ideas gradually gained acceptance.

Exploring the Practice and Context of 'the Other'

Forty student music teachers in Sweden were given the task of writing down their observations of a video, displaying a music class in Canada. One of the goals in our study, when we presented the video recording to the students, was to provide an opportunity for reflection and analysis of the teaching practice of a music teacher. Asking the students to jot down their observations of the music class as the lesson unfolded yielded their initial impressions. This exercise contributed to the experience of the teaching professional's reflection-in-action, at the moment of occurrence of the action. Specific cases provide explicit experiences for analysis and offer a means for student teachers to think critically about the practical implications of teaching and learning theories.

The key questions that guided this study were: What aspects of pedagogical content knowledge would the student music teachers identify? How would experiences from their own cultural context affect their understandings of what could be regarded as relevant and 'proper' knowledge in music education?

Music Lesson in a Grade 1 Class

The video captured a music lesson with 22 students, 6–7 years of age, who participated in 13 distinct but related musical activities. The lesson was organized around thematic links and it was clear from the children's level of participation that most of the materials and activities were familiar to them. Some new materials, activities and configurations were introduced, which expanded upon the familiar materials. The principal activities in the lesson were singing, clapping and dancing. The teacher reinforced musical concepts through gestures, singing, clapping and dancing. She introduced notation of patterns previously experienced through the use of icons and symbols which the children clapped and manipulated physically, and she encouraged the children's aural memory through pitch matching. The teacher used a variety of spatial configurations, such as moving physically from sitting in a circle with the children to the piano, to the blackboard and then again to the children sitting or standing in a cluster.

This video recording had also been previously analysed in a study by Russell (2000, 2005) in terms of its content, its structure and the teacher's pace. Russell interpreted the findings in terms of the individual, the institutional and the cultural contexts. The results suggest that the subject matter, the characteristics of students, the teacher's institutional choices and social factors are essential components of, and fundamental for, an effective classroom management strategy.

Three Scenes: Equality, Inclusion and the Unfamiliar

This section introduces three scenarios that are based on key features that became evident in the student music teachers' reflection on the video recording. Three themes emerged while we were analysing the Swedish students' accounts: *equality*, *inclusion* and *the unfamiliar*. The first two themes strongly accentuate democratic principles in education while the third one is more related to the dynamic of the music lesson itself. These include the social conditions of the classroom and the reinforcement of the United Nations' Convention on the Rights of the Child, including all children's right to receive education without discrimination, together with respect for the children's views (UNICEF 2011).

Some of the key ideas within the area of education underline the preparation of pupils for democratic participation in their society. This is done by highlighting democratic principles both as content knowledge and practical skills in their education. Education *through* democracy is a means to educate *for* a democratic society (Biesta 2003). These ideas are reflected in the steering document *Curriculum for the Compulsory School System, the Pre-School Class and the Leisure-Time Centre Lpo 94* (Skolverket 1994/2006, p. 13), where, under the heading 'Responsibility and influence of pupils', it states that:

> The democratic principles of being able to influence, take responsibility and be involved should embrace all pupils. Development of pupils' knowledge and social awareness requires that they take increasingly greater responsibility for their own work as well as for the school environment and that they are also able to exercise real influence over their education.

The third scene, *the unfamiliar*, highlights the student music teachers' consideration of something that is not yet recognizable or known to them, yet which may appear to be fascinating. Gustavsson (2003) discusses this encounter as a *Bildung* process which also entails the prospect of developing new interpretations and understandings of the familiar after having encountered the unfamiliar and unknown. In an educational and social context, there is an important potential in approaching the perspective of 'the other' in order to develop new knowledge. Georgii-Hemming and Westvall (2010a) state the importance of the encounter of, and the balance between, the familiar and the unfamiliar for a music learner – an encounter and balance which are just as important for a music teacher.

Scene 1: Equality

> The class starts with the students singing familiar greeting songs. The children are sitting on the floor in a circle in the centre of the room, and the teacher first stands, then sits down by the piano, playing the accompaniment of the songs. Then the teacher moves and sits down on a chair in the circle with the children and the class continues with more songs. The children sing together in pairs and small groups. This three-minute introduction consists of a sequential musical dialogue between the teacher and children, based on the interval of a minor third. At the same time, as Russell analysed (2000, p. 12), 'this approach signalled the start of the lesson, established a sense of purpose, warmed up the children's singing voices, and began the process of socializing the children into thinking and acting like musicians'.

Ten student music teachers noted that the teacher sat on a chair while the children were sitting on the floor. When we read the student music teachers' accounts, this particular description of the teacher's behaviour drew our attention because at other times the teacher moved in other ways: kneeling beside children when they were working in small groups on the floor and dancing with a child who did not have a partner, for example. Interestingly, such actions by the teacher were not remarked on by the participants. So, what does the fact that the teacher sits on a chair and the children on the floor mean for the Swedish student music teachers? The following data excerpts are representative of the student music teachers' concerns in relation to ideas of equality, status and authority:

> Why is the teacher sitting on a chair while the children sit on the floor? Inequality? Status? The school seems to be different from the school in Sweden. Just the fact that the children call their teacher Mrs reveals something about the system and different status.
>
> The teacher on a chair, not on the floor as the children. Authority? Generally the students show great respect for their teacher. The teacher makes most decisions but the children are still included. I believe this music class would have been

difficult to perform in Sweden as we do not pay the same respect to authorities (the teacher).

For the Canadian teacher the act of sitting on a chair may have no relation to these concepts of status and authority. For the Swedish student music teachers in this study, however, the teacher's behaviour carries social meanings, which leads them to reflect on the difference in the status between teacher and student. Moreover, that difference is reaffirmed for them when the children call their teacher 'Mrs'. For them, respect for a difference in status is marked by symbolism, such as: (a) equality of conditions – 'I am used to everybody, students and teachers, sitting on the same level'; (b) equal treatment – 'This music class would have been difficult to perform in Sweden as we do not to pay the same respect to the authorities (the teacher)'; (c) representation of authority – 'Teacher's position on a chair represents authority'.

Such symbolism has other implications. In the videotaped lesson the teacher makes nearly all the decisions. The lesson is, therefore, according to the student music teachers, focused on the teacher; that is, the music lesson is entirely teacher-directed. The role of the children is to carry out the tasks presented by the teacher. They do not participate in other ways, such as choosing a song to sing or a game to play. All the ideas come from the teacher; no opportunities are provided for the children to exhibit initiative. Nor is it possible for the children to express themselves spontaneously. There is a certain distance between the teacher and children, with regard to both the one-way treatment of the children by the teacher and the symbolism of physical location, represented in this case by the chair. As one student teacher noted: 'The lesson is well planned and she [the teacher] is nice to the children, but she distances herself by sitting on a chair while the children are on the floor.'

Scene 2: Inclusion

> During the 30 minutes of the music class the children participated actively in the proposed activities. Rarely did we observe any child being inattentive, distracted or disinterested. The intensity with which the teacher focused on each activity stimulated the children to respond in a very engaged way. She also motivated the children by praising their efforts and by suggesting techniques to those who could not, for example, sing in the correct pitch. She maintained intense eye contact with each child and invited everyone to participate in the activities. A few minutes before the class ended a student arrived late. She was asked to sit and watch the other children until the class ended.

Inclusion was a word frequently used by the Swedish student music teachers in their comments on the videotaped lesson. They observed that the teacher was able to develop a 'good class', including engaging all the children intensely: 'The teacher had the children's attention most of the time by using her voice in talking and singing. She included the children a lot.' In a way, this surprised the student music teachers because the group comprised 22 first-grade children. The student music teachers were impressed by the teacher's ability to consistently engage a large group of young children throughout the lesson.

> The teacher captures the students' attention immediately. She addresses them by name and they are all included. The teacher kept the students engaged in a very inspiring way. She did not treat the children like they should be younger than they actually are. She did not make the music lesson into something 'unnecessary'. Instead, she took advantage of the children's wishes to learn and included a lot of theory. Clever!

It was clear to the student music teachers that the teacher knew all the children very well, because she called everyone by name. One student music teacher wondered how much time the students spent in music classes each week, adding: 'The teacher seems to know the children well in the class: is she their ordinary class teacher or does she only teach them music?' At the time of the videotaping, the children had classes with this music teacher twice a week, with 30 minutes per class. The ability of the teacher to address each student by name facilitated interaction between them. Likewise, the teacher showed respect for her students and it was clear that she knew how to handle children in this age group.

The way the teacher planned and structured the lesson, which was filled with songs, games and dances, also encouraged and promoted the participation of the children. All the children seemed to be engaged in each activity. One of the student music teachers referred to the class as 'an experience' thus justifying the need for the engagement of all: 'The lesson has the form of an experience in which the students are participating.' Moreover, this experience was performed in enjoyable way by both teacher and children, as another student music teacher noted: 'Both teacher and students seem to be participating with sense of engagement and energy.'

The fact that one child came late to the music class and was not included in the activities was noted by several student music teachers. One of them said: 'It must have been boring for the girl who came late to the class not to be included.' Another one asked: 'The girl who came late was put on a chair during the rest of the lesson. Why? Could she not or was she not allowed to participate in the class? Is this an including school?' The attention that the student music teachers gave to the concept of inclusion is really interesting. It is related to a debate around human values and democratic principles established in the schools and by the schools. It is, beyond doubt, a cultural aspect based on the democratic dimensions of the curriculum.

Something that the student music teachers did not seem to have noticed on the video-recording was that the teacher said to the person who brought the child to the class: 'It's OK. She can stay here.' This comment indicates that the child was not a member of this class but needed a place to stay until the end of the session. On the face of it, it seems that the student music teachers assumed from a superficial analysis of the videotape that the child was deliberately excluded. This points to the importance of seeking more information to explain a social phenomenon. As researchers running this study, we are aware of the ease with which actions can be misunderstood when one does not have important information and the full context.

Scene 3: The Unfamiliar

> Thirteen musical activities constituted the 30-minute lesson. The children sang a total of nine songs which were linked thematically by the minor third interval and the ♫♫ pattern. The children sang, listened, danced and performed body movements, clapped and wrote rhythmic patterns. Concepts and musical skills were both introduced and strengthened by the teacher through the presentation of the various musical tasks, and resource materials such as piano, blackboard, records and popsicle sticks supported their development.

The diversity of activities and the dynamics of the class were greatly lauded by the Swedish student music teachers. They especially noted the actions of the Canadian teacher, commenting on the various modalities she used to present the same content, explore different teaching materials and provide the children with diverse ways of learning and experiencing musical concepts through practical experience. No doubt there were many activities in little time, as was pointed out by a student music teacher: 'The teacher includes a lot in a short time.' However, the student music teachers recognized the lesson as one which was very well planned with coherent and interlinked activities which were presented gradually in a logical sequence.

When the student music teachers wrote about the pace of the lesson they reflected on the behaviour and attitudes of the teacher and her students. They concluded that the lesson was successful because the teacher managed to maintain discipline and the interest of the children. She chose activities that were appropriate to their age group and adapted the tasks to the abilities and skills of the children. She also knew how to change activities at the moment it was prudent to move on. The teacher lost no time with excessive explanations and had clear objectives for the lesson. The student music teachers recognized the Canadian teacher's extensive teaching experience and understood that this helped her actions in the classroom. They commented:

> A music class with a high intensity level … Both teacher and student seem to be participating with a sense of engagement and energy. It is a lively atmosphere in the class. The teacher gives the impression that she is experienced and used to the situation. The teacher is skilful and does not get distracted. Without any problem keeps a high tempo with lots of instructions.
>
> The teacher had the children's attention most of the time by using her voice in talking and singing. She included the children a lot. One section was followed by the next section and so on. This leads to good, and 'tight', planning. The teacher knew exactly what she was going to do.

> Lots of singing. Full activity throughout the lesson. The teacher introduces many activities and they are linked together. The teacher gives direct comments like 'good' or 'nearly right'. The teacher does not tell the students to stop doing things they are not supposed to. Instead she redirects their attention.

Concerning the pace of the class of the Canadian music teacher, Russell (2000, p. 14) notes that 'while a large number of activities in itself does not point to good pacing, it does imply a fast pace'. A good number of the Swedish student music teachers observed that the music lesson was really fast-paced; beyond the points already stressed earlier, they also reflected upon the possible consequences for such a pace on children's learning processes. One student music teacher observed that the children had no time to 'breathe': 'No time for breaks. Feels like you are holding your breath during the class.' Another student suggested that the children had no time to think about what they were doing: 'No thinking but action all the time.'

We are not certain why the student music teachers commented on the pace and what these comments stand for. Is 'a fast pace' something negative or positive? They did not develop their comments further; neither did they reflect upon whether the pace of delivery was related to content, subject matter, goals of the lesson, the students or the classroom dynamics. We acknowledge the complexity of the issue of pace in teaching. But how can pace be appraised and assessed? Could the students' statements have any relation to educational culture? Are music lessons and/or other disciplines in Sweden given at a slower pace? Due to the role of music education in the Swedish curriculum, the music student teachers' might well lack experience of teaching music to young children. Consequently, they will overlook the possibility that the learning pace of young children might differ from that of teenagers.

'It was quite a high tempo during the class. It is good because you have the time to do many things, but can students incorporate more information after such an intensive lesson like this?' This student music teacher raises an important point. The lesson was centred on the subject matter; that is, it focused on the learning of musical concepts such as intervals; rhythmic patterns; formal structure of musical phrases; high, middle and low pitch; and ascending and descending scales. The amount of information was extensive, and according to the student music teachers it was not possible to see if the students were learning or only performing one task after another automatically.

According to Russell (2000, p. 18) 'in the province of Québec, the curriculum is organized around concepts. For instance, children are expected to recognize differences in pitch, timbre, duration and volume. Exploration of musical sounds and composition is encouraged and no specific repertoire or method teaching is prescribed.' In Sweden the discipline of music in schools has different goals. The class is centred on the individual rather than on the content. In their study of the current discourses of music education in Sweden Georgii-Hemming and Westvall (2010a, p. 24) explain that:

Music as a phenomenon is not focused on, and music is certainly not seen as an autonomous object. However, the meaning of music is perceived as a unique source for personal and social development. Therefore every student must be respected, learn to cooperate, be given opportunities to find their identity and become a fulfilled human being with self-confidence. They must also be aware of – and take responsibility for – what he or she learns, discover their own abilities and the potential value of aesthetic knowledge.

We believe that it was from this perspective that the Swedish student music teachers found the Canadian music lesson somewhat unfamiliar. Although they were unanimous in their opinion that it was 'a good music lesson', their responses to the video lead us to the conclusion that some student music teachers in this study believed that they could not give a similar lesson in Swedish schools.

Concluding Reflections

Reflecting upon *what* to teach and *how* to teach it is undoubtedly crucial in the education of any teacher. Both the courses in the pedagogy of music and the periods of practice during teacher education programmes should aim for the development of skills and reflection so that future teachers will be prepared to successfully integrate content knowledge (what) and pedagogical content knowledge (how) in their practice. This educational process requires musical expertise, knowledge of various methods and approaches to music education, and reflection on the pedagogical practices of professionals, as well as on their own practice as a teacher in the classroom.

In this chapter we have discussed how cultural and educational dimensions affect a student teacher's ideas of what will be considered 'right' or expected knowledge in teaching music. The subject content of music was discussed by the Swedish student music teachers, but their responses mainly touched on democratic principles in relation to equality, status, authority and inclusion. This supports Shulman's argument that the norms of propositional knowledge guide the work of a teacher in terms of ideological and philosophical ideas in the classroom. This, in turn, could be due to the fact that these are key concepts that have been an integrated part of their own education and that represent the long tradition of democracy, equality and active citizenship in the Swedish educational context.

One presumption could be that the social meaning of actions and expressions as well as the ways of implementing democratic principles in music education are different in the Canadian and Swedish educational systems (this would include conventions relating to equal treatment, equal conditions, equal opportunities and the representation of authority). However, another possibility might be that the student music teachers, in their interpretations, are balanced between their familiar understandings, and an unfamiliar application of democratic principles.

This case study suggests that fixed opinions do not necessarily have to stay so. By examining the practices of others we can learn to challenge and critically consider our own customs and attitudes; this enables an internalization of new and different perspectives and approaches. As educators we need to be prepared to meet students and peers who hold a diversity of different cultural and social experiences as well as different understandings of learning and teaching music. It is crucial for the education of music teachers in a global society to set the processes of 'expanding perspectives' in motion. By doing so we can broaden personal, educational and societal repertoires within the world of music, music educators and education.

Questions for Reflection

1. How would you describe the principles that underlie your knowledge and ideas of music teaching?
2. What has influenced these principles?
3. Do you make interesting discoveries when you examine your own 'familiar' understandings of professional knowledge through a different perspective, or the lens of another?

References

Biesta, Gert (2003). Demokrati – ett problem för utbildning eller ett utbildningsproblem? *Utbildning & Demokrati*, 12(1), 59–80.

Burnard, Pamela; Dillion Steve; Rusinek, Gabriel; and Sæther, Eva (2008). Inclusive Pedagogies in Music Education: A Comparative Study of Music Teachers' Perspectives from Four Countries. *International Journal of Music Education*, 26, 109–126.

Froehlich, Hildegard (2007). *Sociology for Music Teachers: Perspectives for Practice*, Upper Saddle River, NJ: Pearson Education.

Georgii-Hemming, Eva and Westvall, Maria (2010a). Music Education: A Personal Matter? Examining the Current Discourses of Music Education in Sweden, *British Journal of Music Education*, 27(1), 21–33.

— (2010b). Teaching Music in Our Time: Student Music Teachers' Reflections on Music Education, Teacher Education and Becoming a Teacher, *Music Education Research*, 12(4), 353–67.

Gustavsson, Bernt (2003). Bildning och demokrati Att förmedla det partikulära och det universella? *Utbildning & Demokrati*, 12(1), 39–58.

Kertz-Welzel, Alexandra (2008). Music Education in the Twenty-First Century: A Cross-Cultural Comparison of German and American Music Education Towards a New Concept of International Dialogue, *Music Education Research*, 10(4), 439–49.

Kushner, Saville (2008). Uma paradoja de la educación. In José Luis Aróstegui and Juan Bautista Martínez Rodríguez (eds), *Globalización, posmodernidad y educación: la calidad como coartada neoliberal*. Madrid: Akal, 225–46.

Lundberg, Dan; Malm, Krister; and Ronström, Ove (2000). *Musik, medier, mångkultur: förändringar i svenska musiklandskap*. Hedemora: Gidlund i samarbete med Riksbankens jubileumsfond. Online version *Music, Media, Multiculture: changing musicscapes* (2003): http://www.visarkiv.se/online/mmm/index_mmm.html

O'Flynn, John (2005). Re-Appraising Ideas of Musicality in Intercultural Contexts of Music Education, *International Journal of Music Education*, 23(3), 191–203.

Olsson, Bengt (2001). Scandinavia. In David J. Hargreaves and Adrian North (eds), *Musical Development and Learning: The International Perspective*. London: Continuum, 175–86.

Russell, Joan (2000). Contexts of Music Classroom Management. *Arts and Learning Research Journal*, 16, 195–225.

— (2005). Estrutura, conteúdo e andamento em uma aula de música na primeira série do ensino fundamental: Um estudo de caso sobre a gestão de sala de aula [trans. Beatriz Ilari], *Revista da ABEM*, 12, 73–88.

Ryner, Birgitta (2004). *Vad ska vi sjunga?: en musikpedagogisk diskurs om tiden mellan två världskrig*. Stockholm: KMH förlag.

Sandberg, Ralf (2006). Skolan som kulturell mötesplats. In Ulf P. Lundgren (ed.), *Uttryck, intryck, avtryck: lärande, estetiska uttrycksformer och forskning*. Stockholm: Vetenskapsrådet, 35–65.

Schön, Donald A. (1983). *The Reflective Practitioner: How Professionals Think in Action*, London: Temple Smith.

Shulman, Lee (1986). Those Who Understand: Knowledge Growth in Teaching, *Educational Researcher*, 15(2), 4–14.

— (1987). Knowledge and Teaching: Foundations of the New Reform, *Harvard Educational Review*, 57, 1–22.

Skolverket [The Swedish National Agency for Education] (1994/2006). *Curriculum for the Compulsory School System, Pre-School Class and Leisure-Time Centre. Lpo 94*. Retrieved from: www.skolverket.se/publikationer?id=1070, accessed on 17 September 2012.

— (2000). *Syllabuses for the Compulsory School (music)*. Retrieved from: www3.skolverket.se/ki/eng/comp.pdf, accessed on 17 September 2012.

SOU (2000). *En hållbar demokrati! Politik för folkstyrelse på 2000-talet*. Demokratiutredningens betänkande Stockholm: Regeringskansliet.

Spindler, Louise S. and Spindler, George Dearborn (2000). *Fifty years of Anthropology and Education, 1950–2000: A Splindler Anthology*. Mahwah, NJ: Erlbaum.

Stålhammar, Börje (1995). *Samspel. Grundskola – musikskola i samverkan: en studie av den pedagogiska och musikaliska interaktionen i en klassrumssituation*. Dissertation, Göteborg University.

— (2006). *Musical Identities and Music Education*. Aachen: Shaker.

Sundin, Bertil (1988). *Musiken i människan: om tradition och förnyelse inom det estetiska områdets pedagogik.* Stockholm: Natur och kultur.

Swanwick, Keith (1999). *Teaching Music Musically.* London: Routledge.

Tate, Philip (2001). Comparative Perspectives. In Chris Philpott and Charles Plummeridge (eds), *Issues in Music Education.* London: Routledge Falmer, 224–37.

Thorsén, Stig-Magnus (2002). Addressing Cultural Identity in Music Education, *Talking Drum*, 84, 1–7.

UNICEF (2011). *Convention on the Rights of the Child*, retrieved from www.unicef.org/crc, accessed on 28 October 2011.

Westvall, Maria (2007). Webs of Musical Significance: A Study of Student Teachers' Musical Socialisation in Ireland and Sweden. Dissertation, Drumcondra, St Patrick's College.

Chapter 10

School and Conservatoire Music Teachers' 'Vocational Habitus': Lessons for Music Teacher Education

Rosie Perkins and Angeliki Triantafyllaki

Introduction

This chapter explores music teachers' professional knowledge as a form of embodied know-how specific to, and constructed within, particular workplace contexts. Beginning with an argument for thinking of professional knowledge as *socially constructed know-how*, we evoke a sociological frame of reference that includes the cultural practices of teachers' workplaces, their vocational cultures, and their active and negotiated identities. Following Britzman (2003), we argue that teaching is about coming to terms with particular orientations towards knowledge, power and identity. We know, for example, that instrumental teachers construct their identities and teaching practices in response to the dominant values of their workplace (Triantafyllaki 2010a). In this process, certain definitions of know-how are adopted by teachers and subsequently enacted, re-constructed and developed. In the first part of the chapter, we examine the nature of this socially constructed know-how and the ways in which teachers take it up and negotiate it in accordance with their biographies, circumstances and workplace cultures.

Recognizing the interplay between personal and social, the chapter then moves to introduce the thinking of Bourdieu. Drawing on his work as a means of bringing together agency and structure, we present the notion of *vocational habitus*, positing that teachers' know-how is constructed as they orient towards certain dispositions of the 'right person for the job' of music teacher (Colley et al. 2003, p. 488). We develop and work with this idea through two case studies, exploring how 'vocational habitus' operates in two diverse UK settings, focusing, first, on professional instrumental teachers working in a conservatoire and, second, on secondary classroom music teachers. Our aim is to illuminate the different ways in which professional know-how is socially constructed in the two settings, and to demonstrate the role that vocational habitus plays in this process. Building on both theoretical and evidence-based arguments, the chapter concludes with a discussion of the implications of this sociological approach for music teacher education.

The Social Construction of Teachers' 'Know-How'

Epistemological issues relating to knowledge and learning in music teacher education are becoming increasingly important (Froehlich 2007; Ferm 2008). From a sociological viewpoint, in order to understand the nature of music teachers' practices we need to understand the various types of knowledge dominant in workplace contexts. Traditionally, two broad types of knowledge are distinguished in educational theory: propositional and process knowledge (Eraut 1994; Paavola and Hakkarainen 2005). Eraut (1994) argues that while the former will be publicly available and is largely codified, the latter consists of 'knowing how to conduct the various processes that contribute to professional action' (p. 107). Much earlier, Ryle (1949) described this latter form of knowledge as 'knowing how' as opposed to 'knowing that'. Akin to theories of 'know-how' knowledge are theories that pay attention to the professional knowledge teachers acquire in their daily practice, elsewhere termed 'craft knowledge' (Brown and McIntyre 1992). This is acquired primarily through practical classroom experience, which is 'for the most part not articulated in words and which is brought to bear spontaneously, routinely and sometimes unconsciously on their teaching' (p. 39). An important characteristic of 'know-how' knowledge is that it is often regarded as a source of valid theory in its own right (Goodson and Hargreaves 1996, p. 11). For example, in a study of an instrumental music teacher's practice in a UK conservatoire, Persson (1996) describes how the teaching 'tends to rely largely on self-devised strategies, commonsense and tradition' (p. 25). Yet, this know-how does not exist in a vacuum, but, rather, is constructed within particular settings and arises through an interactive process of participating in various cultural practices that structure and shape activity (Lave and Wenger 1991).

Accordingly, a sociological viewpoint focuses attention not so much on *what* is taught ('propositional' knowledge) but rather on *why* and *how* it is taught ('know-how' or 'craft' knowledge), understanding teachers' practices as the result of larger cultural, political and economic constellations that shape societal values and traditions (Froehlich 2007). In any culture – understood as a 'way of life' constituted of cultural practices (James et al. 2007) – certain values, norms, behaviours and, thus, forms of know-how will be dominant. Indeed, know-how can be thought of as *shaped* by the cultural practices of any particular workplace, so that certain forms of action become accepted while others become marginalized. Yet, such knowledge-shaping processes are subjected also to agentic negotiation on behalf of the teacher. Indeed, instrumental teachers have been found to exercise varying degrees of agency in positioning themselves within the plurality of resources available to them in workplace values, discourses and expectations (Triantafyllaki 2010b).

The social construction of teachers' know-how and the inevitable tensions it induces is further taken up by Nerland (2008), who advances a two-fold argument. First, she posits that 'professional knowledge cultures are collective mentalities that … express themselves in certain practices' because the organization of knowledge associated with those cultures is related to specific 'styles of reasoning, believing and acting' (p. 53). In other words, professional know-how is *culturally constructed* and related to certain culturally mediated ways of thinking, being and doing. Second, she maintains that forms of work-based learning are characterized by a tension between the *regulative* (i.e. adherence to standards) and the *agentic* (i.e. practitioners' relation to know-how and knowledge objects). Thus, the enacting of professional know-how in any situation is an ongoing process of trying to make sense of oneself and what one is doing while interacting with a particular cultural arena.

It is this interplay between personal and social that steers our thinking towards Bourdieu, whose work attempted to overcome the duality of structure (objectivism) and agency (subjectivism) (Bourdieu 1998; Reay 2004). For Bourdieu, social space is a space of positions, all of which are defined *in relation* to each other (Bourdieu 1989). This means that people are positioned in relation to their workplace contexts, and that workplace contexts are positioned in relation to the wider fields in which they operate. Social space thus becomes conceptualized as at one and the same time socially objective and subjective: 'no doubt agents do have an active apprehension of the world. No doubt they do construct their vision of the world. But this construction is carried out under structural constraints' (Bourdieu 1989, p. 18). The structural constraints of knowledge construction are no more evident than in literature that discusses the dilemmas and conflicts that novice classroom music teachers encounter during the transition from their teacher education courses to their first school post, as they struggle to align their personal biographies, beliefs and developing identities with local school cultures and wider policy-driven professional standards (McNally et al. 2008). The construction of professional know-how, then, cannot be thought of as a completely 'free' construction, but rather a construction shaped by the interaction between agent (teacher) and structural (particularly, in our case, workplace) positions.

In order to further explore the argument that professional know-how is inevitably culturally constructed yet at the same negotiated by teachers, we draw on Colley et al.'s (2003) extension of Bourdieu's theory and particularly their notion of vocational habitus.

Vocational Habitus and Music Teaching

It is through the notion of habitus, as will now be explained, that Bourdieu strove to reconcile objective and subjective (Grenfell et al. 1998). Habitus can be thought of as an orientation towards action that reflects a position in social space (Bourdieu 1998), or as a set of dispositions that develop 'from our social positions, and through our lives' (Hodkinson, Biesta and James 2008, p. 38). Habitus thus reflects the structural conditions in which people operate, recognizing that – for example – members of different social classes internalize their position in society to construct certain forms of actions, choices and practices (Bourdieu 1989). In other words, habitus recognizes that people do not act entirely randomly, rather acting according to the structural conditions – such as class, gender, profession – in which they are positioned. Importantly, habitus is embodied, manifesting itself as 'practical sense' for how (or how not to) behave in a particular social reality (Bourdieu 1998, p. 25).

Returning to *professional* know-how, Colley et al. (2003) have extended the notion of habitus to *vocational habitus*. In any professional field, Colley et al. argue, certain collective dispositions serve to construct 'a sense of what makes "the right person for the job"' (p. 488):

> *Vocational habitus* proposes that the learner [or teacher] aspires to a certain combination of dispositions demanded by the vocational culture. It operates in disciplinary ways to dictate how one should properly feel, look and act, as well as the values, attitudes and beliefs that one should espouse. As such, it is affective and embodied, and calls upon the innermost aspects of learners' own habitus. (Colley et al. 2003, p. 488)

Described in this way, vocational habitus is a 'process of orientation to a particular identity' (p. 488), reflecting the workplace cultures in which teachers work. Each workplace will 'demand' a different way of working, forming as it does a social position that will shape and construct teachers' practices and identities. A primary (junior) school, for example, occupies a very different position – in terms of its purpose, values and identities – from a university, calling upon teachers to come to know and operationalize very different know-how. As Colley et al. point out, however, orienting to vocational habitus is not a case of 'passive absorption into a community of practice' (p. 488). Rather, it also reflects the ways in which teachers construct their identities on the basis of their backgrounds, preferences and experiences. Vocational habitus thus brings into play workplace cultures *and* teacher identities, drawing on both to understand the embodied know-how that teachers construct in their work.

In *music* teaching, vocational habitus reflects knowing-how to teach music in particular settings, where know-how comes about through orientation to the dispositions of the 'right person for the job' of music teacher. Know-how in this context may include, for example, knowing how to engage pupils through appropriate choice of repertoire or knowing how to position oneself in terms of identifying as a performer, teacher and/or performer-teacher. Indeed, know-how must be negotiated between what Colley et al. (2003) term idealized and realized habitus, where idealized habitus reflects the *ideal* know-how of being a music teacher and realized habitus the know-how needed to cope with the *realities* of being a music teacher. Inevitably, such habitus are workplace-specific, so that the ideal habitus of teaching music to secondary school students – as we shall see – will differ from the ideal habitus of teaching music to aspiring performers. Each workplace thus interacts with each teacher to form different constructions of professional know-how.

Vocational Habitus in Action: Examples from Diverse Settings

What vocational habitus, then, exist within music teaching? What do teachers learn about the 'right person for the job' of music teaching, and what know-how does the 'right' music teacher have? We move now to explore how vocational habitus operates in two workplace contexts, differentiating the professional know-how constructed by, first, a conservatoire instrumental teacher and, second, a secondary classroom music teacher. Our aim is to demonstrate the role that vocational habitus can play in thinking about the construction of professional know-how, bringing together aspects of structure and agency to explore how collective dispositions of ideal and realized habitus interact with individual teachers.

Case Study I: A Conservatoire Instrumental Teacher

The first of our case study teachers – Henry – is a woodwind instrumental teacher at a UK conservatoire,[1] where he has taught for sixteen years. Henry was interviewed as part of a larger study focusing on the 'learning cultures' of conservatoires (see Burt-Perkins 2009). He is selected as indicative of a conservatoire teacher who – in the interplay between his practices as a musician, his practices as a teacher and his workplace – reveals aspects of vocational habitus in his embodiment of being and becoming the 'right person' for the job. Henry's professional know-how reflects two broadly defined themes: knowing *how to perform* and knowing *how to be a professional musician*.

Knowing How to Perform
In describing the professional know-how that he makes use of in his teaching, Henry draws attention to the dominance of experiential knowledge, reporting that he 'learnt to teach by experience; I had my first students when I was fourteen'. This is common practice in the conservatoire tradition, with UK instrumental teachers not required to have a formal teaching qualification. Instead, knowledge of *performance* becomes the criterion for selection (Persson 1996), and it is Henry's knowledge as a performer that enables him to operate in the conservatoire context:

> One of the problems I found here is that the students didn't know how to behave professionally, and so one of the things that, my ensemble in association here, so we're working with the students collaboratively, so they'd play concerts with us, the good ones, and they'll learn in that, and that's the best way, because you can stand in a performance class and say this is how you behave, you always arrive early to a rehearsal, you don't answer back, you make sure you tune quietly and

---

[1] In the UK, a conservatoire of music is a higher education (tertiary) institution that awards undergraduate and postgraduate degrees in music. Conservatoires provide a specialized education for performers and composers, with students receiving practical one-to-one lessons alongside their broader programme of academic studies.

quickly, and that's easy to say and give them a list, but actually in practical terms that makes no difference whatsoever.

Here, Henry links his know-how as a performer with his know-how as a teacher, arguing that he teaches – and students learn – through the act of performance. In fact, his performing know-how as a teacher enables students to reach understandings that may otherwise not be possible; performance *itself* provides a 'practical sense' (Bourdieu 1998) of how to act in a conservatoire teaching situation that calls upon the know-how of the teacher as performer.

Taking this further, Henry's dispositions towards performance appear to reflect a conservatoire culture that privileges 'those who do' (Nettl 1995), so that conservatoire teachers are *required* to perform to high standards; it is a prerequisite for the job. As such, performing know-how is important both for Henry's teaching and for his development and identity as a musician:

> Personally I want to keep performing and that's why all my students come to, we play six Wigmore Hall concerts a year, and I get them tickets to the concerts, 'cos I think it's important they see me on the stage doing the stuff sometimes that I tell them not to do, but hopefully as a source of inspiration for them, that, you know, fifteen years after finishing [conservatoire] you can still be striving to achieve the highest level.

Here, Henry positions himself as a performer at the 'highest level', making reference to a performance venue – Wigmore Hall – that is respected as offering a platform for renowned performers. In doing so, he not only reinforces his own identity and know-how as a performer but also reinforces the importance of students learning through observing performance (a point also made by Nielsen 2006). Henry brings into view a vocational habitus that positions high-quality performing know-how, and the sorts of teaching that this enables, as central to the 'ideal' know-how of a conservatoire teacher. He appears to be a 'fish in water' (Bourdieu in Wacquant 1989, p. 43) in his workplace, with the identity of conservatoire teacher being 'choosable' for him (Colley et al. 2003, p. 488) as his own dispositions towards performance 'fit' with the dispositions of the conservatoire in which he works.

Knowing How to Be a Professional Musician

Closely linked with the construction of Henry's performing know-how is his knowledge of how to be a *professional musician*. This centres on being able to make and maintain a career in music, an objective typically held by the conservatoire students whom he teaches:

> There isn't enough work for everybody out there, but you can create your own work and there are, there are all sorts of possibilities, especially through chamber music of making a living, certainly I make a living as a chamber musician, you

know, I don't have a regular, this college job is my first regular job I've ever had, and that's sort of sixteen years in the business.

Positioning himself here as a portfolio musician, juggling his chamber group and his teaching, Henry appears to embody a 'realized' vocational habitus that situates professional musicians (including teachers) as *needing* to be diverse and flexible. This identity is reinforced by the conservatoire's emphasis on preparing students for careers in music, positioning teachers as expert professionals from whom students can learn how to be and become a professional musician.

This is also reflected in Henry's dispositions towards teaching, revealed in his belief that 'if we can't turn out students who are capable of doing quite a few things then I think we're not producing the goods for the students'. Rejecting notions of teaching that 'try and turn [students] into a replica of the teacher', Henry mobilizes his own know-how of creating a career in music to foreground the importance of individuality. Crucially, Henry is positioned here as an 'expert' professional, or in other words someone who has forged a sustainable career in music. The know-how that he has accumulated in this process becomes an important component of his teaching practice, as he draws on it in order to teach others the importance of flexibility in 'surviving' in the music business. The 'right' person for the job in this conservatoire thus becomes a teacher who can negotiate performance know-how ('ideal' vocational habitus) with the know-how of building and maintaining a career in music ('realized' vocational habitus).

Case Study II: An Inductee Classroom Music Teacher

This data derives from a larger study, exploring the key transformations in professional identities and knowledge of four British secondary classroom music teachers during their induction year (Triantafyllaki 2011).[2] The narrative of one such teacher – Mark – was selected for this paper as it was indicative of successfully negotiating idealized and realized identities in orienting towards particular forms of vocational habitus. Mark was able to do this by drawing on both his personal biography and his history of engaging with music, as well as the culture of his school and its wider community. His first teaching post was in an all-boys school with a high percentage of disengaged and special education needs (SEN) children, having a strong 'band' culture and an emphasis on music technology. Mark's professional know-how reflects two broadly defined themes: knowing how to *engage young people* musically and knowing how to *be a classroom teacher*.

---

[2]   The induction year in the UK is a three-term period of assessment, completed full- or part-time that comes immediately after and aims to build upon what teachers learnt during their initial teacher education. It includes (a) a personalized programme of professional development and support and (b) an assessment against the core professional standards for teachers. More information can be found at: http://www.tda.gov.uk/get-into-teaching/life-as-a-teacher/induction-year.aspx.

Knowing How to Engage Young People

A recurring form of professional know-how that Mark employs in his work as a classroom teacher is knowing how to engage young people in music. In foregrounding this form of know-how, Mark draws attention to his extensive experience of performing with bands, which he brings into his teaching. In doing so, Mark is able to ground his teaching practice in the 'real world' and also align his know-how with both his students' and the local community's culture:

> I kind of knew how to approach them. Especially in terms of music, I know the artists they listen to and I've worked with some of the artists they've listened to in the past. So just little things, they are easily impressed by. I would use the scheme of work they are working on so they would have to develop some melodies and I'd use the music they like listening to, to demonstrate to them that whatever music you listen to, artists always develop melodies in a certain way. They were impressed by the fact that I could understand the kind of music they'd listen to and I could adapt the lesson around that kind of music.

Here, Mark brings together his know-how in engaging young people with his former experiences of music-making in bands by incorporating his students' musical preferences into his teaching.

Moreover, forms of behaviour in group music-making are modelled on the classroom environment and, at times, act as a tool for managing his students' challenging behaviour:

> I always encourage students to think as musicians, to listen, to think as members of a big ensembles or an orchestra so always encourage them to use musical terms. Understand the basics of being a good musician. Of listening to one another, remembering that we are all part of the same group ... I think the aspect of being a musician is really important to me so that I'm not always dealing with behaviour management or simply being a teacher. I feel that that musical aspect is important to keep alive so they can be engaged more in the music.

Mark considers it important to sustain this musical side of his professional know-how, 'mainly if we are bringing new ideas, if we want to change some of our units based on our experiences in the music world'. This disposition towards student engagement seems to reflect a wider professional culture in British classroom music teaching that tends to privilege the provision of authentic music learning experiences for pupils and supports stronger links between formal and informal or out-of-school music learning (Green 2008).

A recurring theme in Mark's narrative was the 'good match' between the values and practices of music-making in his school and his own biography and history of musical learning:

> We do a lot of work with bands, you get them to work together, to work in a team. You get them engaged with music technology which is my background, I am really good in music technology, I've done it since I was in secondary school. That, and getting engaged with instruments, and learning different kinds of music around the world with guitars and things. I think what I've done in the past is suited to these kinds of students.

To some extent, therefore, one of the reasons Mark was able to orient towards the idealized habitus within this particular workplace is that it fell within his 'horizon for action' (Colley et al. 2003, p. 488). Mark's educational background in music technology, his individual musical preferences and life experiences in working with bands predisposed him to orient to the idealized vocational habitus for his school and become, as Colley et al. put it, 'right for the job'.

Knowing How to Be a Classroom Teacher
Interlinked with his know-how in engaging students is Mark's disposition towards particular images of being a classroom teacher, which he demonstrates initially through asserting himself as an established member of staff:

> I mean the first week I was, 'my name is X, I am not a support teacher, I am the teacher of the year, I expect the same thing from you. These are the rules…' It was tough at first, they are still getting used to me, they have warmed to me though.

> I was new and didn't want students to take advantage that I was new. I feel I've developed skills to engage them. Even if I do have to use behaviour management, they would always think there was a relationship there, that they still respect me and see me as a teacher that cares about their development as young people.

Here, Mark positions himself as an established member of staff in demanding good behaviour from his students. In doing so, he seems to embody an 'ideal' vocational habitus that situates classroom teachers as having the ability to deal with behavioural issues in the classroom. Yet, in his second quote, Mark also embodies the culturally established image of the 'caring' teacher (Britzman 2003); it is this affective side of his vocational habitus that embodies the 'realized' image of being a classroom teacher. He continues to negotiate this space between 'realized' and 'ideal' vocational habitus by foregrounding in his narrative the need to be available to his students beyond the required lesson time:

> There was a young drummer in Year 9 who before this year did not show any interest in music. And after this year has been really interested in music. I think it's the first year he's had a music teacher who's worked with him after work, encouraged him to listen to other music. Now he's really evolved in music, he's a kid who would never listen to other kinds of music. Now he listens to all kinds

of music, he's involved in a band, he loves music in general rather than only what he listens to.

Here, Mark positions himself as the 'caring' professional (McNally et al. 2008) who cares for his students' musical development, embodying a vocational habitus that is disposed towards encouraging students to engage in music beyond the actual lessons, with the support of their teacher. This identity is reinforced as much by his school's culture of supporting disengaged and SEN students, as it relates to Mark's own disposition of what a school teacher should be like. Throughout his narrative he talks vividly about the determining influence of his own teacher – 'we'd stay at school till school closed. And he'd take an interest and listen to us play and just nurture our talents' – and the impact this had on his later musical development.

In Mark's school, therefore, the 'right' person for the job becomes someone who can negotiate successfully the know-how of engaging students and the know-how of asserting oneself as a classroom teacher ('ideal' vocational habitus) with the necessary affective side of his vocational habitus ('realized') that makes himself available to students beyond the normal lesson hours and cares for their musical development.

Implications for Music Teacher Education

Through the lens of 'vocational habitus', this chapter has explored the ways in which know-how is embodied in teachers' practices. Know-how has been conceptualized as *culturally constructed* as teachers orient towards idealized and realized identities of the 'right person' for the job of music teacher in different workplace contexts. We have seen Henry and Mark embody very different types of know-how as they negotiate the different cultures of conservatoires and school workplaces. In both case studies, know-how can be viewed as an interplay between the teachers' musical backgrounds and experiences and the cultural practices of the workplaces in which their know-how must be enacted. To understand teachers' professional knowledge, then, calls for an understanding of the know-how that is positioned as *possible* within any workplace context, and the complex ways in which teachers orient towards this know-how.

Thinking of professional know-how in this way brings into view a host of implications, of which three are particularly pertinent for music teacher education. First is the importance of recognizing the continually shifting nature of being a music teacher, in which know-how must be constantly negotiated according to each workplace. Teachers need to be equipped with the skills to adapt their know-how in order to become the 'right person' for the multiplicity of roles they are likely to undertake in their professional lives. Second, there is a need to recognize that teachers must juggle idealized and realized identities, knowing how to be the 'right person' for the job but also knowing how to survive and function in that job. Acknowledging this interplay, and the necessity of realized identities in making teaching possible, can be seen as an important component of preparing and supporting teachers for their profession. Third is the need to recognize the blend of structure and agency that is manifested in vocational habitus, taking into account teachers' dispositions and their interaction with workplace contexts. While the case study teachers appear to move as 'fish in water' (Bourdieu in Wacquant 1989, p. 43) within their workplaces, this will not always be the case, bringing into question the ways in which teachers are prepared for the contexts in which they will be placed professionally.

Based on these three implications, we pose three 'questions for reflection' for music teacher educators and music teachers. These questions are offered to the field of music teacher education as a catalyst for discussions that bring into view the necessary complexity of both teacher agency and workplace structure in the construction of professional know-how.

Questions for Reflection

1. For music teacher educators: How can music teachers be best prepared to adapt their professional know-how as they move within different workplace contexts in their professional lives? An example of this would be the introduction of culturally specific reflection exercises that encourage music teachers to recognize the different know-how required in different teaching contexts.
2. For beginning and experienced music teachers: What do you consider to be the distinctions between idealized and realized identities in your workplace? How do you enact your professional know-how in order to be both the right person for the job and someone able to function and hold down that job?
3. For beginning and experienced music teachers: To what extent do you consider your own musical and teaching background complements your workplace culture? In what ways are you able to negotiate conflicts in order to enact the know-how that you consider important? What are the barriers that prevent you from doing this?

Acknowledgements

The authors would like to thank the participating teachers for generously providing their time and sharing their practices. The second author gratefully acknowledges the British Academy Visiting Scholars Scheme for funding the larger research inquiry of which Case Study II is part.

References

Bourdieu, Pierre (1989). Social Space and Symbolic Power, *Sociological Theory*, 7(4), 14–25.

— (1998). *Practical Reason,* Cambridge: Polity Press.

Britzman, Deborah (2003). *Practice Makes Practice: A Critical Study of Learning to Teach*, Albany: State University of New York Press.

Brown, Sally and McIntyre, Donald (1992). *Making Sense of Teaching*, Buckingham: Open University Press.

Burt-Perkins, Rosie (2009). The Learning Cultures of Performance: Applying a Cultural Theory of Learning to Conservatoire Research. In Aaron Williamon, Sharman Pretty and Ralph Buck (eds), *Proceedings of the International Symposium on Performance Science*, Utrecht: European Association of Conservatoires, 249–54.

Colley, Helen; James, David; Tedder, Michael; and Diment, Kim (2003). Learning as Becoming in Vocational Education and Training: Class, Gender and the Role of Vocational Habitus, *Journal of Vocational Education and Training*, 55(4), 471–97.

Eraut, Michael (1994). *Developing Professional Knowledge and Competence*, London: Falmer Press.

Ferm, Cecilia (2008). Playing to Teach Music: Embodiment and Identity-Making in Musikdidaktik, *Music Education Research*, 10(3), 361–72.

Froehlich, Hildegard (2007). *Sociology for Music Teachers*, Upper Saddle River, NJ: Pearson Education.

Goodson, Ivor and Hargreaves, Andy (1996). *Teachers' Professional Lives*, London: Falmer Press.

Green, Lucy (2008). *Music, Informal Learning and the School: A New Classroom Pedagogy*, Aldershot: Ashgate.

Grenfell, Michael; James, David; Hodkinson, Phil; Reay, Diane; and Robbins, Derek (1998). *Bourdieu and Education: Acts of Practical Theory*. Abingdon: RoutledgeFalmer.

Hodkinson, Phil; Biesta, Gert; and James, David (2008). Understanding Learning Culturally: Overcoming the Dualism between Social and Individual Views of Learning, *Vocations and Learning*, 1, 27–47.

James, David; Biesta, Gert; Colley, Helen; Davies, Jennie; Gleeson, Denis; Hodkinson, Phil; Maull, Wendy; Posthlethwaite, Keith and Wahlberg, Madeleine (2007). *Improving Learning Cultures in Further Education*, London: Routledge.

Lave, Jean and Wenger, Etienne (1991). *Situated Learning: Legitimate Peripheral Participation*, New York: Cambridge University Press.

McNally, Jim; Blake, Allan; Corbin, Brian; and Gray, Peter (2008). Finding an Identity and Meeting a Standard: Connecting the Conflicting in Teacher Induction, *Journal of Educational Policy*, 23(3), 287–98.

Nerland, Monica (2008). Knowledge Cultures and the Shaping of Work-Based Learning: The Case of Computer Engineering, *Vocations and Learning*, 1(1), 49–69.

Nettl, Bruno (1995). *Heartland Excursions: Ethnomusicological Reflections on Schools of Music*, Urbana and Chicago: University of Illinois Press.

Nielsen, Klaus (2006). Apprenticeship at the Academy of Music, *International Journal of Education & the Arts*, 7(4), www.ijea.org/v7n4.

Paavola, Sami and Hakkarainen, Kai (2005). The Knowledge Creation Metaphor: An Emergent Epistemological Approach to Learning, *Science and Education*, 14, 535–57.

Persson, Roland (1996). Brilliant Performers as Teachers: A Case Study of Commonsense Teaching in a Conservatoire Setting, *International Journal of Music Education*, 28, 25–36.

Reay, Diane (2004). It's All Becoming a Habitus: Beyond the Habitual Use of Habitus in Educational Research, *British Journal of Sociology of Education*, 25(4), 431–44.

Ryle, Gilbert (1949). *The Concept of Mind*, London: Hutchinson.

Triantafyllaki, Angeliki (2010a). Performance Teachers' Identity and Professional Knowledge in Advanced Music Teaching, *Music Education Research*, 12(1), 71–88.

— (2010b). Advanced Music Training Institutions in Greece as "Workplace Landscapes" in the Construction of Performance Teachers' Professional Identity, *British Journal of Music Education*, 27(2), 185–201.

— (2011). Professional Identity and Learning During the Induction Year: Newly Qualified Teachers Talking. Paper presented at the British Educational Research Association Conference. Institute of Education, University of London, September 2011.

Wacquant, Loic (1989). Towards a Reflexive Sociology: A Workshop with Pierre Bourdieu, *Sociological Theory*, 7(1), 26–63.

PART III
Re-Thinking Professionalism in Music Teacher Education

Chapter 11

Different Types of Knowledges Forming Professionalism: A Vision of Post-Millennial Music Teacher Education

Sven-Erik Holgersen and Pamela Burnard

Introduction: Different Accounts of 'Professionalism'

A recurring question in this volume concerns the role of different kinds of knowledges to support the continuous development and self-renewal of better music teachers and teaching. And this process of knowledge creation and training for creative professionalism in music teacher education (MTE) and teaching practice must be a continuous one, since society continues to change very fast, constantly making new demands on the education service. In this chapter, we argue that the agenda of music education renewal (as with other problems argued in previous chapters), now needs to become more radical. Transforming our music education systems requires more than a rhetoric of greater professionalism but radical solutions to problems, as have been amplified in previous chapters – some points of which will be summarized here. Before turning to the roles of different kinds of knowledges, however, the scope for an enhanced form of professionalism will be briefly discussed.

The following definition of 'professional knowledge' was suggested in Chapter 2: according to Benner (2010), 'professional knowledge' is needed when everyday knowledge is no longer sufficient to deal with the increasing complexity of professional demands on teachers, especially in relation to working with other professions and in their accountability to parents and the community and situations in everyday practice. The imperative difference between professional and everyday practice is that the first draws on scientific knowledge, whereas everyday practice does not. Professional practice bridges everyday practice and scientific practice as it combines knowledge from both. Thus, the three areas are seen as being coupled with different types of knowledge and constitute three areas of practice and knowledge:

1. everyday practice and experience
2. professional practice and professional knowledge
3. scientific practice and scientific knowledge.

Accordingly, professional practice draws on both experiential and scientific knowledge, and the challenge for teacher education is to integrate these different areas of knowledge.

The double design experiment with music teachers in schools and music schools described by Holgersen and Holst (Chapter 3 in this volume), revealed that the relevant subject knowledge and general pedagogical knowledge in the two different music pedagogical genres were distinctly different, whereas most of the relevant didactic theory (didactology, as explained in Chapter 3) was shared in common between the genres. Thus, results suggested that, in professional practice, scientific knowledge has much in common across different pedagogical genres.

It seems reasonable also to consider that music education has a longstanding tradition for apprenticeship learning. How does this tradition fit into our discussion about professionalism? In communities of practice (Wenger 1998), professional knowledge is developed in and through practice, and, in effect, professionalism is a social phenomenon rather than a kind of de-personalized skill or expertise (see also Perkins and Triantafyllaki, Chapter 10 in this volume). This account of professionalism is closely connected with experiential knowledge, yet it is silent about the distinction between everyday practice and scientific practice. Furthermore, determining metaphors in this tradition may not be very helpful: for example, maintaining that teaching is about passing on the artistic and educational tradition, or that learning is about copying the master. Such metaphors tend to hide the fact that all learning (apart from root learning) involves at least some degree of reflection. Apparently, apprenticeship learning in a community of practice is in opposition to the definition of 'professionalism' by Benner (2010). A determining feature of modern information and media society is, however, that nearly everyone has access to scientific knowledge, and the most significant difference between Benner's account and apprenticeship learning, then, is the extent to which scientific knowledge informs reflection in and on practice. In other words, communities of practice may draw on scientific knowledge as well and this seems to be the case for teachers sharing theoretical knowledge in pre-service or in-service courses (Burton, Chapter 6 in this volume).

Developing Professional Knowledge

Music education tends to be conservative and stick to conventional ways of teaching the subject, and more often this is the case for both teacher education and teaching practices in different institutions. A relevant question therefore is: what are some of the most effective ways to develop professional knowledge in music teacher education and teaching practices? The drivers of educational change are not always those of governmental policy; rather, it is rapid and continual change in the wider society that makes an impact on music education. The quality of music education always hinges, however, on effective teaching and learning. As the pace of change is high, music teachers, as with all teachers, must now be helped to *create* the professional knowledge in music teacher education and teaching practice that is needed. In all previous chapters, the importance of professional knowledge creation – with its emphasis on knowledge validation, which eschews a 'do-as-you-please' philosophy and insists on a tightly focused and disciplined framework for developing and diffusing high-quality professional practices – is acknowledged. Every profession – every 'job', for that matter – has its own knowledge base. But as David H. Hargreaves (1999) rightly argues, 'to be content with current knowledge and practice is to be left behind' (p. 122). In knowledge-creating music classrooms, the teachers require courage and imagination, virtues in amply supply in the music profession, but which have been drawn upon too rarely as exemplification of professional knowledge creation in teaching and learning music.

Through the previous chapters, it has been clear that different types of knowledge do not simply add up to 'professionalism'; rather, the crucial point is the ways in which specific types and a plurality of knowledges are brought into dialogue with each other through didactic reflection. In this respect, the multifaceted *pedagogical content knowledge* has been widely accepted as a prerequisite of professionalism and of professional knowledge about what works in schools and classrooms (Shulman 1986 and 1987; see also Chapters 2, 5, 6, 7, 9 and 12 in this volume). It is pointless for music teachers to preach about a future musical community that is belied by the structure and character of the community that currently exists in school. Music teachers help the young to appreciate their cultural heritage. In this chapter we present a vision for music teacher education where educators now prepare music teachers for a world in which some new skills are at a premium. Music teacher educators need to model people who are team-playing, networking and community-supporting, with an ability to be continually creative in a world in which, by definition, fresh problems unfold but must be solved quickly and locally.

Another aspect, then, concerns how to make pedagogical designs and planning that further pedagogical reflection. Since Lawrence Stenhouse in the 1970s coined the term 'teacher-as-researcher', a rich tradition of collaborative research has developed. Many educational researchers (and authors in this book) have suggested that student teachers may benefit from engaging in research activity as part of their preparation for future teaching, and in a wider sense that the teacher-as-researcher perspective may further teachers' pedagogical and creative professionalism (Maclean and Mohr 1999; Jank and Meyer 2002). Here is a vision of how networks of student teachers and teacher researchers within and between schools could promote professional knowledge creation within the individual school and in the education service as a whole, via a web of interlinked knowledge-creating music classrooms.

Hammerness, Darling-Hammond and Shulman (2002) suggested a specific pedagogical method of case-writing to further students' learning to think like a teacher. The scaffolded procedure included writing cases about problems in teaching practice, reading theory, discussing with peer students, making multiple revisions and getting feedback.[1] The aim was not to publish a research article but to gain professional knowledge through the same process. Here is a vision for music teacher education that creative case-writing would make possible the ever closer interaction of theoretical and practical knowledge in music teacher education and networks within and between schools which could promote professional knowledge creation.

Fink-Jensen (Chapter 8 in this volume) argues that student teachers should conduct research of teaching practice as teacher-researchers. Implementing the research strategy called 'astonishing practices' in a university course provided an opportunity for the teacher students to observe, describe, analyse and reflect on a music teaching practice appreciating the differences of the insider's and the outsider's perspective.

Referring to the outcomes of a research methodology course, Holgersen (2006) suggested that student teachers' engaging in pedagogical research become aware of differences between the perspectives of the practitioner and the researcher, and that this awareness noticeably enhanced students' capability of pedagogical reflection. Here is a vision – one that shatters the stereotype of students as passive recipients of new knowledge but champions rather student teacher collaborations in which creative industry or cultural know-how is critical; where the student's level of technological sophistication is positively correlated with the a number of industry alliances (perhaps they or their peers work as sound engineers or original band producers or some network knowledge with credible sources with new knowledge and know-how to apply it); where knowledge creation occurs in the context of an inter-organizational network, and where, as a result of this reciprocal learning, both school-level and industry-level practices are evolved.

The Scope of Knowledge in Music Education

Pedagogical knowledge in music teacher education may be defined and explained in many different ways according to educational traditions and theoretical perspectives. Educational concepts and traditions discussed in the present volume refer to different cultures, different institutional settings (school, teacher training college, university, conservatoire) and different professional aims (music teacher in schools or music major, instrumental teacher or musician). As to theoretical perspectives, the scope of reference theories includes ancient Greek philosophy as well as modern philosophy, anthropological and social/sociological theories as well as psychological, pedagogical and didactical theories about (music) education.

---

[1]   An identical pedagogical design has successfully been implemented in MA programmes at Aarhus University in a course called 'general didactics' which forms the initial course in a group of subject-oriented programmes. One of these programmes is music education.

At the very heart of the discussion of knowledge in music education is the justification of the subject – in schools as well as in further education. Varkøy (Chapter 2) advocates the value of philosophical reflection asking for the justification for music education. It seems to be a trend that music education in general schools is justified by referring to its usefulness for general education or other subject matters (see also Georgii-Hemming, Chapter 12 in this volume). Varkøy criticizes the modern technical rationality for overlooking the intrinsic value of music as a profound human form of knowledge. A similar point is made by Lehmann-Wermser (Chapter 7 in this volume) who describes two different objectives for education, one directed towards specific requirements of the labour market and another aiming at *Bildung*, the first of which can be measured whereas the latter cannot. Referring to Heidegger, Varkøy claims that the true value of music as artwork is its world-opening force and its potential to realize the truth of being. Likewise, Stephens (Chapter 3), referring to Gadamer, emphasizes the hermeneutic openness of artistic knowledge in music education. These views of music as an artform unfolding in human practice can be traced back to the Aristotelian concept of 'techne', which is brought to our attention in the double sense of art and craft.

Aristotelian philosophy, and in particular the concepts of *episteme, techne* and *phronesis*, provides a framework for discussing knowledge in music education without reducing it to the level of practice versus theory, art versus craft, verbal versus tacit, and so on (Georgii-Hemming, Chapter 1 in this volume). In continuation of this non-reductionist view, Stephens (Chapter 4 in this volume) discusses the fact that professional knowledge in music teaching today includes a wide 'range of contextual and generic aspects beyond that of subject knowledge and application'. Stephens points to moral and ethical dimensions of artistic knowledge that provide a necessary corrective to technical goals in education, and he advocates a model of teaching and learning music that is very much in line with the notion of communities of practice: 'The ancient apprenticeship model of master and pupil, exemplified in many indigenous musical traditions (whether one-to one, as in Indian sitar training, or individual and communal, as in Ghanaian Ewe drumming) offers an alternative and integrated model for the construction of musical and professional knowledge'. This view is in line with the 'rehabilitation of apprenticeship learning' that has been occurring since the late 1980s (Lave and Wenger 1991; Kvale 1993).

Nevertheless, apprenticeship learning is still being criticized for being conservative. As Lehmann-Wermser describes it, the training of instrumental teachers in conservatoires is provided by artists, who are also training performing musicians. The artists do not include pedagogical or didactical knowledge about teaching in schools, yet this is accepted because pedagogical proficiency is regarded as integrated knowledge in the holistic approach called *Bildung*. A dichotomy between education for competencies and *Bildung* dominates the educational discourse, as mentioned above. Professionalism in music teaching in classes requires competences as to cross-link different aspects of knowledge, yet these competences are not supported in German music teacher education. As a result, music teachers have difficulties in linking their identity as musicians with that of a music teacher.

The formation of identity as music teachers is described in a less problematic way as seen from an anthropological perspective where the educational process takes place within a community of practice (Perkins and Triantafyllaki in Chapter 10 in this volume). Music teachers' professional knowledge is described as a form of embodied know-how which is forming the 'vocational habitus' of the teacher. Know-how knowledge is often regarded as a source of valid theory; an assumption that appears to be shared with the theory of communities of practice (Lave and Wenger 1991). Interestingly, knowledge is consequently referred to as know-how. It is stated that professional know-how is culturally constructed and related to certain culturally mediated ways of thinking, being and doing. The kind of theory referred to here may be described as everyday practice-theory.

A particular strength of the anthropological perspective is that it offers teacher students the opportunity to understand how experiences from their own culture affect their understandings of what could be regarded as relevant and 'proper' knowledge in music education (Mateiro and Westvall, Chapter 9). By examining the practices of others, we can learn to challenge and critically consider our own customs and attitudes. This general anthropological insight can hardly be overestimated, and it forms the basis for many pedagogical studies (see also Fink-Jensen in Chapter 8).

In authentic contexts, pre-service music teachers may develop expertise and specialized knowledge about music teaching and learning, which otherwise would have been provided only in the form of theory-based knowledge. With assistance from the instructor, the pre-service teacher may navigate in this environment like in the 'zone of proximal development', developing metacognitive skills and gradually getting less dependent on the facilitator (Burton, Chapter 6 in this volume). Students' ability to reflect in and reflect on their teaching practice appears to be a very important objective of in-service training.

As described above, the strategy of engaging in practice as a teacher-researcher may prove extremely valuable for student teachers. The aim of the strategy called 'astonishing practices' (Fink-Jensen in Chapter 8 in this volume) was twofold: first, to observe a chosen music teaching practice in order to describe a problem and, second, to analyse this problem using music pedagogical theory. In this way, students are forced to make the necessary connections between theory and practice as they learn to do so in a research environment.

The transfer of practical knowledge between professionals involves far more than telling or simply providing information. Creativity as a tool for the knowledge creation and for developing and diffusing high-quality professional practices is central to the development of reflection competence in music education.

Within innovative knowledge communities, knowledge-creation approaches examine learning in terms of creating social structures and collaborative processes that support knowledge advancement and innovation (Paavola and Hakkarainen

2005, p. 540). Likewise, in the creativity literature since the early 2000s there has been a shift in emphasis toward characterizing, recognizing complexity, focusing increasingly on the collective and collaborative, and increasingly recognizing the situatedness of activity rather than seeing creativity as 'universalized' (Craft 2005). Innovation is then rarely a solitary individual creation. Instead, creativity is deeply social, with the most important creative insights typically emerging from collaborative teams and creative circles (Sawyer 2006, p. 42). Yet, at the same time, by attempting to describe the dynamics of innovation, models of innovative knowledge communities emphasize the importance of individual competencies and initiative, thereby bringing together individual expertise and communal knowledge in developing a common object of activity (Paavola and Hakkarainen 2005, p. 546).

One such model of knowledge creation that focuses on the activity surrounding the creation of knowledge rather than the knowledge itself, as well as the development of common objects of activity (or artefacts) is presented in Nonaka and Takeuchi's (1995) work on organizational innovation. In this model, new knowledge is created when there is a continual cycling from tacit (personal, context-specific knowledge that is difficult to communicate and formalize) to explicit (cognitive patterning, technical knowledge and subjective insights) knowledge (see Stehr 1994, p. 347). A 'knowledge spiral' is created whereby knowledge is converted from tacit to tacit (socialization); tacit to explicit (externalization), explicit to explicit (combination) and explicit to tacit (internalization) knowledge (see Littleton, Rojas-Drummond and Miell 2008, pp. 175–6). This dynamic model for the creation of new knowledge begins with tacit understanding, continues through the explication of this vague creative force in the form of an innovative product (or artefact) and ends with the reabsorption of new knowledge into the organization as a whole (Eneroth 2008, p. 230).

This type of knowledge-creation activity and others like it (e.g. Engeström's (1987) theory of expansive learning, or Scardamalia and Bereiter's (2006) knowledge-building approach) are based on the premise that innovative practices (a) continuously strive for new and advanced ways of knowing, (b) happen at the communal (rather than individual) level and are focused on the collaborative development of conceptual and material artefacts, and (c) although fundamentally social, emphasize the importance of individual competencies and initiative (Paavola, Lipponen and Hakkarainen 2004; Paavola and Hakkarainen 2005). Within such knowledge-creation activity, learning is understood as a collaborative effort directed toward developing some mediated artefacts, broadly defined as including knowledge, ideas, practices and material or conceptual artefacts (Paavola, Lipponen and Hakkarainen 2004, pp. 569–70). Moreover, the interaction among different forms of knowledge or between knowledge and other activities is emphasized as a requirement for this kind of innovativeness in learning and knowledge creation (Seltzer and Bentley 1999).

A Model of Didactic Reflection

A particular challenge for music teacher training is to prepare teachers for any possible future context. Music teachers working in changing contexts and times, accordingly, must be able to develop their pedagogical knowledge. This requires a process in which musical and pedagogical knowledge is deconstructed, yet not in the sense that knowledge is atomized. Deconstruction refers to the use of theoretical and practical knowledge at different levels of reflection as a prerequisite of developing pedagogical professionalism. Kattmann (1997) has developed the term 'didactic reconstruction' to conceptualize the transformation of subject knowledge from scientific disciplines into school curricula. In the present context, the transformation refers to pedagogical content knowledge in music teacher education and teaching practice. In continuation of 'didactic reconstruction' (Kattmann 1997), I shall suggest three concepts representing different levels of deconstruction, namely didactic pre-construction, co-construction and re-construction.

In short: knowledge about music teaching is pre-constructed in teacher education when detached from teaching practice, co-constructed through everyday teaching practice and re-constructed in professional practice.

Didactic Pre-Construction

As described by Lehmann-Wermser (Chapter 7), the pedagogical culture of music academies is grounded in a very strong identity connected with artistic practices. This strong identity may be considered a strength as well as a weakness of music teacher training at conservatories, the general criticism being that the institutions tend to preserve their artistic culture and resist theoretical reflection and pedagogical innovation. A persistent view among teachers at music conservatories has been – and to some degree still is – that the most important or even the only prerequisite for being a good music teacher is to be a good musician. The rationale of learning behind this view is that mimicry is the general pathway to learning. This is not necessarily a bad position; it may, for example, give way to intense musical communication and musical peak experiences, and insiders in this culture may describe pedagogical knowledge as inherent and embodied (Stephens in Chapter 3). On the other hand, this position does not further pedagogical development. Educational practices and pedagogical knowledge at music conservatories may not have changed very much over many decades, and many teachers try to solve problems in practice using the pedagogical as well as the musical knowledge they have adapted through their education.

Resistance against theoretical knowledge in education may, of course, exist in other educational contexts, only the artistic culture is a very obvious example. Music teacher training and teaching practice tend to be considered *detached fields*. This position implies no de-construction of music or pedagogy, and the term *didactic pre-construction* is suggested to describe this kind of pedagogical knowledge.

Didactic Co-Construction

A distinctive feature of music teacher practice is the constant need for new pedagogical ideas and musical material as the students improve – and especially if they do not improve. This problem is the same when teaching two-year-olds and advanced students. Similar problems occur over time in any educational context as teachers experience that what they learned through teacher training does not fit into the actual teaching practice with challenges such as globalization and new technologies. This situation is reminiscent of a general problem in teaching (not only music), namely that the pedagogical content knowledge in teacher training is different from that required in teaching practice. Many music teachers deal with this problem by copying methods and material from colleagues and courses. This 'hand-to-mouth' pedagogical practice may function very well for a long time; many teachers pursue this pedagogical strategy for their entire career. On the other hand, teachers may also burn out because they have no knowledge of how to develop reflective and theoretically based pedagogical thinking.

Pre-service training and in-service courses may contribute to communicate pedagogical content knowledge between teacher education and teaching practice, even if scientific knowledge only to a very limited extent is included and reflected in teaching practice.

The situation described here is that music teacher education and music teaching practice are considered *juxtaposed fields*. Teachers may engage in pedagogical reflection based on their own and their colleagues' everyday theoretical knowledge, and in this way a (community of) reflective practice can contribute to the development of the pedagogical practice. To the extent that this pedagogical practice implies some degree of de-construction of pedagogical content knowledge, it may be described as *didactic co-construction*.

Didactic Re-Construction

Following the definition of pedagogical professionalism proposed in this chapter, the most important prerequisite for the continued development of professionalism in music teaching is the integration of practice knowledge and scientific knowledge. Both kinds of knowledge are necessary tools for a reflective practice, yet all teachers have first-hand practical knowledge.

Drawing on scientific knowledge of music pedagogy (a body of knowledge as described in Chapter 2), teachers may be able to reconstruct knowledge from the context of teacher training into that of changing teaching practices. In order to develop their practices, teachers must be able to deconstruct knowledge of music and pedagogy, and this may only be possible if music teacher training and teaching practice are considered *interdependent fields*. Music teacher training and teaching practice are mutually changing fields of education, because what happens in musical everyday life must inevitably be reflected in both contexts.

The notion of teacher-researcher, as mentioned above, describes very well the dialectic way of thinking and acting that is required of a person concerned with the development of professional knowledge applicable to changing practices (Jank and Meyer 2002).

Conclusion

The aim of the present chapter has been to discuss different concepts of knowledge in music teacher education and their implications for the development of professionalism in music teaching. On the one hand, different kinds of knowledge must be acknowledged. On the other hand, it is a general assumption that music teacher training may not adequately prepare music teachers for their future work.

Different kinds of knowledge in music teacher education may be said to mutually constitute a basis for professionalism and, though different educational contexts may call for different emphasis, didactic reflection is suggested an imperative prerequisite for creative professionalism in music teaching. To be effective in music education, we need this process of knowledge creation and application (as creative professionalism) to support continuous development and self-renewal of better teachers and teaching. The answer, we argue, lies in a new model of professionalism, a particularly creative professional, developing new conceptions of school effectiveness, school improvement and professional development to meet the needs of the knowledge society.

How we may understand the connections between professional knowledge and creative professionalism in music teaching depends very much on how we understand the term 'creativity'. Tom Bentley offers a helpful way forward with his definition of creativity in education, as follows: 'Creativity is the application of knowledge and skills in new ways to achieve a valued goal' (Bentley 2001, p. 136). He emphasizes that creativity is a set of capacities that 'can be learned' to develop creative teachers and for teaching creatively, which is of course a helpful approach for music educators, in contrast to those definitions which see creativity as some fixed and 'endowed' capacity. In exploring what this may mean for music teacher education and educators, he makes a point which is deeply salient to this chapter and resonates with all contributors' chapters, that we cannot expect learners to become creative in an environment where teachers do not share the same opportunities to develop their own creativity. In an education system for a knowledge economy, he argues,

> Teachers will need to model the kinds of learning behaviour which they are seeking to develop among students and be able to apply their professional knowledge in contexts other than the classroom. (Bentley 2001, p. 138)

In this chapter, a number of areas were identified that could be developed to enhance the overall professionalism of music teachers' work. In conclusion, we now reiterate these and suggest what music teachers would benefit and may all contribute to the re-emergence of a confident creative professionalism among music teachers that will be congruent with a reconstructed professional identity better suited to the twenty-first century by being trained as practitioner-researchers and being engaged in:

- teacher collaboration
- teacher reflection and enquiry in music teaching practice
- cultural and creative partnerships
- exploiting new technologies.

With inspiration from Kattmann (1997), the concepts of didactic pre-construction, co-construction and re-construction are suggested to designate different levels of reflection in music education.

When didactic reflection is part of music teacher education to only a very limited extent, teaching practice may very often replicate subject knowledge. The teachers' pedagogical content knowledge is deconstructed to only a very limited degree. The teaching practice may be characterized in terms of didactic pre-construction.

Teachers may, however, develop some degree of didactic reflection as they participate in a community of reflective building on everyday didactic knowledge. The teachers' pedagogical knowledge content knowledge is to some degree deconstructed. The teaching practice may be characterized in terms of didactic co-construction.

Teacher education may prepare for reflective practice when didactic knowledge is building on scientific knowledge an integrated part of the education, and teachers may continue to develop this kind of professional knowledge in practice. The teachers' pedagogical content knowledge is deconstructed to a great extent. The teaching practice may be characterized in terms of didactic re-construction.

While acknowledging the need for government policy agendas in their work, music teacher educators may also celebrate this new professionalism as being one that is based upon a recognition of their distinctive contribution to society through the education of new and developing teachers.

Questions for Reflection

1. How can music teacher education best support the turning of music teaching into a profession with the best possible opportunities for teachers to develop creative practices?
2. From a music teacher's perspective, what would you recommend be emphasized in music teacher education to shape the attitudes and actions needed to ease the transition of the music education service into the knowledge society?
3. How can music teacher education contribute to the revitalization of the music education service and to bridging the gap between music education today and the music education of the future?

References

Benner, Dietrich (2010). *Allgemeine Pädagogik*. Weinheim: Juventa.

Bentley, Tom (2001). The Creative Society: Reuniting Schools and Lifelong Learning'. In Michael Fielding (ed.), *Taking Education Really Seriously: Four Years' Hard Labour*, London: Routledge/Falmer.

Craft, Anna (2005). *Creativity in Schools: Tensions and Dilemmas*, London: Routledge.

Eneroth, Bo (2008). Knowledge, Sentience and Receptivity: A Paradigm of Lifelong Learning, *European Journal of Education*, 43(2), 229–40.

Engeström, Yrjo (1987). *Learning by Expanding: An Activity-Theoretical Approach to Developmental Research*. Helsinki: Orienta-Konsultit.

Hammerness, Karen; Darling-Hammond, Linda; and Shulman, Lee (2002). Toward Expert Thinking: How Curriculum Case-Writing Prompts the Development of Theory-Based Professional Knowledge in Student Teachers. *Teaching Education: 'The Pedagogy of Cases in Teacher Education'*, [special issue] 13(2), 219–43.

Hargreaves, David H. (1999). The Knowledge-Creating School, *British Journal of Educational Studies*, 47(2), 122–44.

Holgersen, Sven-Erik (2006). Mellem fag og forskning. In Irene Christiansen and Tine Fristrup (eds), *Universitetspædagogiske refleksioner: Om overførslen af viden i undervisning og uddannelse*. [*Reflections on University Pedagogy: On the Transmission of Knowledge in Teaching and Education*], Copenhagen: Danmarks Pædagogiske Universitets Forlag.

Jank, Werner and Meyer, Hilbert (2002). *Didaktische Modelle*. Berlin: Cornelsen Scriptor.

Kattmann, Ulrich; Duit, Reinders; Gropengieber, Harald; and Komorek, Michael (1997). Das Model der didaktischen Rekonstruktion: Ein Rahmen für naturwissenschaftsdidaktische Forschung und Entwicklung, *Zeitschrift für Didaktik der Naturwissenschaften*, 3(3), 3–18.

Kvale, Steinar (1993). En pædagogisk rehabilitering af mesterlæren? *Dansk Pædagogisk Tidsskrift*, 41(1), 9–18.

Lave, Jean and Wenger, Etienne (1991). *Situated Learning: Legitimate Peripheral Participation*, Cambridge: Cambridge University Press.

Littleton, Karen; Rojas-Drummond, Sylvia; and Miell, Dorothy (2008). Introduction to the Special Issue 'Collaborative Creativity: Socio-Cultural Perspectives', *Thinking Skills and Creativity*, 3(3), 175–6.

MacLean, Marion S. and Mohr, Marian M. (1999). *Teacher-Researchers at Work*, Berkeley, CA: National Writing Project.

Nonaka, Ikujiro and Takeuchi, Hirotaka (1995). *the Knowledge-Creating Company*. New York: Oxford University Press.

Paavola, Sami and Hakkarainen, Kai (2005). The Knowledge Creation Metaphor: An Emergent Epistemological Approach to Learning, *Science and Education*, 14, 535–57.

Paavola, Sami; Lipponen, Lasse; and Hakkarainen, Kai (2004). Models of Innovative Knowledge Communities and Three Metaphors of Learning', *Review of Educational Research*, 74(4), 557–76.

Sawyer, R. Keith (2006). Educating for Innovation, *Thinking Skills and Creativity*, 1, 41–8.

Scardamalia, Marlene and Bereiter, Carl (2006). Knowledge Building: Theory, Pedagogy, and Technology. In Keith R. Sawyer (ed.), *Cambridge Handbook of the Learning Sciences*, New York: Cambridge University Press, 97–118.

Seltzer, Kimberly and Bentley, Tom (1999). *The Creative Age: Knowledge and Skills for the New Economy*, London: Demos.

Shulman, Lee (1986). Those Who Understand: Knowledge Growth in Teaching, *Educational Researcher*, 15(2), 4–14.

— (1987). Knowledge and Teaching: Foundations of the New Reform, *Harvard Educational Review*, 57(1), 1–22.

Stehr, Nico (1994). *Knowledge Societies*, London: Sage.

Wenger, Etienne (1998). *Communities of Practice: Learning, Meaning, and Identity*, Cambridge: Cambridge University Press.

Chapter 12

Meeting the Challenges of Music Teacher Education

Eva Georgii-Hemming

Introduction

This chapter discusses the value to professional teachers of being able to relate teaching to pedagogical thinking as well as to broader social and philosophical perspectives. The text focuses on some of the challenges that are faced by music education in schools. Those who are about to face these challenges have been trained within the music teacher education system, so that these issues are also directly relevant to music teacher education. The challenges vary from country to country, according to their different educational systems and conditions. However, there are generic and basic music educational challenges that are common to most countries.

In the early sections of this chapter we explore: (i) music teaching as a *profession*; (ii) the *professionalization* of the job; and (iii) *professional knowledge* in the sense of a critical and reflective approach to teaching. Following this are three sections which gradually develop the arguments of earlier sections from a general perspective to a more specific one. It is important for professional educators to be able to relate their teaching to theoretical and philosophical considerations in order to be able to participate in the general debate on education. Moreover, at a more specific music educational level, such knowledge is crucial in order to be able to make informed choices and decisions; this is important both for the status and legitimacy of the subject and for music educational practice.

My goal is to suggest ways for music teachers to face current and future challenges by connecting aspects of the central arguments in this book.

Professions

This chapter examines the concept of *professional knowledge* – the ability to perform work with competence and skill. However, the concept needs to be examined in detail and related to the idea of a *profession*, since the professionalization of the music teacher's role is one of the most important challenges faced by music teacher education.

Occupations are viewed as professions based on certain criteria, which stem from a model that was developed in the 1960s. The criteria include: (i) extensive education leading to an officially approved degree or title; (ii) having clients – students in the case of teachers – who use the expertise of the professional; (iii) autonomy in practising their job – colleagues perform quality control; (iv) control over the development of knowledge within the occupation; and (v) control over who is accepted into or expelled from the profession (Åmark, Burrage and Torstendahl 1990).

One could say that professions are developed around their own 'body of knowledge'. They have a specific knowledge base including theoretical as well as practical skills, which are renewed, developed and formalized (authorized) within professional programmes (Freidson 2001). A successful profession enjoys power and influence, which demands a great deal of trust from both the public and authorities. Collectively, this leads to respect and status for the profession.

The status of teaching is generally low, and few young people are attracted to it. In Europe, all countries apart from Finland struggle to recruit students to teaching education (Carlgren 2010). There is a debate about whether to allow people without qualifications to teach, and also about who should evaluate the quality of the teaching – colleagues, students, parents, politicians or, perhaps, administrators (Liedman 2011). In terms of the criteria mentioned above, teaching must be defined as a semi-profession, in the sense that teachers do not have clear autonomy in relation to their employer, nor do they have clear authority in relation to their clients.

Professionalization and De-Professionalization

Teaching is a semi-profession, striving to become a profession. The social process that takes place when an occupational group, through collective mobilization, raises its status and achieves a higher position in society is known as professionalization. A strategy for this process is to obtain more control over knowledge production (i.e. carry out research) within its own field (Pembrook and Craig 2002). The struggle to academize teacher training qualifications is not new; however, it seems difficult to agree on *what* exactly is the knowledge base on which research efforts can be built. The emphasis is sometimes on teachers' subject-specific knowledge, and sometimes on knowledge of teaching methods or of children. Even though each of these is an example of important knowledge for teachers, they are not necessarily teacher-specific (Carlgren 2010).

Professionalization relates to de-professionalization. Both concepts are connected to the changing regulatory frameworks for education which have emerged over the last couple of decades around the world (Lindblad and Popkewitz 2004; Carlgren and Klette 2008). Increased decentralization, as well as controlling goals and results – as opposed to detailed instructions and regulations – have been motivated by the idea that 'professionals' should make their own decisions based on their professional knowledge. Researchers who speak of the de-professionalization of teaching are referring to increased control 'from the outside'.

Along with the freedom to design activities locally come increasing demands for reporting and controlling results and for schools to meet their targets. This also applies to higher music education, which is in the process of being evaluated worldwide (Ferm and Johansen 2007). The power relation between internal and external control therefore becomes of greater importance for the development of the schools as well as for teaching. The stronger the external control in relation to the internal, the more relevant it is to talk about de-professionalization. Currently it appears as if the internal, professional control is weaker than the external. Even more established professions (e.g. medical professions) become less independent when so much needs to be documented in a way that supports quantitative measurements and quality control from outside (Liedman 2011).

Within the idea of applying quality control and quality assurance through quantitative measurements in education and professional work lies a confusion of two opposing concepts. Quantity deals with questions such as 'how much?', whereas quality deals with questions like 'what kind?'. Quantitative evaluations of music education can possibly provide information on whether music education is perceived as good or bad, but they tell us nothing of its *qualities* (Liedman 2011). There are those who, without any significant success, have tried to use mathematical calculations to judge art (Birkhoff 1933), but few people today ask critical questions about whether human actions should be the subject of quantitative calculations. The problems with this confusion of quantitative units and qualitative qualities are too numerous to be discussed further within this context. However, the problems link to an instrumental way of thinking and the idea of technological rationality, which is further discussed by Varkøy (Chapter 2).

Ways of thinking and speaking of the quality of education illustrate an underlying view of knowledge, also found in ongoing educational reforms around the world. By referring to concepts like employability and competitiveness (European Union 2006; Ferm and Johansen 2007), exams and grades are being accredited with a more important role, schools performing badly are being punished and the pedagogical forces are concentrated on core subjects like maths and English (Liedman 2011). This development has led to the impoverishment of other subjects (Ravitch 2010), yet differences between economic production values and ethical or aesthetic values are seldom acknowledged (Liedman 2011). This development places great demands on the professional knowledge of music teachers.

The Professional Knowledge of Teachers

Professional music-pedagogical knowledge includes several dimensions and levels. Music teachers need to have knowledge of music (both practical and theoretical), appropriate methods of teaching (including when certain aspects are best taught), how students learn, how schools work, and so on (Shulman 1986).

Music teaching is not only a practical and concrete activity, but also theoretical, reflective and ethical.[1]

If teachers were to engage only in practical aspects of teaching, they would inevitably contribute to the implementation and the acceptance of initiatives coming from above in the hierarchy, or from the outside. Pedagogical practice cannot be limited to how others define it. Teachers need to create a counter-culture to initiatives and perspectives from outside (Borko 2004). Music teachers should therefore possess critical thinking skills and a reflective approach, which would allow them to react at a micro-political level. Music teacher education has an urgent theoretical and critical task ahead if it is to prevent pedagogical activities for future music teachers from being confined to adaptation to government directives and political and organizational changes, following and submitting to new guidelines and policies, and delivering only what is expected (Hargreaves 2003; Hargreaves and Shirley 2010; Lindblad and Goodson 2011). The ability to contribute to an alternative music pedagogical discourse, through conscious and argued approaches about music and the role of education, is a part of phronetic knowledge.[2] This means standing up against external forces, especially when these are at odds with perceptions within the profession about what is the best for people in the long run.

In the following sections I discuss aspects of the philosophically founded dimensions of pedagogical knowledge. These aspects relate to ways of viewing the value of music and music education. Reflecting on this is an essential exercise in order to face external as well as internal challenges.

The Philosophical Dimensions of Pedagogical Knowledge

Questions of the value of aesthetic education are being brought to the fore in an era in which education tends to be justified in relation to usefulness, employability and technological rationality.[3] When 'useful' knowledge is being prioritized, human and aesthetic knowledge risk becoming marginalized.

The condition and status of music education vary from country to country. Music education is currently being affected by hefty budget cuts in several countries (Väkevä and Westerlund 2007; Nielsen 2010; Butera 2011). In other countries the number of music teacher programmes are decreasing, and in some countries music education is at risk of disappearing altogether from the general curriculum. However, in some countries the subject has a relatively stable position in terms of time in the curriculum. Regardless of such differences, official documents show

---

[1]   The reflective nature of teaching is discussed in several chapters in this book, such as Fink Jensen, Chapter 8; Lehmann-Wermser, Chapter 7; Mateiro and Westvall, Chapter 9. For ethical considerations, see Georgii-Hemming, Chapter 1.

[2]   Georgii-Hemming, Chapter 1.

[3]   Varkøy, Chapter 2.

that the educational priorities of politicians seem to remain the same (European Union 2006; Ravitch 2010; Liedman 2011).

In order to meet *external* challenges through participation in the educational debate at several levels, music-teachers-to-be need professional knowledge and insights that: (i) contribute to thinking of and discussing knowledge forms within music (such insights as well as views of music that have been reflected on are also needed in order to meet *internal* music educational challenges); (ii) verbalize the over-arching aims of music as a subject; and (iii) to be able to make conscious and well-founded decisions relating to teaching.

The following sections about the philosophical dimensions of pedagogical knowledge illustrate these three aspects.

The Value of Music

Questions about the value of music – what music *is good for* – are related to philosophical questions about aesthetics and what music *is*. On the one hand, such questions are so numerous that they can fill several books. On the other hand, they are crucial to the professional knowledge of music teachers. Therefore, I have decided to mention, ever so briefly, some different ways of thinking about the value of music. I hope that this can lead to further discussions and literature reviews.

When we speak of the value of music, it can be related to several more or less music-centred criteria. The value of music can point inwards – to the unique and aesthetic qualities of music – as well as outwards – to musical events and contexts.

The perceived inner, aesthetic dimensions involve people's emotional and existential experiences. Aesthetic experiences can create insight and an understanding of one's own life as well as that of others. When people share aesthetic experiences, they share what is essential in all human experiences, which leads to an increased self-perception that enriches the quality of life (Reimer 1989). Critics argue that the stream of thought resulting from 'aesthetic listening' involves adopting hidden ideologies and an oppressive culture stemming from 'dead, white, male imperialists' (Elliott 1995, p. 193).

That the value of 'musicing' (Elliott 1995, 2005) is its connection to people's lives is also argued by those who believe that music pedagogical activities should focus on usefulness, action and activity. Musical experiences lead to personal development on a psychological and cognitive level and are a source of self-growth and self-knowledge (Elliott 1995). This perspective also includes an idea that the value of music lies in how people, *in a certain culture* or *social context*, can make sense of impressions and expressions relating to places and people (Elliott 1995).

The danger with this perspective seems to be that music is not valued for anything other than its usefulness in a particular context. Critics (e.g. Swanwick 1999) suggest that music education should also be liberating by being able to illustrate differences. The goal ought to be that students become captivated by the familiar, but also 'feel 'at home' in the wider world' (Swanwick 1999, p. 41).

Small coined the concept of *musicking* (1998) and, like Elliott, he connects the value of music to musical activities in interaction with the environment. Differences between their ways of thinking are still being discussed (Cohen 2010), and Elliott (2011) is continually developing his idea of 'musicing'. However, from Small's perspective, the sounding music emerges together with social components in a more integrated way, compared to Elliott. Activities such as composing, performance, listening and singing are not only connected to the actual social environment. To participate in 'musicking' also means that thoughts, actions and experiences are closely connected and tied to human relationships. By participating, people experiment with and create their identities (Small 1998). This perspective has existential undertones, since people not only form everyday relationships through 'musicking', but also bring desired relationships into virtual existence (Small 1998).

To summarize, we can say that the recurring question is whether the value of music lies in the internal, aesthetic domain or in the external, social and cultural domain. If we over-emphasize the sounding music, we risk separating music from people and contexts. If we over-emphasize the social and cultural context, we risk eliminating music as an identifiable phenomenon in its own right.

Several music-sociologists therefore argue that the relationship between music and people is moving in both directions. The era and its cultural context are fundamental for how we experience music, what it is, and how it can be valued. For example, Frith (2008) suggests that musical events cannot only be understood or valued through illuminating social or ethnic factors. Individuals or groups of people can express their identities through music, but music can also generate values and assist with the formation of identities. Through musical actions, individuals can comment on, acquire and challenge a particular culture, which will therefore change (Hall and du Gay 1996; Lundberg, Malm and Ronström 2003). Music can be transported from one place to another and still function, which means that the relationship between music and people has a multi-directional connection in which music also has its own existence. The value of music therefore lies in it being a part of the current fabric of society.

The Foundations of Legitimating the Music Subject

The status, organization and content of music teacher education as well as of music education differs between countries; this influences the conditions for music-pedagogical efforts (Lamont and Maton 2010). However, there is one thing in common: it is necessary to reflect on these activities[4] in order for them to develop, but also in order to face the political and pedagogical challenges that lie ahead for music education.

Well-founded and verbalized insights about where music education can and should lead, as well as why it is, and should be, part of the school curriculum,

---

[4]   Burton, Chapter 6; Fink Jensen, Chapter 8.

create opportunities to argue these issues for students, parents, school staff and politicians alike (Hughes, Paton and Schwab 2005). It is sometimes argued that music teachers have difficulties in legitimizing their subject, and that their view of what can be achieved through music lessons is too pretentious and diffuse. Such shortcomings cannot lead to success. To be a professional music teacher is to have a personal, nuanced and articulated view of the value of the subject and its mission – which, in the long run, strengthens the subject status and positioning.

From a *critical perspective of society*, music education can be legitimized through the fact that it contributes to a critical awareness of gender roles and uses of music in media. Democratical music pedagogy can also increase understanding of other people and unfamiliar musical, geographical or ethnic cultures (Allsup 2007; Bladh and Heimonen 2007; Georgii-Hemming and Westvall 2010).

Music as a subject can also be legitimized by placing its cultural-historical importance at the centre of the argument. This perspective has several angles: one contains the idea of a *cultural heritage* – a musical canon – but there are also ideas of different ways of socializing through music – all of which, for several reasons, should be transferred to the next generation.

Focusing on the *human being* and the *individual*, music can be seen as a means for developing social skills, creativity and the ability to concentrate or develop an identity. Other common legitimization arguments are the development of motor skills or the use of music as therapy, where music itself and the aesthetics are not necessarily central aspects.

View of Music and Music Educational Choices in Practice

All music teachers have perceptions of the value of music, musical knowledge and musical activities, and this also influence their choices in the classroom. However, music teachers are not always aware of these perceptions. The perceptions are based on their own experiences, education, the traditions within the subject and its collective conventions. Thus, a teacher's personal perceptions of the value of music do not always correspond to their view of the value of music education (Georgii-Hemming 2011). Since the music-pedagogical choices will enable a particular production of knowledge, and hence exclude others, it is vital for the professionalism of music pedagogy to develop a critical view of music.

The music subject includes many challenges. The knowledge base, for example, contains artistic, scientific, practical and bodily dimensions,[5] which music teachers (or teachers-to-be) need to relate to intellectually, pedagogically and practically. Music education needs to face, as well as relate to, a plethora of historical and current musical and cultural practices that are all a part of today's globalized society (cf. Mouffe 2005), in order to support the development of students into (musical) individuals as well as responsible citizens.

---

[5]   Georgii-Hemming, Chapter 1; Stephens, Chapter 4; Varkøy, Chapter 2.

If we combine all these dimensions with national pedagogical circumstances, we can see that music education can take many different forms and foci: musical skills, competence, creativity, or social or critical skills. The core of professionalism is to be able to consider the opportunities and to make wise and well-considered decisions.

An urgent challenge is to develop cultural tolerance and recognition (Karlsen and Westerlund 2010). Therefore, many teachers are prioritizing the ability to deal with different music cultural attitudes, and ethnic and musical expressions, through verbal dialogues as well as through musical activities. Teachers are (also) striving to connect to students' everyday experiences with the intention that learning should lead to participation and inclusion. In this way, music education can contribute to identity development and recognition of historical and cultural belonging (Georgii-Hemming and Westvall 2010). Previous cultural hierarchies of 'high' and 'low' have, if not dissolved, taken on a different form. Discussions about which genres and cultural values should be a part of cultural life and education in society[6] (Bourdieu 1993) are still a pedagogical challenge, particularly when we relate these questions to identity, gender, ethnicity and social belonging. Music is abstract, but through resonating with music creators and listeners it shapes identity (Frith 2008). Through musical experiences – also in schools and education – we place ourselves (or are placed) in certain social positions (e.g. gender roles) (Green 1997). Such examples illustrate the importance of critical reflection on culture and social life within music (teacher) education.

Conclusion

Ideas of what constitutes good music and good music education are formed and conveyed within music teacher education, among other places. Music teacher education thus has an important mission: to educate professional music teachers. In order to do so, important issues are: well-founded pedagogical knowledge; reflections and thoughts on values and how these are expressed in relation to gender, cultural diversity and power; and interpretation precedence. However, it is also important to develop the potential of music within the local area, through both sound and pedagogy. Teachers-to-be can, and must, be trained to see and understand educational political rhetoric and pedagogical ideology and their consequences for schools and, more widely, education.[7]

The connections between a general music philosophy and fundamental music-pedagogical considerations can appear elusive for a music teacher in training. However, I would argue that a carefully considered music-pedagogical philosophy is necessary to develop professional knowledge for the individual music teacher, as well as for music-pedagogical activities and the music teacher profession as a whole.

---

[6]   Burnard, Chapter 5; Perkins and Triantafyllaki, Chapter 10.

[7]   Mateiro and Westvall, Chapter 9.

Questions for Reflection

1. How can the music teacher profession be understood in terms of different aspects of professional knowledge?
2. Express the values you personally see in, and associated to, different forms of music and musical activities.
3. In what ways are these values expressed in your/a music educational practical context?

References

Allsup, Randall E. (2007). Democracy and One Hundred Years of Music Education, *Music Educators Journal*, 93(5), 52–7.

Åmark, Klas; Burrage, Michael; and Torstendahl, Rolf (eds) (1990). *Professions in Theory and History: Rethinking the Study of the Professions*, London: Sage.

Birkhoff, George D. (1933). *Aesthetic Measure*, Cambridge, MA: Harvard University Press.

Bladh, Stephan and Heimonen, Marja (2007). Music Education and Deliberative Democracy, *Action, Criticism, and Theory for Music Education*, 6(1). Retrieved from http://act.maydaygroup.org/articles/Bladh_Heimonen6_1.pdf, accessed on 18 September 2012.

Borko, Hilda (2004). Professional Development and Teacher Learning: Mapping the Terrain, *Educational Researcher*, 33(8), 3–15.

Bourdieu, Pierre (1993). The Field of Cultural Production: Essays on Art and Literature, New York: Columbia University Press.

Butera, Michael A. (2011). *Music Education and the National Funding Crisis.* Retrieved from http://advocacy.nafme.org/webinar/music-education-an-the-national-funding-crisis, accessed on 18 September 2012.

Carlgren, Ingrid (2010). *Lärarna i kunskapssamhället.* Retrieved from www.lararnashistoria.se/article/lararna_i_kunskapssamhallet, accessed on 10 November 2011.

Carlgren, Ingrid and Klette, Kirsti (2008). Reconstructions of Nordic Teachers: Reform Policies and Teachers' Work During the 1990s, *Scandinavian Journal of Educational Research*, 52(2), 117–33, doi 10.1080/00313830801915754.

Cohen, Mary L. (2010). Christopher Small: A Biographical Profile of His Life, *Journal of Historical Research in Music Education*, 31(2), 132–50.

Elliott, David J. (1995). *Music Matters: A New Philosophy of Music Education*, New York: Oxford University Press.

— (ed.) (2005). *Praxial Music Education: Reflections and Dialogues*, New York: Oxford University Press.

— (2011). Personal website. Retrieved from www.davidelliottmusic.com, accessed on 5 December 2011.

European Union (2006). *Recommendation of the European Parliament and of the Council of 18 December 2006 on Key Competences for Lifelong Learning*. Document 32006H0962. Retrieved from http://eur-lex.europa.eu, accessed on 10 October 2011.

Ferm, Cecilia and Johansen, Geir (2007). Relations of Quality and Competence: Some Reflections Regarding Educational Quality in Music Teacher Education, *Musiikkikasvatus: Finnish Journal of Music Education*, 9(1–2), 65–82.

Freidson, Eliot (2001). *Professionalism: The Third Logic*, Chicago: University of Chicago Press.

Frith, Simon (2008). *Taking Popular Music Seriously: Selected Essays*, Aldershot: Ashgate.

Georgii-Hemming, Eva (2011). Shaping a Music Teacher Identity. In Lucy Green (ed.), *Learning, Teaching, and Musical Identity: Voices Across Cultures*, Bloomington: Indiana University Press, 197–209.

Georgii-Hemming Eva and Westvall, Maria (2010). Music Education: A Personal Matter? Examining the Current Discourses of Music Education in Sweden, *British Journal of Music Education*, 27(1), 21–33.

Green, Lucy (1997). *Music, Gender, Education*, Cambridge: Cambridge University Press.

Hall, Stuart and du Gay, Paul (eds) (1996). *Questions of Cultural Identity*, London: Sage.

Hargreaves, Andy (2003). *Teaching in the Knowledge Society: Education in the Age of Insecurity*, Maidenhead: Open University.

Hargreaves, Andy and Shirley, Dennis (2010). *Den fjärde vägen: en inspirerande framtid för utbildningsförändring* [The fourth way: the inspiring future for educational change], Lund: Studentlitteratur.

Hughes, Nora; Paton, Anne; and Schwab Irene (2005). Theory, Practice and Professionalism in Teacher Education, *Reflect*, 4 (October). Retrieved from www.nrdc.org.uk/content.asp?CategoryID=912&ArticleID=750, accessed on 29 November 2011.

Karlsen, Sidsel and Westerlund, Heidi (2010). Immigrant Students' Development of Musical Agency: Exploring Democracy in Music Education, *British Journal of Music Education*, 27(3), 225–39.

Lamont, Alexandra and Maton, Karl (2010). Unpopular Music: Beliefs and Behaviours towards Music in Education. In Ruth Wright (ed.), *Sociology and Music Education*, Basingstoke: Ashgate, 63–80.

Liedman, Sven-Eric (2011). *Hets!: en bok om skolan* [Torment!: a book on school]. Stockholm: Bonnier.

Lindblad, Sverker and Goodson, Ivor F. (eds) (2011). *Professional Knowledge and Educational Restructuring in Europe*, Rotterdam: Sense.

Lindblad, Sverker and Popkewitz, Thomas S. (eds) (2004). *Educational Restructuring: International Perspectives on Traveling Policies*, Greenwich, CN: Information Age Publishing.

Lundberg, Dan; Malm, Krister; and Ronström, Owe (2003). *Music, Media, Multiculture: Changing Musicscapes*, Stockholm: Svenskt visarkiv.

Mouffe, Chantal (2005). *On the Political*, London: Routledge.

Nielsen, Frede V. (ed.) (2010). *Musikfaget i undervisning og uddannelse: status og perspektiv 2010* [Music in teaching and education: status and perspectives 2010]. Copenhagen: Danmarks Pædagogiske Universitetsskole, Faglig Enhed Musikpædagogik.

Pembrook, Randall and Craig, Cheryl (2002). Teaching as a Profession: Two Variations on a Theme. In Richard Colwell and Carol P. Richardson (eds), *The New Handbook of Research on Music Teaching and Learning: A Project of the Music Educators National Conference*, Oxford: Oxford University Press, 786–817.

Ravitch, Diane (2010). *The Death and Life of the Great American School System: How Testing and Choice are Undermining Education*, New York: Basic Books.

Reimer, Bennett (1989). *A Philosophy of Music Education*, second edition, Englewood Cliffs, NJ: Prentice Hall.

Shulman, Lee S. (1986). Those Who Understand: Knowledge Growth in Teaching, *Educational Researcher*, 15(2), 4–14.

Small, Christopher (1998). *Musicking: The Meanings of Performing and Listening*, Hanover, NH: University Press of New England.

Swanwick, Keith (1999). *Teaching Music Musically*, London: Routledge.

Väkevä, Lauri and Westerlund, Heidi (2007). The 'Method' of Democracy in Music Education, *Action, Criticism, and Theory for Music Education*, 6(4), 96–108. Retrieved from http://act.maydaygroup.org/articles/Vakeva_Westerlund6_4.pdf, accessed pm 23 November 2011.

Index